The Paranormal and the Politics of Truth

The Paranormal and the Politics of Truth

A Sociological Account

Jeremy Northcote

imprint-academic.com

Published in the UK by
Imprint Academic, PO Box 200, Exeter EX5 5YX, UK

Published in the USA by
Imprint Academic, Philosophy Documentation Center
PO Box 7147, Charlottesville, VA 22906-7147, USA

ISBN 978 184540 0712

A CIP catalogue record for this book is available from the
British Library and US Library of Congress

Dedicated to the memory of

Simon Harvey-Wilson

a fellow seeker on the great journey of life

Contents

Figures and Tables

Preface

Topics such as psychic powers, flying saucers and ghosts have become popular in the media and with the general public in recent years. This book is a sociological examination of the controversies that surround paranormal topics. I trace the development of these controversies from the medieval Church's crusade against the occult and Enlightenment intellectuals' condemnation of pseudoscience, to the disputes that collectively constitute the contemporary paranormal debate.

A major aim of this book is to provide a sociological account of the processes that underlie this debate. Through a detailed examination of the participants, issues, strategies and underlying factors that constitute the politics of disputes over the paranormal, I show how the debate is inextricably bound to wider discursive formations that underlie Western thinking generally. These discursive formations constitute the "truths" that define knowledge of ourselves, of the reality that we experience, and the values that guide us. I also show how participants involved in such disputes serve as vehicles for the expression and proliferation of these wider discourses, and how the debate as a whole functions in terms of processes of wider sociocultural continuity and change.

The intention of this book is to help the reader understand why certain phenomena — and those who study them — come to be viewed as deviant. There is, however, no attempt to persuade the reader to accept one version of reality over another, for this would be to serve as an agent of the discourses that define the ideological positions of the paranormal debate. What this book ultimately hopes to achieve is to assist in nullifying the destructive politics of truth that continually thwarts a healthy debate on this matter — or indeed any controversial topic — through the achievement of such an understanding. Having said that, overcoming such a negative form of politics is, as this book demonstrates, no easy matter.

Glossary

Bracketing	The suspension of certain truth-claims (at least for the duration of discussion).
Civil Dialogue	Dialogue that is conducted in a respectful, fair-minded manner.
Democratic Dialogue	A participatory form of dialogue in which anyone who wishes to become involved can do so.
Discourse	The tacit assumptions or "truths" that underlie our understandings of self, society, and reality generally. (Not to be confused with its alternative definition as 'a mode of dialogue between people,' as understood by those who study "discourse analysis").
Epistemology	A set of ideas regarding the foundations of knowledge.
Emic	The participant's perspective.
Etic	The analyst's perspective.
Ideology	A set of ideas concerning how people think and act in relation to the social world. (Not to be confused with the more specific, hegemonic connotations implied by Marxists when they use the term)
Ontology	A set of understandings on the nature of reality, also referred to as a "cosmology."
Pan-narrative	A discursive "blueprint" that relates two or more discourses to one another in a relationship of contiguity or opposition.
Paradigm	A framework for investigating and interpreting reality
Paranormal	A category of alleged phenomena that are held to operate beyond the normal understandings of reality and the universe.
Paranormal Debate	A set of disputes concerning the existence of paranormal-type phenomena.

Paranormal Scene	The setting where people pursue their interest in paranormal topics, including participation in debates and other dealings with fellow participants.
Politics of Truth	A term coined by Foucault, which refers to the discursively based "power" struggles that surround the production of ideas, even at the level of everyday interaction.
Positive Dialogue	Dialogue that is productive, civil and democratic in nature.
Productive Dialogue	Dialogue where participants cooperatively endeavour to achieve mutual understanding.
Reflexivity	The practice of subjecting one's own truth-claims to critical examination.
Schema	A framework for viewing relationships between objects, people or phenomena.
Worldview	The view or image that an individual subjectively forms of his/her world.

Introduction

It was on a winter night, and I and a friend (we were both fifteen years old) were lugging some crates of wild rabbits — jack rabbits — out of the town in which I was born. We released them and we started to walk back the couple of miles to the town, and by this time the snow was very dense, very heavy — it was almost a blizzard condition, very cold. And out of this heavy veil of snow came two red lights drifting toward us. They just passed right overhead, and disappeared into the snowfall going north. We stood there stunned, watching. There was not a sound, absolutely not a sound. These lights were very low, maybe no more than fifty to one hundred feet above us. It was no aircraft — no pilot would have been able to fly that low in those kind of conditions.

Paranormal writer Curt Sutherly was vividly describing an experience he had as a lad. It was October 1996, and we were seated on a comfortable lounge in the lobby of the Sheraton hotel in St Paul/Minneapolis with a national UFO conference in full swing below. I was nearing the end of a five-month research trip, in which I had travelled half way around the world from my home in Australia to experience first-hand the paranormal enthusiast scene in Europe and the United States. I had only just met Curt at the conference, but we had got chatting and I perceived him to be an intelligent person with a genuine nature — not someone whose word you would normally take lightly.

But strange lights flying low and silently overhead? Could it have been a low flying glider, or a plane whose engines could not be heard through the blizzard? Perhaps it was a new ultra-secret stealth military aircraft? Perhaps Curt Sutherly did not experience anything at all, and was simply making the story up? Perhaps it was all a hallucination, or a misperception? Or maybe it was what most people at the conference would have me believe — a spaceship from another planet or an apparition from another dimension!

From all the stories that I have heard over the years, from paranormal enthusiasts all over the world, the same fundamental question keeps emerging: do strange phenomena abound that have thus far eluded the mainstream intellectuals and authorities who tend to define what is possible and real in our universe? It is a question that people sometimes ask me when they hear about my research interest in the paranormal scene. It is a question, in fact, that I have often asked myself. Having been raised by parents with an avid interest in such matters, I have had a quiet interest in matters of the paranormal since my teenage years. But with the exception of a solitary yet intense mystical experience in my early 20s — the significance of which remains unclear to me to this day — I must confess that my cautious disposition (ingrained in me from years of academic study) has left me undecided, perhaps slightly sceptical, of paranormal claims.

As a social analyst, however, I cannot pretend to know the answer to the question of whether the paranormal is real or not. I find it intriguing, however, that there are so many people who do claim to know the answer, with access to little more supportive or countervailing evidence or personal experiences than what you or I have available. What is more, people tend to differ widely in their views on the matter, and are often prepared to defend their viewpoints vigorously against those who would disagree. It is such disputes, carried out in various forums throughout Western society, and what I will collectively refer to as the "paranormal debate", that will be explored in this book.

One hypothesis that I seriously considered when I first began studying the paranormal debate back in 1996 was that the paranormal debate serves as an open forum for a productive discussion of fundamental ontological, epistemological and ideological issues, perhaps resembling what some analysts have labelled a "micro-public sphere." Social analyst L. A. Kauffman writes:

> There are, today, tiny-to-middling public spheres for hob-
> byists and enthusiasts of all kinds, for believers in this or
> that creed or this or that cause — small networks of public
> interaction marked by a level of vibrancy and engagement
> wholly lacking in the ... Public Sphere (1995:155).

Ideally, such discussions in "micro-public spheres" are carried out in a manner unencumbered by bias or restrictions on freedom of speech. They also possess the other qualities defined by social theorist Jurgen Habermas' model of the "ideal speech situation", such as a bracketing of the disputed issues and the exclusion of all motives "except that of the cooperative search for truth" (1976: 108). Indeed, each participant in the paranormal debate would almost certainly see their involvement as conforming to these criteria, and would argue that it is only the agendas and biases of detractors of their point of view that undermine the positive potential of the debate.

As I became more familiar with the paranormal debate, however, a somewhat different picture emerged — one of a debate that is characterised by intransigency on all sides — factors that would seem to work against reaching any lasting — indeed, even temporary — consensus in the debate. Further, such characteristics appeared not to be the result of either hegemonic interests (that is, a desire to preserve a position of power or authority) or ontological differences (that is, the inability to understand alternative points of view due to fundamental differences in the way reality is understood). Rather, the intransigency seemed to be the result of discursive factors that were tied to demonised notions of the "Other."

Within a demonised outlook, opponents are not simply viewed as "mistaken", but are typically seen as ontological, moral or social threats to the "proper" order of things. For example, Skeptics (those who question the existence of paranormal phenomena) often associate the pro-paranormal position with religious dogmatism or primitive, mythical thinking that is fraudulently parading as science — a threat that tends to be framed in terms of a battle between the forces of Reason and Unreason.[1] Hence, from the Skeptics' point of view, ths issue is not so much that they are unable to understand the pro-paranormal position (as the "incommensurability" thesis suggests), even though this may be true to some extent. The heart of the issue is that paranormal proponents fulfil the role of the "demonised Other" — in this case, that of an irrational, gullible "Believer" who, if their beliefs spread to others, would ultimately bring about the downfall of Rational society.

Participants' commitment to keep the "Other" at bay is reinforced by certain notions about what will happen at the individual level, and to the social and/or cosmic order as a whole, if cherished ideals are not preserved. For example, from the Skeptic perspective, if orthodox logico-scientific ideals do not prevail, society might once again be plagued by the crazed and irrational element that flourished in the early witch-hunting days.[2] In a similar vein, some UFO proponents perceive a danger to humanity from malevolent aliens if their views do not prevail, or a global catastrophe if the warnings of wise, benevolent aliens are not heeded. For some Christian fundamentalists, who view the paranormal as Satanic, if people do not strictly follow the Christian path they will aid the "forces of darkness" and lead many down a path to destruction that will take place in the "final days." Such ontological orientations not only lead participants to act against "outsiders" regarded as deviant, but also against

---

[1]   Skeptics tend to refer to themselves using a "k" (the American spelling), even in England and Australia (where the word "sceptic" is spelt with a "c"). Some Skeptics, as I will explain in Chapter Four, also tend to employ a capital "S" rather than a small "s", in order to designate themselves as a distinct group. The form of scepticism that this group expresses is not related to the Academic and Pyrrhonian scepticism that philosophers employ when questioning the basis of all knowledge claims.   Rather, it is a suspicion of only those knowledge claims that are categorised as pseudoscientific in nature.
[2]   Similarly, social analyst Brian Wynne argues that attempts by scientists to downplay tensions within their community are motivated by an attempt to preserve the "intricate social delicacy of consensus in science" in light of "the fearful proximity of cognitive and social anarchy" (1979:81).

fellow members who may be seen to stray from the group's ideals.

As my research continued to probe the depths of the paranormal scene, the debate increasingly appeared to be an arena for constructing difference and engaging in factional conflict, producing a rather "negative" dialogue in which opponents tended to be dismissed without a fair hearing.[3] Consequently, my original hypothesis that the scene resembled a "micro-public sphere" for consensus building and fruitful disagreement gave way to a view that more closely resembled what anthropologist David Hess (1993) has referred to as an "ideological arena", where ideational differences between groups are reinforced rather than overcome.

Hess also argued that the paranormal "arena" is intimately connected to the wider society — a view that also resonated with the general perspective I increasingly leaned towards. It seemed increasingly apparent that wider issues and concerns that were not specific to paranormal matters at all were driving the pattern of interaction between participants in the debate. In this respect, my approach departed from those social analysts who tend to regard the debate as either a marginal or trivial social phenomenon with little relevance to the fundamental processes shaping our Western society or, to the extent that it is relevant, as an indication of instability or dysfunction in those processes. Unfortunately, the tendency of social analysts and laypeople alike to portray paranormal interest as marginal or "deviant" has obscured the way in which paranormal interest constitutes a fundamental continuity with the wider culture and the central workings of society (Goode 2000:3). As

---

[3] My notion of a "positive dialogue" and a "negative dialogue" differs from early formulations that, as Gurevitch (2000) has noted, tended to view all dialogue as inherently positive. The erroneous assumption made by these theorists is that unfamiliarity breeds distortion, suspicion, and fear of the Other, whereas familiarity through dialogue inevitably leads to trust, tolerance and understanding.

social analyst Arthur Parsons remarks with regard to prophetic movements:

> ... if the scholarly or public debate over specific prophetic movements becomes articulated in terms of their deviance from or rejection of conventional secular society, we fail to appreciate that their appeal and power are derived from the cultural and social fabric of their host societies. Indeed, at the core of innovative movements, in their fundamental moral principles and in their most ritualized social practices, we find components of secular society that have not been rejected but elaborated and intensified (1989: 223).

My research indicated that the paranormal debate reveals the same interrelationship with "secular society", being concerned with issues that underlie the scientific and religious frameworks that shape knowledge and values in contemporary society, and with the place of humankind in society, the world around us, and the wider cosmos. In fact, going beyond Hess's cultural contextualisation theory, I will show how the issues of contention within the debate are seen to concern the fundamentals of knowledge-construction in Western society generally.[4] In particular, I want to make transparent the "politics of truth" surrounding the paranormal subject — that is, the discursive processes involved in defining the validity and value of paranormal ideas in Western society as but one class of a more general system of knowledge or 'truth' production.

The reader may well be wondering what is meant by the term "discursive". As a concept taken from the social philosophical writings of Michel Foucault, it refers to a set of assumptions or truth claims that tacitly underlie people's understanding of reality, society, and self. My Foucaultian use of the term "discourse" is not to be confused with the

---

[4]   When I use the term "the West" or "Western society", I am not referring to a socio-economic bloc as distinct from "the East." I use this term simply to refer to a culturally related group of nations of a distinctly European heritage that have historically be labelled "the West", comprising such countries as England, France, the United States, Canada, Germany, Holland, Australia, and New Zealand. I should point out, however, that some analysts reject the notion of "the West" as a meaningful classification (see, for example, Dean 1998), and I would not dispute this position.

more general sociological usage of the term that refers to discourse as modes of written or verbal speech (the study of which is referred to as "discourse analysis").[5] Some theorists, such as Jean-Francois Lyotard (1984), refer to discourses as "metanarratives", as they are seen to constitute grand narratives or "stories" about how reality works. Foucault and Lyotard hold that discourses serve to legitimise certain interpretations of events and situations through a self-referential appeal to truth - that is, by appealing to so-called "facts" that are themselves merely discursive notions. These "truths" define such things as the essential qualities of an event, the reasons for why that event has come about, and how that event should be appropriately dealt with.

Let us take the event described by Curt Sutherly as an illustrative example of the discursive concept. Discourse would refer to the set of interpretations that were made about the event, such as Sutherly's designation of the experience as "paranormal" in nature, or to those who would seek to explain his experience as being otherwise, such as a hallucination. Discourse also refers to the set of assumptions that define the paranormal concept in the first place, and that mark it off as different in some way from orthodox scientific and religious concepts. Discourse also refers to the way such perceived differences are seen to be harmful, and the strategies aimed at "correcting" such deviations and affirming the proper order of things. In short, discourse refers to the set of "truths" that shape the way people think and behave.

Unfortunately, theorists such as Lyotard and Foucault have tended to take a rather sceptical approach to knowledge claims in their own discursive approaches. For Lyotard, knowledge consists of a "myth" that is not grounded in an objective or universal structure. For this reason, the discursive perspective is often described as "poststructural", because it does not support the idea that

---

[5]   In this respect, social analyst Teri Walker describes the Foucaultian conceptualisation as "Discourse within discourse" (1988:55).

there is an objective reality that fixes the structure of ideas, practices and meanings. Instead, knowledge-claims within discursive formations are seen to be governed by changing relationships of contiguity, opposition and mutual exclusion with respect to one another — for example, the normal/paranormal dichotomy.

One point I am keen to stress is that a discursive perspective need not rule out the possibility that there is (at least) some degree of correspondence between truth formulations and some objective reality. As I have said, I cannot claim to know whether the paranormal is real or not. All that I can say is that, for the purposes of this study, the issue of the reality or otherwise of paranormal phenomena will be left open in the analysis. Likewise, postmodernists cannot reasonably claim that amongst the various truth claims that circulate, that there is not some component of objective reality present at some level.[6] It is simply that, as social analysts, we must assume that we are not fully in a position to know at what level objective reality operates (if any), and how much of a constitutive role it has in the knowledge that we take to be true.

Having said that, I have made the point elsewhere (Northcote, 2004) that leaving aside such validity issues — what is generally referred to as a "bracketing" approach — in itself constitutes a distinct form of ontological bias. Such bracketing is a form of bias because it effectively rules out the possibility that paranormal phenomena or irrational tendencies can fully or mostly account for the social processes involved in producing the paranormal debate. For example, some UFO proponents claim that the growing 'movement' of popular interest in UFOs is being orchestrated by extraterrestrials in order to prepare the citizens of Earth for official extraterrestrial contact. Meanwhile, some Christian evangelists (or fundamentalists) attribute popular interest in spiritual and occult matters to

---

[6]   I am reminded here of folklorist Thomas E. Bullard's (2000) distinction between the mythic components of UFO beliefs and the possible (although by no means certain) factual basis behind encounter claims.

demonic manipulation - part of Satan's ongoing battle with God. Skeptics, for their part, view irrational psychological propensities as the basis for people's interest in, and defence of, paranormal ideas.

Putting aside the question of the reality or otherwise of paranormal phenomena means that such explanations, *ipso facto*, are ruled out as total explanations for the social processes underlying the debate itself, because sociological explanations have been accorded a privileged place in the account. Sociologist Erich Goode (2000:145) recognises the problem in his study of beliefs in UFOs when he states that sociological generalizations about UFO reports depend on the falsity of at least most sighting claims. Otherwise, the applicability of a "sociology of belief" to understanding UFO beliefs would not be relevant. The same problem concerns my own study of the ways paranormal beliefs are contested.

Such bias, however, is unavoidable, being the very basis upon which social scientific inquiry is made possible. Nevertheless, I am very much aware that the position I advance in this book excludes certain explanations about the factors underlying the paranormal debate, and that, as a consequence, participants in the debate on all sides might contest the theoretical position that I have taken.

As a consequence of taking a discursive approach to the paranormal debate, which puts to one side the issue of whether paranormal phenomena exist or not, I am essentially stating that the disputes that take place over the paranormal are more political in character rather than scientific - that is, matters of ideology rather than of evidence. Further, I contend that such political processes are not guided by aliens, demons or psychiatric tendencies, but by sociological processes of truth construction (this perspective constituting my particular ontological bias in this study). My use of the term "political" with regard to the paranormal debate may seem somewhat unusual, given that politics is usually associated with matters of government. But there has been, as social analysts Nicholas Dirks, Geoff Eley and Sherry Ortner note, "an expanded and more sophisticated understanding of the role and nature of 'the political' in social life" (1994:4). Such an understanding sees "politics" as a mode of contestation and negotiation that is played out in all kinds of everyday social settings and fields of interest such as theology, education, science, sexuality and morality, to name just a few. Increasingly, analysts are seeing the contestation over paranormal knowledge as "political" as well. For example, social analyst Jodi Dean writes with regard to the field of ufology:

> Ufology is political because it is stigmatised. To claim to have seen a UFO, to have been abducted by aliens, or even to believe those who say they have is a political act. It might not be a very big or revolutionary political act, but it contests the status quo (1998:6).

The paranormal debate is political because it challenges the boundaries between "legitimate" and "illegitimate" knowledge that lie at the heart of our "modern" society.

The deep-seated nature of paranormal contestations raises the question of whether such an "ideological arena" lends itself to consensus building or even respectful disagreement in a contemporary "public sphere", or whether people are simply unable to overcome the demonised views they have of one another. The ramifications of this analysis of the "politics" of the paranormal debate might be unsettling for some, for it will highlight the entrenched nature of the differences that characterise beliefs between humans. This has implications not only for the kind of metaphysical disputes over the nature of reality characteristic of the paranormal scene, but also for religious disputes, ideological differences and divisions related to racial, gender and sexual inequalities throughout the world. The issues might be expressed differently, but they are all fundamentally about the inability of people to see past their preconceptions of one another and to overcome their feelings that the Other poses a threat of some kind to the proper order of things.

However, the ability to understand the processes underlying these tensions through a discursive approach to social analysis, and a commitment to address ideational differences through a reflexive, dialogical approach, is intended

to offer a more constructive way of dealing with these differences than the demonising animosity that typically characterises disagreements. The paranormal scene, like many
other social settings that have been rejected as trivial (itself a
result of political demonising), may have something very
important to offer social thinkers in this respect. So, without
further ado, let us begin our exploration of the politics that
characterises the paranormal scene, and see what lessons it
holds for our understanding of knowledge claims and
deviance generally.

Chapter 1

Defining "The Paranormal"

What people commonly term "paranormal" is intrinsically a Western ontological category. The substance of the term rests in its contrast to what is designated "normal." It needs to be kept in mind that phenomena designated as "paranormal" are objects or properties that *appear* to be contrary to normal or established phenomena. For Kant, "phenomena" refers to the conception of objects, not to the objects "in themselves." This is a useful insight to apply to our own understanding of paranormal phenomena. That paranormal objects may not be intrinsically unusual or odd – if indeed they exist in a form resembling what they are claimed to – is something that most proponents of paranormal ideas are only too happy to concede. The term "paranormal" is merely a relative concept.

The term seems to have gained popularity around the late 1930s and early 1940s, superseding another term, "supernormal phenomena", which was popular with psychical researchers in the 1920s (see, for example, Lodge 1927). However, as I will explain in detail in the next chapter, the notion of a category of phenomena (or ideas concerning such phenomena) that lie outside what is considered acceptable knowledge has a long tradition in Western society.

In contrast, in many non-Western countries such as Brazil (Hess 1991) and India (Rao 1994), the paranormal category is generally indistinguishable from mystical, spiritual, and traditional folk magical beliefs. This lack of distinction has facilitated the acceptance of paranormal-related ideas in those countries, without the stigma frequently attached to such beliefs in the West (where dominant scientific paradigms have largely invalidated, and Christian paradigms largely condemned, such ideas). To the extent that conflict over paranormal ideas does occur in countries such as Brazil, the polemics and disagreements are, in comparison to the conflict that takes place in the West, mostly veiled and indirect (Hess 1993:179), and a "debate" as such is, consequently, not readily identifiable.

In Western terms, the "paranormal" can be understood as a category that denotes a range of alleged phenomena judged to be unexplained or inexplicable in terms of "normal" scientific understanding. This categorisation relies heavily on the notion of what is considered "normal" — which itself is a very arbitrary judgement, and leaves the definition of what qualifies as *para*normal open to a wide variety of interpretations and opinions. For example, ex-parapsychologist Susan Blackmore told me: "you can't define the paranormal, no one has come up with an adequate definition of the paranormal" (1996: personal interview). While Blackmore prefers a fairly narrow, paraphysical definition — namely, "something that violates really fundamental physical principles" — she admits that this is purely her "own working definition."

In their examination of the concept of the "occult", Colin Campbell and Shirley McIver (1987) warn against purely negative definitions, pointing out that there are many ideas that fall outside the realm of mainstream science that would not be considered by most people to be "occult" at all. Instead, Campbell and McIver prefer a more substantive definition that places the emphasis on certain features of occult ideas, such as their magical or spiritual quality. The same argument might be applied to definitions of the paranormal. However, it is difficult to define a shared quality that links together the myriad of alleged phenomena that come to be labelled as "paranormal."

At any rate, there are problems in treating any category as possessing certain intrinsic, substantive qualities, as it fails to consider the variable ways in which a category may be defined, and how definitions of that category may change over time. What is more important is that we understand the way that participants in the paranormal debate themselves understand the category, as this will indicate the way that discourses have defined the term and placed it within a particular truth regime.

In its narrower usage, the paranormal category refers to phenomena beyond the laws of currently understood physics (sometimes referred to as "paraphysical" phenomena or "psi"), and includes subjects such as extra-sensory perception (ESP), telepathy (communication via the mind), mediumship (communication with the dead), psychokinesis (affecting objects from a distance) and apparitions (ghosts). Subjects without a clear paraphysical component such as ufology, cryptozoology (the study of unexplained animals) and cryptoarchaeology (the study of ancient mysteries) have tended to be excluded from this somewhat narrow category. These subjects do not necessarily violate, as Blackmore puts it, "fundamental physical principles." The Loch Ness monster and Big Foot, for example, are postulated to be creatures like others that roam (or have roamed) the Earth. Aliens from outer space are supposedly beings that have evolved on other planets. The Lost City of Atlantis is believed to represent a civilisation much like other great ancient cities on Earth, except that it is believed to have existed in a much earlier era. These ideas may question established notions of history and taxonomy, but they do not question basic principles of physics.

However, in the last few decades, the term "paranormal" has been employed in a much broader sense. Hess writes:

> [W]hen parapsychologists use the term "paranormal", they intend for it a considerably narrower scope than do the skeptics and much of the media and general public, for whom "the paranormal" is sometimes synonymous with the "occult" or the "supernatural" (1993:7).

Within this wider definition, "paranormal" tends to refer to all types of reported phenomena considered to be outside the realm of mainstream science, and the term is used interchangeably with terms such as "unexplained," "extraordinary" or "mysterious" phenomena. It is this wider sense of the term that I employ in my study, for two reasons. First, many of the people I studied had an interest in several different paranormal topics that included both physical and paraphysical-type mysteries. Second, many of these topics, regardless of their particular focus, tend to be influenced by the same politics of truth as part of a broader debate surrounding unorthodox ontological claims.

I realise, however, that there will be many within the aforementioned fields who will question my association of their area of inquiry with a broader "paranormal" debate. Normally such associations—quite contrary to the objective of the present study—are motivated by various pejorative or ontological interests aimed at discrediting these fields. For example, lumping parapsychology in with UFOs and Big Foot is seen by psychic researchers to be a means of belittling their field of endeavour, and—rather ironically—the same sort of protest is made by Ufologists when their field is associated with psychic studies. The focus of the present study, at any rate, is not on the subject matter that constitutes any so-called "paranormal" category of knowledge, but on the debate that surrounds subject areas that— whether paranormal proponents like it or not—have become associated with this category. In fact, it is the very indeterminate nature of the paranormal category and the "politics" of its application that is of interest here, and so its use in this book should not be seen as any more than a loose, expedient designation for a type of knowledge claim that is contested in orthodox academic and religious circles on the basis of its marginalised status.

It should also be pointed out that it is on the intellectual aspects of the discourse surrounding people's participation in the paranormal debate (in particular the exchanges between paranormal proponents and opponents) that this book will focus. Participants' intellectual involvement can be usefully contrasted with experiential or performative forms of involvement (including participation in various "occult" practices). Occult practices concern attempts by participants to gain access to (or seek control of) occult/paranormal forces through a variety of experiential and symbolic means. Such practices include witchcraft, sorcery, paganism, meditation, mediumship, and channelling. Some of the ritual aspects of occult practices have been studied by anthropologist Tanya Luhrmann (1989). The focus of the present book is instead on the intellectual mode of involvement. The emphasis on such forms of participation is deliberate, for they most clearly reveal the "truths" that guide paranormal-related thinking and behaviour and the "political" contestations that surround those truths. This is not to say that rituals and other practices do not also express "truths" and "political" orientations, but rather, they often do so in a much more symbolic, subtle manner that is not readily discernable to the analyst (and, hence, requires a more speculative, interpretive approach).

My employment of the term "involvement" needs to be qualified somewhat, given that some analysts (for example, Irwin 1993:12–13) make a distinction between "paranormal belief" and "paranormal involvement." The term "involvement" would normally apply to those enthusiasts who pursue their paranormal interests in a more active manner (such as by reading books, attending meetings and conducting rituals) in contrast to those who merely have an opinion about the paranormal but do not actively participate in the "scene." However, I have found that even those whose paranormal interests stop at merely having an opinion about the subject are, through the formation, expression and defence of that opinion (even to themselves in their own minds), actively involved in the paranormal debate. Consequently, the distinction between "belief" and "involvement" is, in my opinion, rather tenuous. At any rate, the participants I examined in my study are those who are actively engaged in publicly promoting and defending their views at venues such as society meetings, conferences, or Internet discussion groups. These are the participants who might be described as "hard core" and whose belief positions are more enduring and resolute. Consequently, they are those who tend to be most "political" in their involvement.

The belief of people in such phenomenon is not, of course, the focus of this book. Sociologist Erich Goode (2000) devotes a whole study to the sociological basis of paranormal beliefs, and there is no attempt to replicate his examination here. My interest is primarily in the dispute that takes place around paranormal beliefs, and hence I am concerned with explaining behaviour rather than belief systems. There is no suggestion made whatsoever in this book that belief in the paranormal is in need of explanation (sociological or otherwise). In so far as belief systems are addressed in this book, they are done so only as a means for understanding interaction between enthusiasts, as belief and practice are closely intertwined in all human endeavours. For example, the process by which individuals come to adopt a position of belief is, I hold, pivotal to understanding their mode of interaction with opponents, and therefore will be examined quite closely in a later chapter, without suggesting that the nature of that belief system itself can be subjected to the same kind of sociological analysis (although I certainly would not rule this out).

The use of the term "enthusiast" also needs qualification. UFO historian David Jacobs pointed out to me that in the UFO research area, the term "enthusiast" is employed by Skeptics to denigrate UFO researchers as not being truly scientific but, rather, "weak-minded UFO lunatics" (personal communication, 2006). The pejorative connotations of the term are unfortunate, and are not meant to apply to its use in this book. The term "enthusiast" simply denotes a person who has a strong interest in the paranormal area, and includes opponents such as Skeptics and Christian fundamentalists as well as paranormal proponents. It is recognised that many participants recognise themselves as researchers, and when applicable, I refer to authors and investigators as "researchers". However, who gets dubbed "researcher" and who gets dubbed "enthusiast" is itself a somewhat arbitrary and contentious matter. Further, researchers tend to be viewed as a sub-group of the enthusiast category in this book, which they may not be altogether happy with. This is an unfortunate, but unavoidable, state of affairs, and points to the deep-seated politics that characterises the scene, where even seemingly innocuous terminology is not immune to strident challenge.

Beyond delimiting the paranormal category and determining the mode of involvement that I will focus on, it is also necessary to set limits in terms of the scope of the debate that I will address. One problem in this respect is that each paranormal "field" has its own internal debate. For example, participants and social analysts alike will speak of the "UFO debate", the "parapsychology debate", the "crop circle debate", and so on. Further, within each individual field there are even more specific debates, which may centre on controversies surrounding particular methods, theories or sub-fields of interest, such as the alien abduction controversy within Ufology (see Jacobs 2000b), or the Ganzfeld debate within parapsychology (see Palmer 2003). Because my interest is mainly in the wider discursive politics surrounding such subjects, I will focus on the more general controversy surrounding the paranormal category as a whole (and which I hold the more specific debates tend to reflect).

A final task I have set myself is to explain the manner in which different participant types are identified in this book. Beyond the Proponent-Skeptic positions that characterise the basic line of division in the paranormal debate, there a several groups that are seen to converge around various ideational positions, such as New Agers or Christian mystics. However, identifying the particular form of social organisation that characterises each of these types, and delineating their boundaries, is no an easy matter. As Hess writes, "It is difficult to give New Agers, Skeptics, and para-psychologists an unambiguous label such as 'social movements' or 'communities'" (1993:189), because, he argues, their loose-knit and, in some cases, informal modes of organisation differ from what is conventionally understood as a "social movement" or "community." Based on the field work that I have undertaken, I thoroughly agree with Hess's assessment.

In this respect, the paranormal debate is not geographically bound — that is, one does not enter the scene as one would a village, and there is no single, identifiable "community" as such into which a newcomer needs to be accepted. "Community" in the paranormal scene can best be described in terms of the scattered social networks that exist between participants. The scene is also relatively domain specific — being confined to what could be categorised as the "leisure domain." Outside their paranormal-related activities, most participants live normal lives, working in nine-to-five jobs, raising families, and maintaining friendships that are not necessarily based on a shared interest in, or opposition to, paranormal-related subjects. Participants tend to pursue their (pro or anti) paranormal interest in their own time by means of reading paranormal-related newsletters, magazines and books, and viewing television programs and films related to the subject. Sometimes, though not always, they also talk to family, friends and acquaintances about their views, and some even attend meetings, lectures and conferences on paranormal-related topics, or participate in one or more of the various paranormal-related Internet group discussions. I say "sometimes", because some participants are very much alone in their paranormal-related interests.

Because of the fragmented, amorphous, translocal and privatised nature of the scene as a whole, the paranormal arena presented certain challenges in terms of conducting fieldwork for a sociologist such as myself with a background in ethnographic research methods. I realised very early on, for example, that to cover the range of participants and situations that constitute the paranormal debate, a form of ethnography was required that would resemble what anthropologist George Marcus (1995) refers to as "multi-sited ethnography." According to Marcus, multi-sited ethnography:

> ... moves out from the single sites and local situations of conventional ethnographic research designs to examine

the circulation of cultural meanings, objects, and identities
in diffuse time-space (1995:96).

Consequently, in my discussion, I will move back and
forward between particular individuals, groups and settings, and between these micro-level "sites" and the wider
"paranormal debate." There is a risk involved in this
approach that assertions and behaviour that are produced
within a localised context may be taken out of context when
applied to the paranormal debate as a whole. Certainly,
people's perspectives must be understood as contextualised
ones that are shaped by localised factors to some degree. On
the other hand, there is a general politics of truth at work in
the paranormal debate that frames localised manifestations
of thinking and discussion on the topic. These factors are
widely discursive in nature and historically emergent,
being greater than any particular dispute among protagonists. In fact, an understanding of the present-day paranormal debate is not possible without an understanding of the
history of the development of ideas surrounding the paranormal category of knowledge in Western society, and it is
to this history that we next turn.

Chapter 2

A History of Struggle

Introduction

The contemporary paranormal debate, and the politics that underlie it, have emerged historically out of discourses that have shaped Western civilisation for centuries. Not only have these discourses determined the status of paranormal ideas vis-à-vis scientific and religious ideas, but they have also defined the points of similarity and difference between these ideational systems — indeed, their very boundaries. However, the nature of the relationship between these systems has been variously constituted and undergone change within the discursive matrix over time. In fact, the history of paranormal/occult ideas reveals that the boundaries between science, religion and the occult/paranormal have long been fluid, negotiable and contentious (Gieryn 1983; Hess 1993) — a situation that continues to characterise much of the politics surrounding paranormal ideas to this day. Indeed, I will show how discursive changes over time have changed people's perceptions of paranormal ideas in terms of what is accepted and rejected as legitimate knowledge.[1]

While the boundaries of paranormal or "occult" ideas have fluctuated over time, such transformation has been set against a fundamental continuity in the constitution of a certain type of ideas as rejected knowledge. Hence, the per-

---

[1] This emphasis on evolving discourse as the primary factor responsible for the changing status of paranormal ideas over time is in accord with the view put forward by historian Keith Thomas, who argues that the factors affecting societal views on the occult throughout history have been primarily "mental" in nature (1971: 661).

sistence of the occult as an excluded category can be seen to reflect a certain discursive continuity against a background of general discursive change. Why is it that the "occult" category has endured down through the centuries but continued to be excluded by other discourses such as religion and science that have come and gone from pre-eminence? Does both its continuation and exclusion somehow serve a functional role necessary for the maintenance of knowledge forms? Is there a structural dimension to its existence and negation, perhaps based on its role in distinguishing magic from religion, or pseudo-science from science? Is its survival and persecution a consequence of hegemonic struggles, where the occult (a traditional symbol of subversion) is used as a ready-made tool by insurgents and oppressors to further their particular agendas?

These are interesting questions, and the answers might be relevant to understanding a whole range of persecuted groups down through history — ethnic minorities, women, homosexuals — all of whom have been rejected or marginalised in one form or another in the past (and still are in contemporary society). This is despite the fact that the pre-eminent discourses of the societies that have rejected these groups have undergone a great deal of transformation during these periods. Hence, an understanding of the issue of discursive continuity and change with respect to the occult is not just a matter of background interest or theoretical marvel for the present study. Rather, history informs the present in fundamental ways, and it will be shown in this book how present day disputes over the paranormal reproduce disputes that are centuries — even millennia — old.

It should be noted that I am principally dealing here with the status and understandings of the "occult" and "preternatural" as categories of knowledge, and I will pay only cursory attention to the manner in which individual subject areas (such as astrology or necromancy) have become implicated with these wider categories. While the "paranormalisation" of particular subject areas is an interesting issue, this process is too intricate and too unique to each area to warrant a detailed examination here. A focus on the paranormalisation process would additionally divert our attention away from the wider politics that surrounds marginalised knowledge claims. It should be pointed out that the two processes are not distinct, and in fact the larger discursive struggle over paranormal ideas informs the paranormalisation of individual subject areas in very profound ways. Nevertheless, what we are interested in here is the end result of the paranormalisation process (or the starting point perhaps), that is, what happens to knowledge claims once they have already been labelled "occult" or "paranormal" and why should this present such a problem to various groups?

The starting point for an historical examination of the politics surrounding the occult presents an interesting matter, as disputes over the status of the occult are probably almost as old as occult practices themselves. To search for the historical origins of the occult controversy would be to enter a murky labyrinth of speculation and generalisation. There are, however, a number of historical periods that appear as strong candidates for a starting point for such a history: for example, the period of classical Greek civilisation, which heralded intellectuals such as Hippocrates (5th–4th century BCE) who pitted *naturae* (nature) against *magos* (magic).[2] This is an opposition that continued to occupy the minds of Roman thinkers such as Pliny the Elder (AD 23–79) some five centuries later when he called magic "the most fraudulent of arts" (1963[AD 77]: 279).[3] Concomitantly, the early Jews and Christians established the "occult" category and associated it with sin and evil — associations that are still made by the Church today. But it was not until the seventeenth century that opposition to the

---

[2]   Magic or *magia* emerged as a disreputable category in ancient Greece, being associated with practices derived from the Persian magical arts (Kieckhefer 1989:10). Hippocrates rejected divine or occult causes of illness in favour of natural causes. Plato recommends solitary confinement for those who "bewitch" people through the "pretence" of summoning spirits (Laws XI), and clearly designates "diviners and fanatics for all kinds of imposture" as atheists and, hence, non-religious in orientation.

[3]   From his work *Natural History* (Bk. 30, I, 1).

occult took on the familiar form that we see, more or less, in operation today. Consequently, it is the centuries just prior to, and since, this period that will be the focus of this chapter.

1. "Occultism" and the Early Church

I will begin by examining the origins of the Church's perspective on the "occult", which is still applied to paranormal ideas by many Christians today. The "occult" is a Christian category that refers to certain magical practices that are not sanctioned by the Church, as opposed to what the Church views as the proper magical (or from the Church's perspective, "religious") practices carried out by God's chosen representatives on earth — namely, the priests.[4] The Christian outlook on the occult appears to have been influenced primarily by biblical scripture, and one particular passage in the Old Testament was (and still is) cited by Christians to explain why the Church is opposed to occult practices and beliefs. The passage states:

> There shall not be found among you [any one] that maketh his son or his daughter to pass through the fire, [or] that useth divination, [or] an observer of times, or an enchanter, or a witch, or a charmer, or a consulter with familiar spirits, or a wizard, or a necromancer. For all that do these things [are] an abomination unto the LORD (*Deuteronomy* 18:10–12).

The roots of this condemnation lies in the struggles that took place in ancient Palestine (c.7th–4th centuries BCE) concerning the establishment of monotheism among a population still practising magical rites — a struggle that continued with the Christian Church as it spread throughout "heathen" populations in Europe.

It is interesting to note that despite biblical passages such as above, the Church was, for many centuries prior to the thirteenth century, not strongly opposed to many practices that were later labelled "occult". The reason for this indifference partly relates to the fact that, earlier, the Church had

---

[4]   The distinction between magical and religious practices is, I contend, somewhat arbitrary.

tended to favour New Testament over Old Testament teachings, and consequently Old Testament passages such as the one above did not hold the same degree of authority. In fact, because many lay people were attracted to a folk-magical view of the cosmos (which they often syncretised with Church doctrine), the Church itself seemed to have tolerated — and, some analysts argue, even promoted — syncretised "magical" ideas during that earlier period in order to win converts (Cavendish 1977:58ff; Flint 1991). Such ideas went by names such as *miracular*, *mirabilia*, *mysterium* or *gratia* — terminology that, according to historian Valerie Flint, allowed the Church to incorporate magical ideas without associating them with the disreputable category of *magia* (Flint 1991:5). However, even magical practices, or *magia* — although generally described by early theologians or "scholastics" as being superstitious (Clark 1997), misguided (Thomas 1971:76), and disreputable (Kors & Peters 1972:29) — were not, at this early stage, considered heretical or Satanic.

By the late medieval period, however, Church theology had undergone a number of significant changes, and one reflection of this was that the Church's position on magic began to harden, as Old Testament passages such as the one quoted earlier started to take on increasing authority. Out of this came a growing condemnation by the Church of magical practices in general. Scholastics such as Gratian (who lived between the eleventh and twelfth centuries) and Aquinas (who lived 1225–1274) now concluded that magic was an "illusion" manifested by Satan.

Initially, the Church's thinking was that most people were generally unaware of such deception, which made them more victims than sinners. Consequently, Gratian (1897 [c.1140]) recommends in his *Decretum* only that magic practitioners be ejected from the parish.[5] At this point in the development of Church theology, Satan was seen as clever

---

[5]   Pt. II, Caus.26, q.5, c.12. The canon in question, *The Canon (Capitulum) Episcopi*, actually derives from an earlier canon, which Gratian and other medieval writers credit to the "Council of Ancyra."

with his magical tricks and sometimes malicious in his motives, but not a threat in the face of the overwhelming supremacy of God and the Church. Indeed, the Church condemned the Cathari (also known as the Albigensians) in 1215 for their suggestion—amongst other things—that Satan posed a serious threat to God's authority (Volz 1997:139). But this relatively assured stance towards the limits of Satan's powers was to diminish over the coming centuries as the Church's perception of magic and Satan changed, and supernatural dualism (that is, God versus Satan) became central to Church doctrine (Russel 1984:185). This change was reflected in the work of Thomas Aquinas and the emerging Aristotelian philosophy that Aquinas and other scholastics espoused (Clark 1997:45).[6]

2. The New Scholastics and the Satanic Threat

When Thomas Aquinas, a devout Dominican friar and university professor, attempted a systematisation of Christian thought in the thirteenth century, the result was that both magic and the devil were firmly established in Church doctrine as being thoroughly diabolical. Aquinas's opinion on this matter was influenced by Aristotle's views regarding the fundamental importance of contraries, such that every principle was seen to have an antithesis: good could not exist without evil, nor could God exist without Satan. Moreover, Aristotelianism held that there was a zero-sum relationship between such opposites, such that the more of one meant the less of the other. This led Aquinas to conclude that God and Satan, the guardians of good and evil respectively, were locked in an eternal struggle over the fate of human souls. As Aquinas wrote in his *Summa Theologica*:

---

[6]   Keith Thomas remarks: "If the clergy tended to be quicker than some laymen in detecting the hand of the Devil, it was as much because of their university training in Aristotelianism as because of their religion" (1971:256).

> [A]ngels are sent by God to guard man. But demons are not
> sent by God: for the demons' intention is the loss of souls;
> whereas God's is the salvation of souls (1922:140).[7]

It was at this time that the Church came to believe that
people sought the powers offered by Satan because of their
desire to "further adultery, theft, murder and like malefices"
(Aquinas 1975:98).[8] Out of this belief emerged a distinction
between magic that was malevolent in intent and aided the
work of the Devil (referred to as *maleficium*), and magic that
simply made use, in a neutral or even beneficial way, of the
inherent occult properties of nature (Kieckhefer 1989:9).
Those accused of being engaged in *maleficium* came to be
seen as a danger to all God-fearing people, rather than being
seen as merely misguided as they had in the past.[9] Neither
were they any longer excused on the basis of their ignorance
of the "Satanic nature" of magical beliefs and practices,
because by this time, the Church had become such a unify-
ing and influential force in European society (in both a religious and a political sense), that the laity were expected to
be aware of the Church's teachings and requirements of
them.[10] The enforcement of a Satanic perspective on the
occult accompanies the consolidation of the Church's control over the populations of Europe.

Even though the Church still felt that people's magical
powers were "very much transacted upon the Stage of
Imagination", it was now held that because it was Satan
who was creating that illusion and was being empowered
by it, the "effects" were "dreadfully real" (Cotton Mather
1868[1692]:393, quoted in Clark 1997:522). Consequently,

---

[7]   Part 1, question 114, article 1, objection 1.
[8]   *Summa Contra Gentiles*, bk. 3, pt. 2, ch. 106.
[9]   Women – held by medieval scholastics to be the epitome of
      uncontrollable tempers and emotion – tended to be those most
      accused of this *maleficium*. In this respect, some analysts (such as
      Barstow 1988; Goodare 1998; Green 1998) have linked the subsequent
      witchcraft persecutions of the sixteenth and seventeenth centuries to
      the oppression of women in society generally.
[10] Even though individual European countries were governed by their
      respective monarchies, the Church assumed substantial influence
      over the political affairs of Europe, particularly in Spain and France.

the "pact" between witch and demon came to be considered "treason" against God and the Church. Being "in league with the devil" through the practice of magic was to become a crime increasingly punishable by death. This practice began with the efforts of Dominican Inquisitors to persuade successive Popes to declare witches "heretics" as opposed to merely "infidels."[11] Although in 1258 Pope Alexander IV refused the Dominicans' requests, telling them that evidence of heresy above and beyond witchcraft practices had to be established before a trial could take place (Kors & Peters 1972:77), later Popes were more open to such requests. Pope John XXII (who held office 1316–1334) is said to have lived in terror of witches, and actively encouraged their persecution. By the fifteenth century, Inquisitions had been set up all over Europe, and increasing numbers of people were being tried and executed for their alleged occult beliefs and practices.

While initially only magic categorised as *maleficium* was considered a punishable offence, this was also soon to change. In Germany, for example, the introduction of the *Constitutio Criminalis Carolina* in 1532 was to see *all* magic declared punishable, although not as yet a capital offence (Scarre 1987:33). The Saxon code, introduced in 1572, however, went to the extreme of declaring all magical practices a capital offence (Scarre 1987:33).

The conditions that led to the progressive hardening of the Church's position on magic, and the spread of such views throughout European society, are still subject to a great deal of debate by historians. Some historians emphasise the tumultuous social changes and calamities of the period, such as plagues, famines and wars, as being contributing factors — for these events were attributed by many at the time to Satan's interference in worldly affairs (Easlea

---

[11] As historian Wlad Godzich explains: "[A]n infidel is someone who can still be converted to the Christian faith, whereas a heretic, we are told by the Repertorium Inquisitorum of Valencia dating from 1494, is someone who has exercised his or her free will against the true faith and must therefore be severely punished for this lapse" (1992:6).

1980:36). Other historians note the impact of the growing trend towards nationhood taking place in Europe at the time. This trend was accompanied by greater efforts by the Church to integrate diverse ethnic groups, and with this came a growing intolerance towards the laity's equally diverse folk customs, particularly any perceived paganistic components (Godzich 1992). Religion and statehood were working hand-in-hand according to this argument. However, we need to look to the spread and coalescence of different philosophical and discursive developments, such as Aristotelianism and the changing views on the imagination, for a sufficient explanation of the change that took place. These changes were certainly evident in the works of Thomas Aquinas. They were also evident in the disputes that surrounded the views of various Renaissance thinkers who did not share the Church's dire view of magic, which we shall now have a closer look at.

3. The Occult as a Renaissance Passion

While the foundations of Church opposition to the occult were laid during the late medieval period, so too were the foundations of support for the modern occult and paranormal "sciences", for not all prominent thinkers during this period viewed the occult as diabolical. This period, popularly known as the Renaissance, spanning the fourteenth and sixteenth centuries, not only saw a revival in Graeco-Roman philosophy with its emphasis on the pre-eminence of the "individual" (Cavendish 1977:97), but also saw a growing fascination amongst certain intellectuals of the time with the occult arts of the ancient Persians, Jews and Greeks.

The occult interests of these new intellectuals were directed primarily toward *magia naturalis* (natural magic) such as alchemy and astrology, which constituted a "high" or "intellectual" form of magic associated with the higher sciences. These Renaissance thinkers set this form of magic apart from the *magia daemonica* (demonic magic) of witchcraft and sorcery (Thomas 1971:228), which was recognised as the "low" or "popular" magic associated with the allegedly uneducated and fantasy-prone populace. They also set their ideas apart from "mythical" ideas concerning dragons, monsters, and other anomalous creatures and phenomena — subjects equally considered to be the product of a vivid imagination that made the "uneducated" susceptible to the acceptance of unfounded ideas. In contrast, the Renaissance occultists saw themselves as exercising a higher form of "Imagination" that complemented their scientific observation of nature.

According to the historian Wlad Godzich, the Imagination was seen as a place of union between the spheres of the subjective world of experience and the objective world of understanding. This was the basis, he argues, of "the pretensions to totality of astrology, of alchemy, or of mysticism" (1992: 21–22). For the German-Swiss physician and alchemist Paracelsus (who lived 1493–1541), the Imagination was the hidden essence or "soul" of nature. Because the Imagination was the "macrocosmic" equivalent of the human imagination, Paracelsus held that those of pure faith could access nature's hidden realms through it. He wrote: "He who is born in imagination finds out the latent forces of Nature" (1894: 307). Further, given that "the body is ruled by the soul" (1894: 310), Paracelsus argued that people could, through the Imagination, even come to influence the material "body" of nature. For Paracelsus, this was the basis for the efficacy of the magical arts.

Hence, the "Imagination" was vested with a pivotal role in both understanding and influencing the workings of the natural world. Indeed, *magia naturalis* was considered to be an area of rational, scientific inquiry into the "hidden" workings of nature. The fifteenth century Italian philosopher Giovanni Pico della Mirandola (who lived 1470–1533) described magic as:

> The sum of natural wisdom, the practical part of natural science, based on exact and absolute understanding of all natural things (1969 [1557–1573], quoted in C. Webster 1982:58).

This combination of mysticism and science was wide-spread during the Renaissance, and often went hand-in-hand with emerging scientific views.[12] Intellectuals such as the inventor of logarithms, John Napier (who lived 1550–1617), the chemist Van Helmont (who lived 1580–1644), and the physicist Isaac Newton (who lived 1642–1727), were all students of alchemy (Cavendish 1997:113), while the astronomer Johannes Kepler (who lived 1571–1630) was deeply interested in astrology, which he defends in his (1610) paper, "Tertius Interveniens" (Mackay 1841).

There was a great deal of interest in all anomalies of nature during this period, not just "magical" ones (Clark 1997:158). For example, English philosopher Francis Bacon (who lived 1561–1626) urged inquiry into "everything … that is in nature new, rare, and unusual" (1898[1620]:496).[13] Bacon, although suspicious of those "deviating instances" that "depend on superstition" and "are found in the works of writers on natural magic" (*ibid*), was not opposed to the possibility of such phenomena existing *per se*. He wrote:

> Nor would we in this history of wonders have superstitious narrations of sorceries, witchcrafts, dreams, divinations, [and the like,] totally excluded, where there is full evidence of the fact (1898[1605]:80).[14]

Such subjects were not considered "supernatural" but, rather, "preternatural".[15] According to historian Stuart Clark:

> In the late medieval system of nature … events were either natural, supernatural, or preternatural. Natural events occurred as the entirely regular, normal, uninterrupted consequences of the laws of nature, and supernatural ones as manifestations of the divine will acting above nature altogether. Preternatural events were within nature but were abnormal and deviant (1997:262).

---

[12] Some theorists contend that occult ideas (such as those of alchemy) lay at the very basis of the development of science (see Ben-Yehuda 1985:95).

[13] *Novum organum* Bk. II, XXIX.

[14] *Advancement of Learning*, bk. II, ch. II.

[15] The term "supernatural" first appeared in Western Christendom in the ninth century (Benson Saler 1977:46).

Included within the "preternatural" category were subjects such as alchemy, folk magic and rare phenomenon such as monstrous births and unusual animal sightings. The Renaissance intellectuals believed that the investigation of such anomalies offered the greatest opportunity to further their understanding of the natural world. As Bacon put it, such investigation might help in the "deeper disclosure of nature" (1898[1605]:81).[16]

But while the intellectuals of the Renaissance saw their interests in high magic as a new and exciting way of understanding reality, the Church merely saw such ideas as a new manifestation of Satan's ongoing influence over the general populace. The imagination was a dangerous place, and a "free mind" that deviated from Scripture (as selectively interpreted by the Church) was susceptible to Satanic manipulation and lies. In fact, together with the social calamities, plagues and wars that also flourished during this period, this burgeoning occult interest led some within the Church to fear that the "end times" spoken of in the biblical book of Revelation were now imminent. It was this type of thinking that, in 1532, led Frederick Mausea of Weissenfeld to conclude, after pondering why more prodigies were appearing in his age than in any previous one, that it must be because his age was witnessing the last days before the apocalypse (Clark 1997:366).

The Church responded to the increased interest in the occult by branding intellectuals interested in "high" magic as heretics — a practice, in fact, that began very early in the Renaissance period. For example, in the fourteenth century an Italian doctor, Peter of Abano, was tried twice by the Inquisition for his works on magic, prophecy and physiognomy (Cavendish 1977:80), while Cecco D'Ascoli, chair of astrology at Bologna University, was condemned by the Inquisition in 1327 for his "occult" views (Cavendish 1977:80). Such persecution was to continue throughout the Renaissance era. In 1486, Pico della Mirandola was declared

---

[16] *Advancement of Learning*, bk. II, ch. II.

a heretic and was imprisoned for a brief time.[17] The Hermetic magician Giordano Bruno was burnt at the stake in 1600 (Jaki 1975:24).[18]

The Church was to find an unlikely ally in its opposition to occult ideas near the end of this period, in the form of a new breed of intellectuals who emerged in the seventeenth century. These intellectuals (who perhaps ironically had developed many of their ideas from the Renaissance intellectuals who were sympathetic to occult ideas) were to play a major role in shaping early opposition to the paranormal. Moreover, like their contemporaries who supported such ideas, and the medieval Church who opposed them, they too are the predecessors of another group of key ideological players in today's paranormal scene, the Skeptics. I will now trace the emergence of this particular brand of opposition from its inception during the period known as the "Enlightenment".

4. The Enlightenment Era and the Birth of the Modern Skeptic

While there had been a progressive scepticism throughout the Renaissance toward supernatural ideas such as angels, demons, spiritual realms and the like, and also toward "low" magical ideas such as witchcraft and fortune-telling, it was not until the Enlightenment period (from the late seventeenth to the late eighteenth century) that many intellectuals came to view "high" magic in a similarly sceptical manner. Most analysts believe that this emerging scepticism was related to a fundamental change in the way reality was perceived, with the occult ontology of the past being displaced by a more materialist understanding of the world. So great was this ontological change considered to be, in fact, that it has come to be referred to as a "watershed" (Koestler 1960). However, as I have already pointed out,

[17] This charge was absolved in 1493 (Pater 1983[1873]:39).
[18] Bruno drew on Polish astronomer Nicolaus Copernicus's ideas to claim that the universe was populated by humanoid beings, and called for a revival of Egyptian religion and its practices of sun worship.

many of the forerunners and "fathers" of Enlightenment science were also highly interested in, if not actual proponents of, occult ideas, so the term "watershed" is somewhat of an exaggeration.

Michel Foucault (1970) offers his own perspective on the changes which led thinkers to initially accept both occult and scientific ideas as equally valid, but then later to rule out the occult. Foucault argues that initial support for occult ideas came from the view that, "Magic ... permitted the decipherment of the world by revealing the secret resemblances beneath its signs" (1970:48).[19] Implicit in the theory of resemblance was the idea that objects and concepts share an occult essence, and in the scientific application of this theory, intellectuals sought to "know how and by what laws they are linked" (Foucault 1970:29). The emphasis that Renaissance intellectuals placed on resemblance in their occult/scientific thinking meant that they came to "accept magic and erudition on the same level", such that an essentially occult practice like divination was not seen as a rival form of knowledge, but rather as "part of the main body of knowledge itself" (Foucault 1970:32).

According to Foucault, a subsequent shift in scientific thinking away from this view of nature as the manifestation of a "language of signs", marked the first real distinction between occult and scientific inquiry of the type identifiable in our modern age. This shift seemed to centre on a redefinition of the relationship between the various "parts" of the natural world. For example, two of the great Enlightenment thinkers, mathematician, astronomer, and physicist Galileo Galilei (who lived 1564–1642), and philosopher René Descartes (who lived 1596–1650), saw the motion of objects as the result, not of some inner occult essence, but of direct mechanical causation, similar to a system of levers and gears (Wilson, F. 1996). Similarly, Francis Bacon (discussed above) was critical of how the resemblance approach had associated objects, entities, substances and events based on

---

[19] Anthropologist James Frazer (1980[1890]) refers to this as "sympathetic magic."

"superficial" and "superstitious" connections rather than on "real and substantial resemblances" (1898[1620]:494).[20] In this new perspective, nature was considered to be an "open" book to be read literally rather than symbolically (Olson 1994:166). Its processes were now seen to be the localised effects of causes and relationships that could be empirically observed and described, rather than the outward "signs" of hidden relationships that might be understood — even manipulated — according to rules of resemblance.

Certainly, this emphasis on mechanical processes and empirical observation can, to a degree, account for the birth of sceptical attitudes towards *some* occult ideas during the Enlightenment period (namely, those occult ideas based on rules of resemblance). But mechanical philosophy fails to account for scepticism toward these and other occult/preternatural ideas after this period, due to the fact that mechanical philosophy had all but fallen out of favour with scientists by the end of the Enlightenment. It is somewhat ironic in this respect, that even though Descartes and Galileo had laid the foundations of modern mechanical physics by rejecting occult thinking in favour of the mechanical model, it was left to physicist and mathematician Isaac Newton to explain the causes of such motion in terms accepted by scientists today. Further, Newton did so using a theory of gravitation that was based on Kepler's ideas of attractive force — ideas that Galileo had rejected for being too occult (Easlea 1980:89)! Not surprisingly, Newton's ideas themselves were to prove too magical for a number of his mechanically minded contemporaries. Philosopher and mathematician Gottfried Wilhelm Leibniz (who lived 1646–1716), for example, attacked his theory for "going back to qualities which are occult" (1934[1702–3]:163).

Other historians point to the effects of the rise of empirical philosophy as the precursor to widespread scepticism of the occult. However, although empiricism (unlike mechanical philosophy) did survive relatively intact beyond the

[20] *Novum organum*, bk. II, ch. XXVII.

Enlightenment, there was nothing inherent in empiricism itself that actually ruled out occult ideas. Even the "father" of empiricism, Francis Bacon, had, as I have already noted, an interest "in what cases, and how far effects attributed to superstition, depend upon natural causes" (1898[1605]: 80).[21] To Bacon, an acknowledgment and understanding of preternatural phenomena might possibly extend the boundaries of an empirical understanding of the world. His only problem with the idea of occult influences was that, apart from the "practice of such things" by "criminals" (*ibid*), he was not willing to concede their presence without solid empirical evidence. Knowledge-construction, Bacon argued, should be a process of working upwards from an empirical foundation, not downward from metaphysical speculation or rumour. Although later empiricists such as David Hume were highly sceptical of occult claims, Bacon's own open-mindedness suggests that empirical philosophy may not have been intrinsically opposed to, or incompatible with, occult ideas (particularly more empirical-oriented preternatural ideas).

We need to look beyond these particular philosophies to identify the factors that influenced this early scepticism and helped sustain it in the post-Enlightenment period. One such factor was the demotion in the status of the imagination that occurred during the Enlightenment. The historian Ioan Couliano notes:

> ... the transition from a society dominated by magic to a predominantly scientific society is explicable primarily by a change in the imaginary (1987:xviii).

This demotion of the imagination is a development that we can trace back to the late medieval Church, and their tendency to dismiss many people's claims of magical powers on the grounds that they were imaginary. In taking this position, the Church was making a firm distinction between the factual status of reality and the non-factual status of the imagination (the occult being associated with the latter). The Church's reasoning, as I explained earlier, was that,

[21] *Advancement of Learning*, bk. II, ch. II.

with the exception of miracles granted by God, people could not violate God's created order. To the extent that they believed they could, such ideas were seen to be either the result of wishful thinking or an illusion created by a mischievous Satan – both being factors that were associated with an active imagination.

Although the Church itself was to become less sceptical of such claims during the Inquisition (when, as I previously explained, they considered certain aspects of the occult real enough to have alleged practitioners executed), intellectuals of the Renaissance period continued the Church's earlier scepticism of the more "base" preternatural ideas and the "lower" imagination that gave rise to them, even as they embraced the "higher" forms of magic and the "higher" Imagination. By the time of the Enlightenment, however, even the "higher" Imagination had fallen into disrepute.

One of the first Enlightenment thinkers to demote the Imagination was Descartes, who initially seems to have had a strong interest in magic but later became disillusioned and sceptical (Keefer 1996), claiming to have seen through the "promises" of alchemists, the "predictions" of astrologers, and the "impostures" of magicians (1968[1637]:32). He came to see a clear division between the "subjective" imagination and the "objective" reality of the physical world, and believed that the imagination should not play a leading role in attempts to understand the objective world.

Bacon, although intrigued by the possibility of preternatural phenomena, was another Enlightenment thinker who criticised the employment of *vis imaginativa* in inquiries into the natural world (Easlea 1980:127). Bacon was particularly critical of the way that the "school of Paracelsus" and the "pretenders to natural magic" had "almost made the force and apprehension of the imagination equal to the power of [religious] faith, and capable of working miracles" (1898[1605]:176).[22] Rather, to Bacon, the imagination tended to be error-prone – prone, for example,

---

[22] *Advancement of Learning*, Bk. IV, Ch. III.

to "impute accidents and natural operations to witchcraft" (1826[1627]: 491).[23] As Godzich remarks:

> In modernity, banished from its mediating role ... [the Imagination] will be reduced to a combinatory or hallucinatory function, and the phantasm will cease to be the subject of experience to become the object of mental alienation, of magic visions, in short of psychological turbulence if not outright trouble (1992:21–22).

Indeed, the real danger that the intellectuals of the Enlightenment saw in an "undisciplined" imagination was the contribution that they believed it was making to the social ills of the time, such as the "witch craze" and other "irrational" social disturbances. Such Rationalist sentiments were now becoming commonplace even in the population at large. Foucault (1980[1978]) argues that following the calamities of the seventeenth century (such as overpopulation, crime and the great plagues), the wider society began to adopt an increasingly rationalised outlook. Societies were now becoming too large and unmanageable to be completely administered by a central authority such as the Church or Monarchy, so people were increasingly expected to not only take charge of their own lives (their health, moral conduct, etc), but to do so in a practical, "rational" manner. This approach was based on the same spirit of practicality that dictated the emerging sciences, and conformity to it was deemed essential to the maintenance of social order. Foucault may have exaggerated the effect of these discourses, but in a generalised way, the discourses to which he refers certainly began to play a role in a new mentality among governing authorities that changed the societal landscape of post- Renaissance Europe.

In such a climate, the occult, because of its association with a now discredited imagination, did not fair well. In fact, philosophers of the period such as David Hume (who lived 1711–1776) and Immanuel Kant (who lived 1724–1804) directly linked science and its exclusion of

---

[23] *Sylva sylvarum*, Century X.

"pseudoscientific" ideas to the very pursuit of moral and civic order.[24] Hume, for example, wrote that "superstition is an enemy to civil liberty" (1963[1741]:250) and "produces the most cruel disorders in human society" (1963[1741]:249). Similar associations continued to be made by later thinkers. For example, in his (1841) *Memoirs of Extraordinary Popular Delusions*, Charles Mackay indicates something of a "moral panic" with regard to the popular interest in prophecies, astrology, fortune telling, witch-hunting and other fantastic phenomena. He wrote:

> [M]illions of people become simultaneously impressed with one delusion, and run after it, until their attention is caught by some new folly more captivating than the first (1932:xix, quoted in Goode & Ben-Yehuda 1994:1).

It seems that much of the early Rationalists' wariness towards paranormal ideas was (and still is) based on this perceived association between such ideas and irrational "passions".[25] In contrast, supernatural ideas promoted by Christianity and other organised religions were seen to be relatively harmless. Those ideas were long-practiced traditions with established canons of thought that did not seem to invoke the same irrationality and fear-driven behaviour in the populace (with the notable exception of the Church-incited beliefs that underlay the "witch-craze").

In the post-Enlightenment era, then, magic and other anomalous phenomena, associated as they were with the imagination, increasingly came to epitomise the irrational Other, much as magic had come to epitomise the satanic Other in the Church's world view. However, while the Church viewed occult belief as a moral threat to the well being of the cosmos and the early Enlightenment intellectuals viewed such belief as a threat to the epistemological

---

[24] Kant associates alchemy and astrology with "pseudoscience" in his (1950[1783]) *Prolegomena to Any Future Metaphysics*.
[25] It is useful to relate this discourse on "irrational passions" to Mikhail Bakhtin's distinction between the grotesque, uncontrolled "body" of the populace and the refined, controlled "body" of the elite (see Fiske 1993:188 for an application of Bakhtin's concept of the "monstrous" to the paranormal dispute).

foundations of science, post-Enlightenment intellectuals tended to view the occult more as a threat to the well being of the social order. So while Bacon, back in the early Enlightenment period, had only rejected testimonial support for preternatural ideas, his successors rejected the very ideas themselves, because of the "irrational" processes that they had come to represent.

We can see, then, that even though the occult's status, in terms of its objective validity, was progressively diminishing throughout the seventeenth and eighteenth centuries, many people continued to see it as a threat to society, regardless of whether it was viewed as real or not. For example, the French law condemning sorcery (which carried with it the implication that such practices were real) was annulled by Louis XIV's royal ordinance of 1682, although the practice was still considered enough of a social threat to warrant replacing that law with one condemning the *pretence* of possessing magical powers (Scarre 1987:54).

In terms of the severity of State-sanctioned punishment for such offences, by the end of the eighteenth century things were beginning to soften considerably. The emerging Humanism of this period was one the main factors that contributed to this change, and one of its effects was to redefine the value placed on human life, making it "more and more difficult to apply the death penalty" (Foucault 1980[1978]:138). The growing authority of empirical discourse also played its part in altering the State's views on punishment, for empiricism demanded that accusations should be backed by credible evidence rather than rumour and hearsay. The "law of proportion" that empirical discourse promoted also may have impacted on the sentencing process (Foucault 1979). For example, the State no longer considered the torture and execution of suspected witches to be a "measured" response to the crimes for which they were being accused, particularly in the absence of proof of their ill effects in the growing climate of scepticism.[26]

5. The Changing Views of the Church

So what did the Church make of this emerging scepticism towards magic? Although it might seem somewhat ironic given their long persecution of the occult, theologians were initially opposed to any questioning of its reality. Even King James VI/I (who lived 1566–1625) endeavoured to "resolve the doubting harts of many" that "such assaultes of Sathan are most certainly practised" (1597:xi). Indeed, some among the faithful were starting to question, and would before too long make their doubts public. In his 1695 work, *The World Bewitched*, the Dutch pastor Balthasar Bekker (1634–1698) disputed the existence of witches and condemned those clergy who persecuted individuals accused of witchcraft. Bekker was expelled from his church.

It seems the problem for the Church was that in summarily dismissing witchcraft, people might also reject the reality of Satan, and possibly by extension, the reality of God. These were, after all, the early days of atheism – which was a threat judged by some to be even greater to the Church than any threat posed by the occult, or rather, was viewed as another one of Satan's tricks. Not surprisingly, then, the Church also opposed many of the scientific views that accompanied scepticism – views that they believed fostered atheism (and supported Satan) by promoting a reality not reliant on divine causation.[27] One example of such

---

[26] This view was particularly prevalent in countries such as England where, according to social analyst Elliott Currie (1974), the legal system served more as a mediatory mechanism for resolving interpersonal grievances than as a moral sanctioning body.

[27] On the other hand, the Church tolerated any scientific ideas that seemed to confirm their views. For example, thirteenth century Franciscan philosopher Roger Bacon was amongst the first to assert that the Christian faith could be confirmed through experimental knowledge of nature. It was even believed by some theologians that by investigating witches, it was possible to investigate Satan himself, and by investigating Satan, they could, in turn, investigate God (Shermer 1997:106). As King James VI/1 put it: "For since the Devill

opposition can be seen in the fate of Galileo Galilei who, in 1611, came to the attention of the Inquisition for his Copernican views. Galileo was eventually imprisoned for heresy and later placed under house arrest until his death in 1642. In light of Galileo's fate, Descartes delayed publication of his own cosmological views, fearing that he too might be tried for heresy (Tolbert 1999).

Later, however, the Church's attitude to occult/magical beliefs began to become more sceptical, and those holding such beliefs came to be seen as less of a threat. The emergence of Protestantism in the seventeenth century, and its subsequent influence on Church thinking, seems to have played a significant role in bringing about this change of attitude. Although the witch-hunts had dramatically increased during the period immediately following the Protestant Reformation—with Protestants being just as enthusiastic as their Catholic counterparts in encouraging this persecution (Cavendish 1977:125)—in the longer term, however, Protestant influence seems to have hastened the demise of the witch-hunts.

The changes in Church attitudes toward the occult began with calls by Martin Luther (who lived 1483–1546) and Jean Calvin (who lived 1509–1564) for a return to the primacy of New Testament texts over Church tradition. Calvin pointed to passages in the bible that suggested that the cosmic drama between God and Satan had already been divinely scripted, with Satan and his human agents already doomed to ultimate defeat (1960[1559]:177).[28] This was a shift away from the Church's zero-sum view of evil (which posited that the more there was of one contrary, the less there was of the other), and meant that Christians were alleviated of the need to directly combat Satan and his human agents.[29] All that was now required of people was that they follow the

is the verie contrarie opposite to God, there can be no better way to know God, then by the contrarie" (1597:55).

[28]   Bk. I, ch. XIV, 18.
[29]   Stuart Clark also notes the influence of Galilean physics, which emphasised absolute quantity rather than contraries as the basic structure of the natural world (1997:47).

path of Christ and not be tempted by evil (Calvin 1960[1559]:309ff) — a belief that shifted the focus away from the enemy without to the enemy within, with temptation rather than demonic magic becoming the greatest threat.[30]

To avoid temptation and attain salvation, Protestantism encouraged a work ethic, for hard work was seen to instil moral discipline, and it was discipline that kept a person on God's path and Satan at bay. This emphasis on self-discipline was the same discourse that was so important in constituting the new social and scientific worldviews of the time (Weber 1930), and coupled with growing Humanist sentiments amongst more noble-minded Christians, Church opposition to the occult began to soften. This change was reflected in the rapid demise of the witch-hunts towards the end of the seventeenth century.[31]

6. The Paranormal Debate in the Post-Enlightenment Era

Despite the marginalisation of preternatural/occult ideas by scientific and religious circles during the Enlightenment, in the following centuries such ideas were to find new support bases amongst various preternatural/occult circles, and, more generally, amongst the general populace. Much of this support came from post-Enlightenment challenges to science's banishment of magic and the Imagination. The most notable challenge in this respect came from a movement known as Romanticism, which arose in the late eighteenth and early nineteenth centuries.[32] Various societies with elements of occult/mystical philosophies also became

---

[30] Calvin, Bk. II, ch. IV, 1ff.

[31] Occult historian Richard Cavendish argues, however, that the conspiratorial fears that underlay the Church's persecution of suspected witches were, in the eighteenth and nineteenth centuries, simply transferred (minus the Satanic association) to conspiratorial fears regarding secret societies (1977:141).

[32] Psychologist Brian Mackenzie has argued that both the Romantic Movement and psychic research emerged from the "sense of alienation of human experience from the world of scientific fact" (1987:597).

popular during this era, such as the Rosicrucians, Illuminati and Freemasons.

Support for the preternatural/occult also came from intellectuals keen to find a "home" for preternatural phenomena within orthodox science. The theory of animal magnetism proposed by German physician Franz Mesmer towards the end of the eighteenth century, was one such attempt to relate scientific principles to occult ideas, although orthodox medical practitioners at the time rejected the "mesmeric" effect as a "delusion" produced by "the force of imagination" (Flood 1845, quoted in Parssinen 1979:109).[33]

While post-Enlightenment science maintained a firm distinction between the "occult" and "science", it is clear that, as Keith Thomas points out: "common people never formulated a distinction between magic and science" (1971:668). This perspective raises some doubt about just how deep-seated or durable the "Rationalisation" of the general populace actually was during the Enlightenment era. At the very least, it would seem that Rationalisation may not have taken the form that sceptical intellectuals promoting a materialist worldview might have hoped. Indeed, the preternatural seems to have enjoyed a great deal of popularity with the public of this era, largely due to its sensationalist appeal. As Clark observes:

> Printed collections of natural secrets and wonders were … aimed at the private pleasure of readers and at their ability to hold an eloquent and amusing conversation in polite circles (1997:267).

---

[33] Mesmer's theory held that a form of magnetism pervaded the universe, which certain individuals could access and manipulate. Alleged powers such as clairvoyance and thought-transference were attributed to this all-pervasive force.   Although the intellectual community was not receptive to Mesmer's ideas, his inquiries into hypnosis were later to find some legitimacy in the psychological community through the work of Sigmund Freud (Hall & Grant 1978). It is worth noting, however, that, according to renowned psychologist and Freud's close associate, Carl Jung, Freud himself once described occultism as "the black tide of mud" (Jung 1961:150).

Catering to the public's appetite for such material, Robert Cross Smith began publishing a weekly astrological almanac in 1824, and as a result, has been credited by some modern historians as being "the founder of modern popular astrological journalism" (Howe 1967:29, quoted in Cavendish 1977:151).

Further evidence of the increasing appeal of occult-related subjects to the general public was the popularity of the Spiritualist movement, born out of a groundswell of popular interest in clairvoyance, telepathy, necromancy, channelling and hypnotism in the mid-nineteenth century. Historian R. Laurence Moore (1977) writes about the widespread interest in these subjects:

> Often in the public eye during the nineteenth century, they were another source of entertainment for at least two generations of Americans who liked to explore puzzling situations and gathered to witness anything billed as out of the ordinary (1977:5–6).

According to Moore, Spiritualism was for many people something akin to "good theater" (1977:5), and Spiritualist *séances* tended to be set up as spectacles, "designed to give the audience a full sense of participation" (1977:16).

In contrast to the general public's seemingly fad-like interest in paranormal-related subjects, a core group of more committed supporters began to form in the aftermath of the initial Spiritualist "explosion".[34] This group, drawn largely from intellectual circles, was typically composed of religiously inclined individuals seeking a unity between religion (including Eastern religions), Spiritualism and scientific perspectives. They began to form societies dedicated to this goal, perhaps the best known being the Theosophical Society, which was founded by Madame Blavatsky in New York in 1875. Her multi-volume work titled *The Secret Doctrine* (1952), initially published in 1888, became the organi-

---

[34] Social analyst R.G.A. Dolby remarks: "[I]t is common for popular deviant sciences to die away rapidly as fashionable discussion turns to other things. However, in the wake of a phase of fashionable interest, a proportion of those exposed may acquire a more lasting interest" (1979:20).

sation's "bible," and the Theosophical Society quickly expanded into an international organisation with branches in cities throughout the world.

The Society for Psychical Research was another group that grew out of the Spiritualist movement of the nineteenth century. It was founded in England in 1882 (and the American Society for Psychical Research was founded soon after in 1885) by members who were frustrated by scientists' refusal to embrace religious ideas as an integral aspect of science, and by the orthodox Church's refusal to embrace science as an integral aspect of religious knowledge (Gauld 1968:49–56). While not all Society for Psychical Research members were advocates of the paranormal (some members, in fact, were quite sceptical of paranormal claims), other members, who had a dual faith in the validity of both science and religion, believed that if the existence of psychic phenomena could be scientifically demonstrated, then this would be akin to demonstrating the survival of the spirit beyond physical death (thereby authenticating one of Christianity's central doctrines).

There was, however, a progressive stripping away of the religious component from organisations such as the Society for Psychical Research and its American counterpart from the 1930s onwards, as psychic researchers sought to gain academic credibility in an increasingly atheistic scientific community. During this period there was an increasing emphasis on *experimental* psychic research (such as the study of ESP and psychokinesis under controlled, experimental conditions).[35] Meanwhile, the more religiously oriented psychic proponents went elsewhere, establishing Christian paranormal societies such as the Churches' Fellowship of Psychical and Spiritual Studies, which was established in England in 1953, and the Spiritual Frontiers

---

[35] Parapsychologist J.B. Rhine (who lived 1895–1980) of Duke University, Durham, North Carolina, was the main proponent of this approach, which was to receive a great boost in status (or so it seemed at the time) when, in 1969, the Parapsychological Society that he founded (in 1957) was accepted by the American Association for the Advancement of Science as a member organisation (Alcock 1981:5).

Fellowship International, which was established in the United States in 1956.

Many other paranormal organisations and societies began to spring up from the mid-twentieth century onwards. The Fortean Society founded in 1931, for example, examined any phenomena perceived to be of a preternatural nature, such as geophysical oddities, unidentified flying objects (UFOs) and spontaneous combustion, in addition to ghosts and other psychic phenomena normally studied by parapsychologists. Interest in UFOs (initially referred to as "flying saucers") became particularly widespread after the Second World War, and numerous "flying saucer cults" emerged from the 1950s onwards.

Another upsurge of public interest in magical, occult and paranormal phenomena — particularly mysticism — occurred in the late 1960s, in what became known as the "hippie" movement. This movement was essentially a reaction, particularly from the youth of the day, to Western materialism, technological dependency and conservative political values. More liberated attitudes to sexuality, drug experimentation, interest in rock music, "natural" lifestyles, spirituality and opposition to the Vietnam War, all served as focal points for the movement. Acceptance of occult ideas, particularly those associated with Eastern and nativistic mystical and religious philosophies, were part-and-parcel of the alternative worldview. This interest in the "spiritual" (with mystical/occult associations) later became a key element in the New Age movement that arose during the 1970s.

From the late 1970s onwards, more conservative sections of Western society increasingly became fascinated with paranormal ideas, their interest spurred on by Hollywood blockbuster films such as *Close Encounters of the Third Kind* (1977), *Poltergeist* (1982), and *ET — the Extra-terrestrial* (1982). While preternatural/occult ideas have been a favourite subject in popular Western literature since the Renaissance, films such as the above were distinctive in their openly "political" treatment of the struggle between Skeptic and Proponent — a treatment that, more often than not, portrayed the sceptical position as being in error. Pro-paranormal perspectives presented in these movies received further support from popular documentary/expose-type television shows such as *In Search Of* (1976–82). The 1990s were to see a steady increase in the public's appetite for such paranormal-related media content, an interest that was catered to, for example, by the television series *The X-Files* (1993–2002) and more "expose" type programs such as *Sightings* (1992) and *Unsolved Mysteries* (1988–99).[36] In the new millennium, American television serials such as Charmed (1998–2006), *Medium* (2005–) and *Supernatural* (2005–) continue to be popular, while J.K. Rowling's *Harry Potter* book series has attracted a large readership and has been turned into an immensely successful motion picture series.

As public interest in the paranormal and occult has been perceived to grow, efforts by Skeptics to counter its credibility have likewise increased. The Committee for the Scientific Investigation of Claims for the Paranormal (CSICOP) was established in 1976 with the express aim of arresting what was perceived to be an "alarming growth" in paranormal interest (Kurtz 1976). We have already seen how the seeds of such scepticism were being sown as far back as the Enlightenment, and the modern-day Skeptics continued to counter extraordinary claims and the "tyranny of unreason" with calls for "rationality" and "convincing evidence" in much the same way their predecessors did. In the contemporary paranormal debate, CSICOP and similar Skeptic organisations have come to constitute the main sceptical "front" against popular support for paranormal ideas.

Conclusion

The history of the emergence of preternatural/occult/paranormal positions in Western society, and their changing for-

---

[36] During my research, when asked by various people about the subject of my study, I found the easiest explanation was to tell them that I was studying people who are interested in *"X-files* stuff." This nearly always brought a nod of instant recognition and interest.

tunes over time, reveals that the general discursive configuration that characterises the contemporary debate was, more or less, set in place by the seventeenth century. By this time, as we have seen, the basic divisions between what were considered valid perceptions of reality and what were not had been more or less established, and the stage was set for ideological disputes over these divisions that have endured to the present-day.[37]

I have explained how various discourses have defined paranormal ideas at various points in time as "occult", "*magia*", the "preternatural", and so on—categories that were often demonised within religious and scientific circles by associating these ideas and practices with the unruly aspects of existence (such as Satan, the imagination, and the gullible masses). In fact, although individuals and groups who demonised the occult came and went, there were always new opponents to take their place and to reproduce the occult's demonised status, even while other discourses (such as the artistic imagination of the Renaissance) were giving legitimacy to it.

One line of argument that could explain such a trend is that it was primarily power-interests that determined the level of acceptance of occult/preternatural ideas. Pluralist and Marxist-oriented analysts might argue, for example, that the history of conflict over the paranormal has been largely determined by the changing balance of power-rela-

---

[37] The arbitrary nature of these boundaries can perhaps be better appreciated when it is realised that many phenomena that are today taken for granted were, in the past, rejected as ludicrous. For example, prior to the late 18th century, scientists rejected the possibility that rocks fell from the sky ("rocks" that are now referred to as meteorites) and ridiculed witnesses of such falls and those intellectuals who took such claims seriously (Westrum 1978). Conversely, many established scientific "facts" and theories of past eras have since fallen by the wayside. As sociologists Barry Barnes and Donald MacKenzie remark: "if history is any guide, most currently accepted scientific knowledge can expect eventually to be rejected in favour of some alternative, or more precise, conceptualisation." They add: "Science is both a major source of rejected knowledge and the main instrument of its rejection" (1979:49).

tions between groups attempting to maintain a monopoly on the "truth", with the various views on the occult being little more than hegemonic tools in this greater struggle. In one scenario of this kind, the Church can be seen to have embraced occult ideas when it suited them (that is, when it increased its popularity amongst the diverse ethnic groups who held "magical" beliefs), but to have discarded them once they had gained a firm control over the populace (thereby ensuring their authority as the sole guardians of the supernatural realm).[38] Thereafter, breakaway sects and groups who embraced occult/magical ideas did so because they saw them as ideologies of resistance to the Church's monopoly on knowledge and the Church's control over society. The same kind of perspective can be applied to the scientific establishment's initial acceptance, and later rejection, of preternatural/occult ideas. In this respect, occult ideas served as a symbol of subversion — at first welcomed by those seeking to challenge the dominant ideology, then opposed once the challengers themselves gained dominance.

It is doubtful, however, that hegemonic motives were the principal factor in either the Skeptics' and Christian fundamentalists' long-term opposition to, or non-mainstream groups embracement of, preternatural/occult ideas.[39] Rather, the issue is more one of discourse than of hegemony. I have shown, for example, that opposition from the Church to preternatural/occult ideas rose considerably during the thirteenth and fourteenth centuries — a period during which the occult did not pose much of a hegemonic threat to the Church at all. Rather, the thirteenth-fourteenth century demonisation seemed to occur in tandem with a

---

[38] Hence, the shift from viewing occult practitioners as infidels to viewing them as heretics.

[39] In this book I use the term "mainstream" interchangeably with terms such as "dominant" or "orthodox." Such terms have come under attack by some analysts. However, I agree with social analyst R. Laurence Moore who states: "Historical mainstreams, however vague, do exist, and in the course of their careers people do come to believe that they are more or less in or out of them" (1977:xii).

growing theological emphasis on the threat posed by Satan, such as was evident in the writings of Aquinas. In other words, the demonisation coincided with changing *ontological* considerations, which were themselves largely the result of discursive changes (such as the influence of Aristotelianism and a changing epistemological view of the imagination).

Similarly, later opposition to preternatural/occult ideas from intellectuals coincided with discursive changes, including the post-Enlightenment demotion of the imagination, a growing fear of the "passions" of the populace, and the Humanist backlash against the persecution and public hysteria of the "witch craze" era, with which preternatural/occult ideas had become associated. Like the Church's rejection of the occult, scientific rejection seems to have been more an effort to expunge the occult element within its own ranks and within the wider social fabric for the sake of preserving the "proper order of things" than an effort to stamp out hegemonic rivals. While Skeptics would emphasise that Enlightenment thinkers gradually came to see the 'light' regarding the falsity of paranormal ideas, the view presented here is one of increasing influence of a particular notion of responsible thinking that was (rightly or wrongly) seen as antithetical to occult ideas.

To the degree that hegemonic motives were a factor in Church and scientific opposition to the preternatural/occult, this was related to the *ontological* importance that the Church and scientific establishment attached to their authority to guard against error. Historian Geoffrey Scarre makes this point in relation to the Church, when he writes:

> The Church's fear and loathing of religious dissent undoubtedly owed much to the thought that dissenters, or heretics, were *weakening its power to combat the Devil*, and were indeed servants of the great enemy (emphasis mine) (1987:15).

Apart from the Church's desire to stamp out occult supporters in order to protect the cosmic order, they were also trying to protect the social order—indeed, it was through the divine order that society was blessed. In this respect, there is a sense in which the demonisation of the preternatural/occult can be seen to have circulated beyond religious and scientific discourses as part of an discourse of responsible governance that associated the preternatural/occult with anti-social thinking. Once this notion had become ingrained in an discourse of responsible governance, anyone who took up a position of intellectual and/or moral authority in society felt somewhat obliged to subscribe to the view that those who held preternatural/occult ideas constituted a threat to the social order.

Note that in presenting this historical overview, I have not addressed the histories of individual preternatural/occult subjects that became implicated within this discursive configuration. Rather, my interest has been in the emergence of the broader categories of knowledge. This broader focus is in keeping with my main objective, namely, to show how wider discursive processes have been the key factor in constituting the dispute over the paranormal category as a whole. Generally speaking, however, individual subjects came to be labelled "preternatural" or "occult" due to their association, however tenuous, with the imagination or with magic. For example, historian Terry Parssinen (1979) argues that one of the reasons that Mesmerism was rejected by the medical profession was because its practitioners were seen to resemble magico-religious healers and, as is clear from a report produced by the British Medical Association in 1891 (see Parssinen 1979), it was only when hypnotism was distanced from occult theories of animal magnetism and its exhibitionist style of practice that medical professionals took it more seriously.[40]

Conversely, alien abduction researcher Budd Hopkins points out that UFOs were initially seen in the late 1940s as a legitimate physical anomaly worthy of investigation which had little to do with "exotic" spaceman theories (Hopkins 2000:216). Indeed, the United States Air Force carried out an

---

[40] Similarly, sociologist Ron Westrum (1978) contends that the phenomenon of meteorites was initially rejected because of its association with myths concerning supernatural stones that fell during lightning strikes.

ongoing investigation into UFO reports, including the well-known "Project Blue Book" (Swords 2000). It was only when the contactee movement emerged in the 1950s with its occult associations (including claims that extraterrestrials could engage in telepathic communication with contactees), that the UFO area became associated with other discredited paranormal topics and fell into disrepute (Clark 2000). Not surprisingly, Hopkins sees little association between UFO research proper and medieval occult ideas (Hopkins 2006: personal communication).

My task in the next chapter will be to examine how, and to what extent, the various positions taken in the contemporary paranormal debate draw from, and even sustain, the discursive influences that have fuelled the paranormal debate throughout history. As we proceed, we will see how the historical processes examined in this chapter have thoroughly informed the ideological positions taken by contemporary players in the paranormal debate.

Before we proceed with a more contemporary analysis of the debate, however, there is one final point to note in regard to the history of the preternatural/occult/paranormal, namely, that the main ideological parties involved in the contemporary debate — paranormal proponents, Skeptics and Christians — all have their own versions of how their outlook (and the outlooks of their opponents) have emerged historically, and those perspectives would not necessarily accord with the ones I have presented in this chapter.

In fact, my own analysis is admittedly biased in this respect, just as I explained in the previous chapter any social analysis inevitably is. For example, my version of the basis for popular interest in the paranormal did not take into account the following factors that participants themselves might see as relevant, namely: (1) an increasing spiritual maturity in humanity (a New Age perspective); (2) a strengthening of Satan's dominion (a Christian conservative/ fundamentalist perspective); (3) an increase in paranormal experiences among the population and a growing willingness to report them (a scientific-oriented paranormal perspective), or (4) a rising tide of Irrationalism or a failure of the education system (a Skeptical perspective). Instead, what I have attempted to do in this chapter is to examine the emergence of discourses that I feel underlie such perspectives, and in so doing, I realise that my account may have undermined these alternative perspectives to some degree. Such are the biases inherent in any account.

Chapter 3

The Players in the Contemporary Debate

Introduction

The contemporary paranormal debate takes place in a dynamic arena of diverse participant types, positions and fields. But the major players and their ideational positions are fundamentally derivations of the discursively based historical positions outlined in the previous chapter. Consequently, an argument that I intend to develop in this chapter is that the same "politics of truth" that drove the occult/magical disputes of old, continues to drive many key aspects of the paranormal debate today.

1. Supporter and Opponent Positions

A common, but in my view overly simplistic, portrayal by analysts of the contemporary paranormal debate in terms of its main discursive players is that of "Believers" versus "Skeptics." To be fair, participants themselves tend to make a division along somewhat similar lines, although some paranormal proponents would not identify with the term "Believer", because it is seen to indicate a non-scientific, belief-based acceptance of a paranormal reality, which is not how most see their own position (hence the term "proponent" will be employed to refer to these participants). Some paranormal proponents would also consider the term "Skeptic" to be something of a misnomer in its application to those who oppose paranormal ideas — their point being that true scepticism implies a critical, open-minded inquiry, in contrast to what they see as the close-minded, cynical approach of many of their opponents. Hess, commenting on the way these terms have become "somewhat politicized" (1993:190), remarks that certain parapsychologists have suggested to him that he should refer to Skeptics as "critics", because, he explains, "parapsychologists see themselves as the true skeptics." Along similar lines, Caroline Watt, a parapsychologist at Edinburgh University, explained to me why she prefers to use the term "counter-advocates" rather than "Skeptics" to describe parapsychology's opponents:

> With sceptical, it should mean, if you look in the dictionary, "questioning." That means you look at both sides of the evidence, both sides of the question. Now I would draw a distinction between sceptical and counter-advocate, where someone has a belief position. You have people who believe in psi, or people who disbelieve in psi. And quite often, people who call themselves Skeptics are actually counter-advocates (1996: personal interview).

I will have more to say about these disputes over terminology later. But nomenclature aside, the Proponent-Skeptic dichotomy clearly constitutes a discernible line of division within the contemporary paranormal debate.

The Proponent-Skeptic dichotomy should not be seen, however, as a clear-cut one, for the division between those who oppose and those who support paranormal ideas is somewhat arbitrary, with participants in the paranormal debate straddling a continuum between absolute acceptance of paranormal phenomena and absolute rejection. Even some Skeptics have an open mind (to some degree) about the possible existence of some paranormal phenomena, as I will explain in more detail shortly. There are also participants who waver between the two opposing positions (that is, from Proponent to Skeptic, and vice versa), both in the short-term and over the longer term. Hence, I agree with Collins and Pinch, who, in their study of psychic researchers, declare:

> "Believer" and "sceptic" will be used here to apply to very loose social categories: They are not psychological traits.

> Thus, their use is not meant to rule out the possibility that
> members of one category or another might now and again
> have moments, or even days, of doubt about their beliefs
> (1982:45).

The fluidity of the Proponent-Skeptic categories itself creates a degree of tension within the debate, where we see not only conflict between polarised ideational positions, but a disagreement over where the boundaries of those positions actually lie. This point will become clearer as my examination of the paranormal debate progresses. The distinction between Skeptic and Proponent positions is further blurred by the diversity that exists within Skeptic and Proponent camps, where we find a variety of fields and participant types. My task in the remainder of this chapter will be to outline the essential characteristics of the main participant types, and show how they are located in different ways on the Proponent-Skeptic continuum.

2. Participant Types

There are a number of different participant types involved in the paranormal debate, each taking a rather unique approach to the paranormal subject. The following description of a crop circle tour I participated in during the course of my research is a good illustration of some of these types. The bus tour was organised as part of a crop circle conference I attended in Glastonbury, and it took us to a number of crop circles in the southwest of England.

One of the participant types I identified early in the tour was the "New Age" oriented enthusiast—recognisable by the particular activities in which they engaged during the tour. For example, after a short walk up a hillside to the first circle formation, several people seated themselves on the ground in the formation's centre, adopted a meditating posture and proceeded to "tune in" to the site's "spiritual energy". The previous evening, my guesthouse hostess in Glastonbury had told me of her own method of getting "in tune with the circle's energy." She told me that I should walk around a formation in the direction of the swirl, which she interpreted as a metaphor for "going with the flow" in one's life generally. If I did so, she explained, I would feel the energy emanating from the formation and be "one" with the earth's energy. Both my guesthouse hostess and the meditators at the crop circle site represented to me (and possibly would have identified themselves as) the New Age element within the scene.

I followed the contours of the formation as my guesthouse hostess had instructed, but I did not feel any energy. Was it just me? Not according to the readings recorded by one of the tour's Dutch participants, whose hand-held microwave emissions-detector registered nothing either. Meanwhile, our two tour guides were busy explaining some of the scientific characteristics of the formation. They noted how the crop stems had not been broken, which they saw as an indication that the wheat had not been crushed, as one would expect if hoaxers had created the formation. The most likely explanation, in their opinion, was that the crop had flattened of its own accord, probably in response to a high-energy emission from above (possibly from a UFO) or from below (possibly due to Earth "energy"). They also noted how the nodes on the stem were heat damaged, which reinforced their "microwave-emission" theory. Both my Dutch companion with the microwave detector and our tour guides represented to me the "scientific-oriented" paranormal proponent.

Another participant type also became evident on our arrival at this crop circle, when we encountered a farmhand sitting on the fence with a mobile phone pressed against his ear. He instructed us to wait, and ten minutes later a car pulled up, two women got out, and put up a sign requesting one pound a head to visit the site (a donation, the sign informed us, for the local church). The crop circle site we arrived at next, however, was much more organised, with a sign already placed near the main road announcing "Europe's Best Crop Circle" and a farmhand at the gate ready to take our entrance fees. These people represented to me the entrepreneurial element of the scene.

Finally, during our visit to a spectacular crop circle formation near Stonehenge, I noticed, along with some others in the group, hub-like indentations in the centre of the main circles. I had previously read about hoaxers using wooden planks that they rotated around central poles to create the circular patterns, and wondered if it was one of these devices that had created the indentations. Even after one of our guides had explained that the markings were the places where crop circle researchers had taken soil samples, a couple of us remained somewhat unconvinced. This "doubting" element on the tour could perhaps be seen as representative of (albeit in a mild form) the sceptical element in the paranormal scene.

In this one setting, there were scientific-oriented type researchers, spiritual-seeking New Agers, entrepreneurs and moderate skeptics, and perhaps other participant types that were less identifiable. Indeed, there are many participant

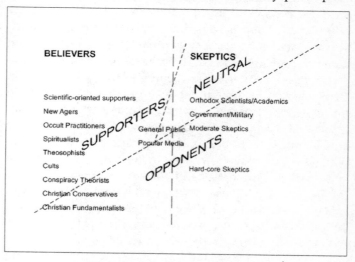

Figure 1: Ideational Positions Within the Debate

Note: The diagram consists of two grids transposed over each other. The first grid, consisting of two columns distinguishes between participant types who affirm the existence of paranormal phenomena and those who are sceptical. This grid can be identified as the *ontological dimension* of positions within the debate. The second grid indicates the level of support given to paranormal ideas—what might be referred to as the *ideological dimension* of positions within the debate.

types that can be identified within the paranormal scene, and in the diagram (Figure 1), I have indicated the main types that I have come across during my travels and reading.

We can see from the diagram how some participant types can be quite uniquely situated in the debate as a result of their particular ontological and ideological orientations, with some participant types even situated ambivalently between different orientations. It should be noted that the participant types and orientations that I have included in the diagram are generally recognised by most participants within the debate, although they are only typifications that in reality are not always so clearly identifiable nor universally agreed upon.

I will now describe the main participant types in some detail. The participant types that I will outline are those that are most prominent in the paranormal debate. There are other types — such as conspiracy theorists, militia enthusiasts, various "cult" groups, Spiritualists, Theosophists, and the entrepreneurs who trade in paranormal/occult paraphernalia — who will also be mentioned from time to time in later chapters. Also not discussed in detail here, but referred to frequently elsewhere, are the various participant types associated with particular paranormal-related fields, such as UFO proponents, parapsychologists and crop circle proponents, all of whom have their own particular ontological and ideological interests and concerns that are subject to debate. These field-based participant types tend to intersect with the broader-based participant types that I will discuss, and many of the issues that concern them tend to overlap with those that concern these broader groups.

2:1 – Scientific-Oriented Paranormal Proponents

Many paranormal proponents have what could be called an intellectual, or "scientific", approach to the paranormal. As Steven Greer, Director of the Center for the Study of Extraterrestrial Intelligence, explains:

> We take an empirical approach to our research. Empirical observation is the mother of all science. It is really the mother of all learning and knowledge (Virato 1996:online).

These paranormal proponents tend to see themselves as researchers or investigators, and view paranormal research as a frontier scientific discipline. They are the contemporary counterparts of those early preternatural proponents examined in the previous chapter, who also framed their interest as being "scientific". Of all the paranormal proponents involved in the paranormal debate, it is the scientific-oriented ones who are perhaps the least critical of orthodox scientific methods — seeking not to overthrow science, but to supplement scientific inquiry with their own paranormal research. But many of those same proponents are critical of the scientific establishment because of its refusal to support paranormal research.[1] As one Australian UFO researcher, Simon Harvey-Wilson, told me:

> I'm not anti-science. In the long run, I think it is science that has to do the work. Nothing is really proven until science has proved it. But science never proves anything if it doesn't bother to do the work (1996: personal interview).

While gaining the support of the scientific mainstream is an important objective for many paranormal researchers, in the absence of such support paranormal researchers have undertaken "to do the work" themselves.[2] Their research methods often borrow from the methods employed by orthodox researchers and investigators (such as the soil-sampling techniques mentioned by my tour guide on the crop circle tour). Paranormal researchers may also employ more unorthodox methods to investigate suspected paranormal phenomena. For example, on a ghost tour of New Orleans in which I participated (organised by the Society for Paranormal Research), our guide explained how the Society employed mediums (such as herself) to detect the presence of spirits. While these are methods that would not

---

[1] See Appelle (2000) for a discussion on the basis of mainstream scientific rejection of UFO research from a paranormal proponent perspective.

[2] It is interesting to note in this respect that, as sociologist R.G.A. Dolby points out: "An amateur, who does not have a career at stake, may be more prepared to take intellectual risks than a career-oriented professional" (1979:24).

be considered "scientific" by conventional scientists, they are considered by some paranormal researchers as legitimate scientific methods. After all, if psychic phenomena are real, then why not use a psychic to detect such phenomena? It makes sense if the notion of a psychic reality is accepted.

These particular paranormal researchers often justify their unorthodox methods on the grounds that the testing procedures deemed appropriate by orthodox science are materially biased, and as such, do not always lend themselves well to the study of alleged paranormal phenomena. They also cite the paranormal's elusive and unpredictable nature as their basis for rejecting a strict scientific protocol.[3] Many of the arguments in the paranormal debate, in fact, revolve around this question of what does and does not constitute the "proper" scientific study of the paranormal, and paranormal researchers are often at the centre of such disputes, vigorously defending their methods as "scientific". Many of the researchers promoting what they feel are more orthodox scientific research procedures also tend to set themselves apart from other researchers and "lay" enthusiasts whose approaches and theories they regard as being less scientific. For example, "experimental parapsychologists" will distinguish themselves from "field parapsychologists", UFO field investigators will distinguish themselves from alien abduction investigators, and so on. Disputes amongst researchers over who is more "professional" or "scientific" within their particular field, and even who is more scientific between fields, are common, and feature prominently in the disputes that surround the paranormal debate.

2:2 – *New Agers*

The New-Age movement continues the alternative approach to reality inaugurated by the hippie movement of

---

[3]   From this perspective, the problem with science is that, as philosopher Karl Popper points out, it is based on "people's faith in the 'principle of the uniformity of nature'..." (1972:252). Social analyst Edward Said (1978:145) contends that science is biased against anomalies that violate such a principle.

the 1960's, and embraces spiritual/religious interests that are often interwoven with paranormal ideas. The perspective of New Agers is rather eclectic, but generally speaking New Agers seek to explore alternative values and ideas to those offered by the "Establishment." They also tend to reject the scientifically oriented, materialistic perspective on nature — at least as a privileged route to acquiring "true" knowledge. Rather than espousing the more traditional scientific view that treats nature as an external reality that can be objectively verified, New Agers tend towards a more subjective, experiential view of reality. To them, nature is intrinsically connected to the Self, and both Self and nature are connected to a greater spiritual reality that the physical senses cannot normally perceive and conventional science (with its emphasis on "machine and method") cannot measure or control. Many New Agers believe, however, that these "hidden" aspects of reality can be intuitively sensed (Heelas 1995; Possamai 2000), and, consequently, they tend to privilege experiential knowledge over empirical validation, and the power of the imagination over the authority of physical reality.

New Agers also tend to obscure the ideological/ontological divide, in that they see people's actions as having a direct effect on nature and the "spiritual realm." Protecting the environment and "Mother Earth" are, therefore, important moral issues for many of them, as is the cultivation of a loving, peaceful temperament that is in harmony with others and with the cosmos as a whole.

New Age enthusiasts are typically attracted to paranormal related subjects that are thought to have a spiritual element. For example, it is not uncommon for New Agers to credit UFOs with a spiritual significance, due to the widespread notion that aliens (who are seen by most UFO proponents — although not all — to be behind the UFO phenomenon) may be advanced spiritual beings or "teachers." Crop circles, ley lines, crystals and pyramids also attract New Age interest due to their perceived connection to Earth/cosmic energies that New Agers can "tune into", while practices of a psychic, magical, and mystical nature attract their interest due to the emphasis New Agers place on a mind/body, spiritual/material synthesis. Some New Age enthusiasts consider themselves to be "white witches", "magicians", "sorcerers" or "pagans", and hence have a strong interest in occult ideas and practices.

The range of paranormal-related ideas that attract contemporary New Age interest extend beyond Western subjects to include Eastern religious-based ideas such as karma and past lives/reincarnation, and also nativistic notions of spirit-guides and healing. New Agers are also interested in matters that, as anthropologist Tanya Luhrmann (1989) remarks, are "far more widespread than the occult." New Agers, she observes, have an interest in "holistic medicine, 'intuitive sciences' like astrology and tarot, ecological and anti-nuclear political issues, and alternative therapies, medicines and philosophers" (1989:30).

New Agers bring to the paranormal debate a fundamental scepticism towards the materialism of academia and the conservative religious doctrine of the churches (which they believe do not adequately address the "true" spiritual nature of reality). However, the attitude of New Agers towards more orthodox scientific and religious ideas is somewhat ambivalent in nature. For example, many New Agers do not seem to be strongly opposed to scientific and religious concepts. For this reason, social analysts often see New Agers as redefining, rather than supplanting, science and religion. Andrew Ross (1991), for example, sees New Agers as representing a kinder, gentler science, while sociologist Thomas Luckmann (1991) sees them as representing a non-institutionalised form of religion.

With their unorthodox mix of scientific, religious and occult ideas, New Agers have become the target of a great deal of criticism from Skeptics and Christians. Skeptics reject what they see as the ideologically based foundation of many New Ager's paranormal-related assertions. This criticism differs from the charge that Skeptics level against scientific-oriented paranormal proponents for making unsubstantiated claims, for they at least are seen to do so in the language of scientific discourse. New Agers, on the other hand, are often seen to be unresponsive to "rational" criticism. This is because the basis of many New Age claims rests on subjective, experientially based intuitions that lie beyond the scope of empirical verification. Meanwhile, Christians reject what they see as the occult basis of many New Age spiritual beliefs. In the chapters to come I will present a number of examples of the type of disputes that arise when New Age ideas are expressed in the course of the debate.

2:3 – *Occult Practitioners and their Clientele*

The term "occult practitioner" can be used to describe a wide range of people with occult-related interests, including those with an interest in magical practices such as fortune telling, clairvoyance, cabalism, voodoo, witchcraft, sorcery, Wicca and a large number of people who "experiment" with alleged magical devices such as Ouija boards, charms and amulets. Fortune-telling practices such as astrology, numerology, tarot readings and palmistry seem to attract the most interest, both in terms of those who regularly practice such "arts" and the clientele who regularly consult fee-charging practitioners in these arts. A 1990 Gallup Poll, for example, revealed that 14% of Americans have consulted a fortune-teller or psychic (Gallup & Newport 1991). In particular, these areas have tended to attract a strong female following, and magazines (aimed primarily at women) cater to this popular interest by featuring regular columns by psychics, astrologers and numerologists.[4] Popular topics covered include romance, relationship issues, health and careers.

The more dedicated individuals who become involved in occult practices tend to view themselves as "initiates" into a realm where forces of "good" and "evil" (or "positive" and "negative") aid or hinder the fortunes of individuals. Ritual

---

[4]   A perusal of popular Australian women's magazines such as *New Idea* and *Woman's Day*, and similar magazines in the United Kingdom and the United States, reveal dozens of advertisements for psychic-lines and other psychic services.

practices aimed at working with or countering these forces are commonly performed either alone or, in some cases, as a group activity (for example, the covens of Wicca gatherings). Many of these practices are either revivals or continuations of older occult traditions that have been passed down via occult literature or through social networks and various occult societies (see Luhrmann 1989).

While some are dedicated practitioners, there are many who just "dabble" in the occult as an occasional leisure-time activity. Some young people, for example, experiment with occult devices such as Ouija boards and spell books as part of a general teenage curiosity (Lowney 1995).[5] The "taboo" nature of the occult is no doubt a large part of its appeal to many young people, particularly to those who have a rebellious streak (Fine & Victor 1994).

2:4 – Christians

Christians are generally rather sceptical of paranormal phenomena that are not referred to in biblical scripture, but give credence to that which is, such as astrology, necromancy, sorcery and witchcraft (Emmons & Sobal 1981b).[6] In this respect, they share with paranormal proponents the belief in the reality of such phenomena. However, in line with the strong stand that the Church has historically taken against occult ideas, many Christians do not share the favourable view that paranormal proponents have of such phenom-

---

[5]   Some youth subcultures, such as Gothicism and Heavy Metal, are strongly attracted to occult ideas and practices.

[6]   In fact, sociologists Charles Emmons and Jeff Sobal (1981b), using data from the 1978 U.S. national Gallup poll, argue that more Christians than non-Christians are sceptical of occult phenomena that are *not* mentioned in the bible (such as the Loch Ness Monster, Big Foot, ESP, and clairvoyance). On the other hand, the study shows that more Christians than non-Christians believe in occult phenomena that are mentioned in the bible (such as life-after-death, angels and devils). Curiously, however, belief that witches can possess magical powers (witches and witchcraft being mentioned in the bible) was significantly lower amongst Christians than non-Christians.

ena.[7] There is, however, considerable variation in what
aspects of the paranormal they most strongly condemn.
Some, for example, are more opposed to the magical and
psychic aspects, such as necromancy and astrology, than
they are to fields such as ufology that concern alleged
anomalous phenomena. In contrast, other Christians associate fields such as ufology with particularly alarming new
trends in society concerning growing depravity and Satanic
influence.

Christian opposition to paranormal ideas is widespread
even though Christian beliefs, and many of their practices,
themselves contain a "supernatural" element. For example,
the Catholic Church recognises miracles such as the tran-
substantiation of bread and wine into Christ's flesh and
blood, visions of Mary and the Saints and stigmata.[8] Other
denominations have a similar interest (or more precisely, a
faith) in miracles and powers. Some Evangelists, for example, claim to use the power of God to identify and heal afflic-
tions — a practice that has a counterpart in the paranormal
scene in the form of "psychic healing." Most Christians,
however, would distinguish the "supernatural" elements
in their own ideas and practices from the "occult" elements
in paranormal-related ideas and practices, by ascribing the
supernatural to God, and the occult to humans and, ultimately, to Satan (working through humans).

The rationale underlying Christian opposition to the
paranormal appears to be based on two levels of perceived
danger. For some Christians, the paranormal is just one of a
number of moral concerns regarding the perceived declin-

---

[7]   Unfortunately, however, in the few surveys carried out on Christian
       beliefs concerning the paranormal (for example, Emmons & Sobal
       1981b; Duncan, Donnelly & Nicholson 1992; Donahue 1993), in cases
       where Christians *do* believe in the paranormal, no distinction has
       been made between those who view it in a positive light and those
       who see it in a negative light. Hence, it is not possible to discern from
       these surveys the degree of opposition by Christians to paranormal
       subjects.

[8]   In fact, as early as the sixteenth century, Calvin was attacking the
       Catholic Church for its "magical" practices of exorcism and the
       Eucharist.

ing morality of contemporary society. Other Christians who
oppose the paranormal, however, tend to single this area
out as being particularly dangerous — seeing it as one of the
key signs of Satan's influence in our modern age. Some even
see it as a sign of impending "Armageddon." Writes one
modern-day fundamentalist/evangelist:

> It is highly probable that in light of the numerous end time
> signs befalling the planet such as the apparitions of Mary,
> UFO sightings, alien abductions, phenomenal weather
> related disasters, earthquakes throughout the world, mass
> consciousness contemplating, dabbling into the occult and
> paganism, etc., we will see those physical demonic mani-
> festations the apostle John mentioned during our life time
> (Ripp 1996:online).

The inclusion of "UFO sightings" and "alien abductions"
in such "end-time" scenarios (not to mention "apparitions
of Mary", which is a not-too-subtle attack on the "occultism" of the Catholic Church that is typically made by
Protestant evangelists), indicates how some Christians
have expanded the traditional occult classification of "wonders performed by the devil." In fact, alleged UFO sightings
and alien abductions tend to be viewed by some Christians
as a particularly dangerous modern-day manifestation of
the Devil or the "Antichrist." As one Christian explained:

> The alien manifestation will convince nearly everyone they
> have no need for a personal saviour. If aliens fulfil an
> antichristian agenda, aren't they part of the working of
> error from Satan himself, setting up the Antichrist? It just
> seems so obvious. Aliens must therefore be agents of Satan,
> the fallen angels (Flynn 1997:online).

Christians have suggested a variety of methods to counter what many of them see as the "danger" of the paranormal, but generally, they suggest maintaining a strong,
disciplined commitment to their faith and simply avoiding
any occult ideas and practices. Along these lines, mathe-
matics professor and devout Christian, Robert Herrmann,
suggests:

> How do we prevent any of these very demonic concepts or
> procedures from entering into our lives or those of our fam-
> ily? One significant procedure is rather obvious. Simply

have absolutely nothing to do with any form of the "Psychic this or that", any form of the occult or occult symbolism no matter where it is presented. Do not read any books relative to it, do not watch any television, movies, Internet, anything associated with such concepts or symbols (1997:online).

Such emphasis on avoidance and discipline rather than direct confrontation has long been a policy of post-Reformist Christian theology, as I explained in the previous chapter. Perhaps as a result of such a policy, and the wider range of moral concerns that Christians today have, Christians tend to be less vocal opponents of the paranormal than, say, Skeptics, and certainly less so than their witch-hunting predecessors in previous eras. However, their opposition is still considerable, and continues to play an important role in the politics that surrounds the paranormal subject.

Not all Christians, however, share such opposition to the paranormal. In fact, some Christians express interest and support for paranormal ideas, either seeing God as the instigator of magical, psychic and supernatural phenomena, or viewing such phenomena as a natural aspect of God's work of Creation. With regard to this latter view, for example, a member of the Churches' Fellowship for Psychical and Spiritual Studies, the Reverend E.G. Moore, writes:

Insofar as we possess it [i.e. psychic ability], it is innate: it is a gift from God, like a gift for music. Like a gift for music, it can lie fallow or it can be developed; but basically it is there (1983:1).

In treating the paranormal/psychic and the miraculous as natural phenomena, these Christians hold that religious concepts can be subject to scientific investigation just as any other natural phenomenon can. For example, a member of the council of the Churches' Fellowship for Psychical and Spiritual Studies told me:

[T]he Fellowship has tried to base its outlook on a more orthodox Christian understanding on the one hand, and linking it up with a careful investigation of the psychical area on the other hand, and trying to find the links between the two. In other words, trying to discover the links between the psychical and the spiritual, but from a standpoint, a firm standpoint, of orthodox Christian insight (1996: personal interview).

Many Christians (particularly those in positions of authority), however, would not identify with such an encouraging attitude towards the paranormal, and would see little similarity between their own ideas and practices and those of paranormal supporters. Consequently, the dominant Christian attitude towards the paranormal (and by dominant I mean most vocal) seems to be that of mistrust, and to the degree that Christians become involved in the paranormal debate, their position typically takes the form of voicing strong opposition.

2:5 – Skeptics

The group who most single-mindedly and vocally oppose paranormal proponents are those who identify themselves as "Skeptics" — their efforts being largely directed towards countering "unreason", just as their Enlightenment predecessors had attempted to do. Most Skeptics' denunciation of the paranormal is based on a rejection of its fundamental logical or empirical validity — a position that is in contrast to that taken by many Christians, who oppose the paranormal but nevertheless accept its reality. Like many Christian opponents, there is considerable variation in what aspects of the paranormal Skeptics most strongly oppose. Some Skeptics, for example, have more doubts about the possibility of paraphysical phenomena (such as ESP) than anomalous phenomena (such as UFOs). As prominent Skeptic, Carl Sagan, comments:

> [T]ravel at very high speeds between the stars, that's by no means out of the question. Walking through walls is a little tough for me. I don't see how it could be done ("Interview with Carl Sagan" 1996:online).

Also, like many Christian opponents, Skeptics should not be thought of as being only opposed to the paranormal, for the paranormal is just one of a number of areas that can concern Skeptics (see Kurtz 1996:6). For example, some of the Skeptics I encountered at conferences I attended also spoke out against Creationist and Evangelical claims, alternative medicine, cults and Scientology, amongst other concerns. The common factor here is the perception by Skeptics that such views constitute a blind faith that is merely parading as a rational, scientifically valid perspective. In this respect, Skeptics frequently criticise paranormal proponents for insisting that their ideas are based on evidence when, in their opinion, their ideas are strictly faith-based. Writes Skeptic Zoran Pazameta:

> It is when someone attempts to mix scientific and religious principles, venturing into the toxic no-man's-land of pseudoscience, that the conflict — and the damage — ensues (1999:38).

Pazameta's mention of "damage" here is indicative of the threat that many Skeptics feel that belief in the paranormal poses to the moral wellbeing of society (a fear that is shared by many Christians). For Skeptics, the social threat lies in a "reversion to primitive forms of magical belief" (Kurtz 1996:7) — a perspective that invokes the Humanistic view that intolerance and injustice arise from primitive, superstitious thinking. Writes journalist Thomas Sutcliffe:

> The habitat of mind in which astrology and mediumship flourish is also a perfect breeding ground for intolerance and injustice — an ecology in which monsters can grow unresisted alongside those "harmless" freaks and clowns (1996:online).

Similar to the evangelical Christian fear of an impending Armageddon, some Skeptics even tend to invoke a vision of a resurgent "Dark Age" (the age prior to the Enlightenment) should paranormal beliefs go unchecked. For example, the initial manifesto of CSICOP reads:

> Perhaps we ought not to assume that the scientific enlightenment will continue indefinitely; for all we know, like the Hellenic civilization, it may be overwhelmed by irrationalism, subjectivism, and obscurantism (Kurtz 1976:28).

To counter the spread of paranormal beliefs, Skeptics encourage the general public to dismiss the claims made by paranormal proponents, and they often engage proponents in public debate in order to demonstrate the error of such views.

Just as we find a small percentage of Christians supporting paranormal ideas, however, so too do we find a small percentage of Skeptics who appear to be open to the possibility that some paranormal-related claims may be valid. These Skeptics might be referred to as "empirical Skeptics" as opposed to "metaphysical Skeptics", as they do not reject paranormal phenomena as a metaphysical possibility, but simply doubt their existence based on the accumulated empirical evidence of reality as it currently stands.[9] These Skeptics demand that paranormal claims withstand a great deal of scrutiny before they are accepted — more scrutiny, in fact, than would be required to prove the validity of phenomena that does not violate the "laws of physics." A common saying of many Skeptics, in fact, is that "extraordinary claims require extraordinary proof."

One Skeptic who claims to be of the more moderate ilk is Susan Blackmore, who at the time of our interview in 1996 was in the unique position of being a committee member of both the Committee for the Scientific Investigation of Claims of the Paranormal and, at the other end of the continuum, the Society for Psychical Research (she has since resigned from both and moved away from the psychical research area). Blackmore distinguishes between Skeptics "who would label themselves with a big 'S'" and who are convinced paranormal phenomena do not exist, and "skeptics spelt with a small 's'" who remain open to its possible existence. Skeptics with a big "S", she explains, are those who have the attitude: "We think science is good, and we think everything to do with the paranormal is anti-science." Skeptics with a little "s", on the other hand, are those who, like herself, "very much doubt the existence of the paranormal phenomena but they're really interested in it, they're

---

[9]   As Kant (1990[1781]: 56) puts it in his *Critique of Pure Reason*, "an empirical judgement never exhibits strict and absolute, but only assumed and comparative universality (by induction); therefore, the most we can say is - so far as we have hitherto observed, there is no exception to this or that rule."

prepared to look at data and so on." It is the hard-line scepticism, however, that tends to dominate the Skeptic organisations, as evidenced by the resignation of moderate Skeptic Marcello Truzzi as co-chairman of CSICOP in 1977 because, according to co-founder Skeptic Paul Kurtz, of CSICOP's increasingly hard-line approach (Kurtz 1996:6).

In summary, it would seem that contemporary Skepticism is very much a continuation of the academic-led Enlightenment scepticism discussed in the previous chapter. In particular, contemporary Skeptics, in their effort to maintain the integrity of scientific and rational inquiry, still condemn the paranormal as an invention of the undisciplined, "irrational" imagination.[10] In terms of how contemporary Skeptics view themselves, they tend to see themselves as guardians of the principles of orthodox Rationality and Empiricism, and of the social order that they believe is held together by such principles. But while many Skeptics claim to speak on behalf of the contemporary academic community, it is not altogether clear whether their views are representative of the academic/scientific community as a whole, as I will discuss next.

2:6 – The Academic/Scientific Community

Although the various participant types discussed so far can be classified at the pro and anti extremes of the paranormal belief continuum, there are a number of other participant types whose positions in the debate are more ambivalent and whose mode of involvement is less direct. The first of these types that I will examine is the academic/scientific community.[11]

---

[10] A study by Brugger & Taylor (2003) attempts to empirically demonstrate that paranormal believers are characterised by a dominant right cerebral hemisphere that gives rise to creative and delusional cognitive impulses.

[11] In the sociology of science there is some disagreement about the use of the term "scientific community" (Tambiah 1990:9). The definition I employ here is one that simply views the scientific community as a population of accredited teaching or research professionals.

As I discussed in the previous chapter, the academic/scientific community have come to wield considerable authority in defining which views concerning the nature of reality are "normal" and "acceptable" and which views are not, and a widespread perception amongst participants in the paranormal debate is that academics are largely sceptical of paranormal claims. However, the few surveys that have been carried out on paranormal support amongst academics indicate that Skepticism is not as widespread as one might expect. For example, in a survey conducted by M. Wagner and M. Monnet (1979), of the almost 50% who responded, 73% of professors from the humanities, arts, and education indicated a belief in ESP, while 55% from the natural sciences and 34% from psychology departments indicated similar support. L. Otis and James Alcock (1982) surveyed humanities and science professors at the University of Michigan and the University of Toronto, and of the 53% who responded, one-third indicated a belief in paranormal phenomena, with no clear difference between the humanities and the sciences (Alcock 1987:554). Commenting on his results, Alcock notes that the figures do not support the general perception of academics as being overly sceptical of paranormal claims or unsupportive of paranormal research. Studies conducted on the level of academic support for UFO research, such as a 1977 survey of members of the American Astronomical Society (Sturrock 1994), also seem to support Alcock's observation.

Regardless, however, of how the rank-and-file academics/scientists view the paranormal, it is the views of the academic/scientific "elite" — the "gatekeepers" of science as some analysts refer to them — that ultimately define what is and is not accepted knowledge (Dolby 1979), and the "elite", it appears, are not nearly as tolerant of paranormal claims as some rank-and-file academics/scientists are.[12] For example, Alcock (1987:554-55) cites a study by James McClenon (1982) in which "elite" scientists such as those

---

[12] For a characterisation of elite scientists as "gatekeepers", see A. Webster (1979:124) and James Alcock (1987:554).

belonging to the American Association for the Advancement of Science council and various related section committees were surveyed on their belief in Extra-Sensory Perception (ESP). Of the 71% who responded (a total of 339 respondents), only 25% believed that ESP is a likely possibility, while 50% felt that its existence is impossible or unlikely.

A visiting medical scientist I spoke to at Harvard University reflected this "gatekeeper" attitude when he expressed a low opinion of paranormal research because, he said, it did not follow the "rules" of science. There are certain rules, he explained to me, which should be followed when conducting valid research. The rules he was referring to are those that scientists generally refer to as the "scientific method", which consist of established procedures that ensure that phenomena are identified and investigated in a reliable manner. Repeatability is a key factor in such methodology, for it allows fellow researchers to independently verify the findings of others. It is this lack of repeatability that philosopher Karl Popper (1972) cites as the reason that mysterious anomalous ideas (Popper uses the case of legends about sea serpents) are not considered "scientific." He writes:

> It follows that any controversy over the question whether events which are in principle unrepeatable and unique ever do occur cannot be decided by science: it would be a metaphysical controversy (1972:105).

Accordingly, the only instances where research on alleged paranormal phenomena have been tolerated (but only *just* tolerated) by scientists is where repeatability has been seen to be rigorously observed. For example, scientists generally consider experimental parapsychology to be a more acceptable research field than subjects such as astrology, because parapsychologists are seen to share something of the commitment to controlled experimentation and repeatability. Consequently, parapsychology has been accepted (albeit somewhat cautiously) into a number of academic institutions such as Duke University and the University of Edinburgh, and also into the American Association for the Advancement of Science.

Other paranormal fields, however, have been less welcome in academia, although it is perhaps true to say that most scientists do not generally display a great deal of hostility towards these fields. Rather, they tend to treat paranormal ideas the same way they treat all suspect ideas and fields, namely, they pay little attention to them. This "low-key" approach is probably indicative of a view amongst the majority of academics and scientists that orthodox science is so well entrenched within academia and the wider society that it is at little risk from paranormal-related ideas. However, under certain circumstances, gate-keeper academics can become markedly hostile to those making paranormal-related claims, particularly when academics themselves speak out in support of paranormal ideas. As social analyst Stephen Murray points out with regard to academic attitudes towards mystical ideas generally: "Only when suspect work does not disappear from scientific discourse, when it is taken seriously by some scientists, does scientific scorn become visible" (1980:201). The kind of reactions of academics to fellow academics who have publicly expressed support for paranormal ideas will be described in Chapter Six, with particular reference to the controversy that surrounded Harvard professor of psychiatry John Mack's claim that alien abductions were a genuine phenomenon.

Generally speaking, then, it would seem that the academic/scientific community has continued the practice of rejecting paranormal claims that began with those early intellectuals of the Enlightenment period. The basis for this rejection has, likewise, changed little over time—with academics continuing to maintain that paranormal claims, theories and explanations do not measure up to the standards of rational inquiry demanded by the logico-empirical method. However, as I have also shown, their degree of opposition may not be as deeply rooted, nor as readily expressed, as is commonly thought.

2:7 – The General Public

In the previous chapter, I traced the growth of public interest in the paranormal up to the current era, noting that popular mediums such as film and literature have fuelled public enthusiasm for the paranormal in past decades. In addition, other public mediums such as the Internet and the popularity of public conventions, fairs, meetings and the like, have all played their part in not only bringing paranormal ideas into popular culture but, conversely, popular ideas into the paranormal debate.

All sides involved in the paranormal debate, particularly paranormal proponents and Skeptics, tend to regard the general public as an important yet largely invisible player in the debate. The general public's position on the paranormal is difficult to gauge, because public attitudes vary considerably and have also fluctuated a great deal over time. Over the longer term, public interest in the paranormal has, as I discussed in the last chapter, tended to waver between periods of scepticism, enthusiasm and indifference. But in the last few decades, public attitudes seem to have swung in favour of the paranormal. Indeed, if we are to accept the figures presented in a 1990 Gallup poll on paranormal belief in the United States, the majority of Americans believe in at least some form of paranormal phenomena. In fact, only seven percent of those polled claimed to have no paranormal beliefs at all (Gallup Jnr & Newport 1991:139). The results of a 2001 Gallup poll indicate that this situation has changed little (see Appendix).

Some social commentators (Taylor 1994; Leonard 1999) have questioned whether this current popular interest is just a passing fad or is indicative of a more deep-seated and lasting shift in public attitudes towards the paranormal. As outlined in the previous chapter, the long history of paranormal interest in Western culture indicates that more deep-seated processes are at work. In later chapters, I will identify what I consider these processes to be, and illustrate how they are related to the politics that drive the paranormal debate.

2:8 – The Media

The final group that has a strong influence on the paranormal debate is the public media. Their influence stems partly from their role as an integrative force that connects the varied and largely dispersed groups discussed above. Thomas Luckmann, for example, notes the "subinstitutional coalescence" of occultism and other "privatised" discourses around "commercial and mass-medial support structures" (1991:170). However, the relationship between the media and the paranormal scene is a symbiotic one – for while the scene may, to a large degree, owe its coherency to the media, the media's own commercial interests are also served by catering to the interests of the burgeoning paranormal following.

There has been little in the way of survey work carried out on media attitudes towards the paranormal. A content analysis of the New York Times carried by Hickman, McConkey and Barrett (1996:224) revealed a "general pattern of profound scepticism on the part of the press", particularly in longer, narrative articles on the topic. But with regard to media treatment of the UFO subject, Charles Emmons states: "There is a tendency to think too stereotypically about mass media, when in fact there has been quite a variety of types of treatment" (1997:27). Indeed, the manner in which various paranormal stories are treated by the media varies between different publications/programs and tends to change over time, ranging from outright cynicism to enthusiastic support.[13] The reason for this variability might relate to the personal perspective of journalists and their editors, but perhaps more importantly to the perceived interest of the target readers/viewers.

According to surveys conducted by Perth's daily newspaper *The West Australian* on the interests of its readers, the daily horoscope "sometimes out-rates the business section

---

[13] Both paranormal proponents and Skeptics tend to regard the media as biased towards their opponents' position. For a critique of sceptical bias in the media, see Jim Speiser (c.1997:online). For a critique of pro-paranormal bias in the media, see Paul Kurtz (1996:7).

and TV guide as the main reason for reading the paper" (Tuesday, 8 August 2000:7). The question is, however, whether it is the public's interest that dictates the media's handling of the paranormal subject, or whether it is the media itself, with its financial and other vested interests, that is largely responsible for generating and sustaining this public interest.

In support of the former position, Walter Sullivan, former science editor of the *New York Times*, writes that, with regard to the media's coverage of UFOs, while the media and press have no doubt "stimulated ... public imagination" over the subject, they only report such stories in the first place because "many American adults believe that UFO's are extraterrestrial visitors", which consequently "makes a UFO report a good story" — one that "the public resonates to" (Sullivan 1972:258).[14] Journalist and film director Bob Couttie, who once produced a radio series on the paranormal titled "Forbidden Knowledge" (1986), also supports the view that media coverage of the paranormal is largely a reflection of public concerns and beliefs (1988:112).

I asked a small-town reporter for a newspaper in the United States who had written about a UFO sighting to explain to me why he bothered to report on the event. He said: "The reason I wrote about the local sighting (and my editor decided to publish) was that we'd gotten some calls about it" (1999: personal interview). He told me: "I've always loosely defined "news" as whatever everyone's talking about, or would be if they knew about it." In this respect, the media seems to rank the newsworthiness of paranormal-related stories according to the entertainment and interest value of paranormal subjects to the general public. My journalist informant explained:

> Most people like a good yarn, and I don't mind spinning one on occasion. So I suppose I view such stories as enter-tainment, with an ancillary purpose of reminding us

---

[14] Sullivan (1972) points out that it was the press itself that invented the term "flying saucer."

that — maybe — the world is a stranger, more absurd place than we can think.

At what point, however, does "spinning a good yarn" and "reminding" readers of a story's possible importance become an act of sensationalism and manipulation, such that the writer is participating in a process of generating public interest rather than merely catering to an existing interest? Many of those opposed to paranormal ideas argue that there is, indeed, a sensationalist tendency in the media, which in turn, has had a significant impact on shaping public interests and attitudes toward the paranormal.

While it is possible to make a case for either the media being constitutive of public interest or the media being reflective of media interest — or, as sociologist Erich Goode (2000:194–204) attempts to do, a case for both — it should be kept in mind that members of the media are also members of the general public, with many of the same interests, desires and tastes that the wider public has. My journalist informant, for example, told me that he has personally been "fascinated by weird stuff" for most of his life. Similarly, Chris Carter, the creator of *The X-Files*, has often spoken in interviews of his curiosity regarding the paranormal and cosmic matters generally (Van Syckle 1995). Consequently, the line between media interest and public interest in the paranormal may be a fine one at times, and it may not always be entirely accurate to portray the media as an autonomous institution influencing an "external" general public, as if the two exist somehow separately.

3. Discursive Commonalities and Differences

In my overview of the various participant types that play a central role in the paranormal debate, I have indicated the main views and interests that characterise each type's ideational position. The positions outlined in this chapter, and the understandings that circulate within the paranormal debate regarding the essential characteristics and differences between these positions, form an important part of what Hess refers to as "paraculture" (1993:15). "Paraculture"

consists of a whole range of typifications concerning arguments, strategies and, of course, ideational positions that,
while being common knowledge to many participants in
the debate, may be unfamiliar to outsiders. In referring to
these typifications as common knowledge, however, I do
not mean to imply that participants universally accept
them. It is important to note that participants tend to have
their own characterisations of the various positions, which
may differ from the ones I have presented here. Nevertheless, participants still make use of the kind of generalised
typology that I have presented in this chapter, adapting it to
their own experience of the various types, and colouring it
with a rhetoric that is shaped by their particular orientation.

While the characteristics discussed have been those that
tend to distinguish each particular type, participants do
share (to varying degrees) a number of common characteristics. These commonalities (which are often unacknowl-
edged by the participants themselves) can be attributed to
certain base discursive formations that permeate Western
society generally and the paranormal debate in particular.
Paranormal researchers, Skeptics and the media, for
example, tend to base their positions on the acceptance of
logico-empirical science, even if they interpret that science
in different ways. Similarly, Christian paranormal proponents obviously share with conventional Christians (conservatives and fundamentalists alike) an appreciation of
Christian concepts and ideals, but the concepts are also
shared by New Agers at a more fundamental, religious level.

Foucault (1972) offers an instructive model for conceptualising such commonalities and differences, which he
refers to as the "tree of enunciative derivation." Foucault
contends that competing positions sometimes share the
same base discourses, consisting of general "governing"
statements that "put into operation rules of formation."
Where these positions differ, he explains, is at their "summit", where each discursive formation is "more delicately
articulated, more clearly delimited and localized in its
extension" (1972:147). Employing this model, we can see
how, for example, scientific-oriented paranormal research

may be regarded as a subversive branch of the same enunciative discursive base from which Skepticism is derived — both positions valuing Rationalist ideals such as objectivity, logic and provability, but expressing them in different ways.

Of course, in applying Foucault's "tree" to any ideational position within the paranormal debate, we must take into account that such positions tend to have multiple discursive bases. New Age ideas, for example, are not only heavily influenced by Christianity, but have also been influenced by science, philosophy, occult traditions and Eastern spirituality.[15]

As I proceed in the following chapters to examine the contemporary paranormal debate itself, Foucault's model of base commonalities and summit differences will be a useful model for conceptualising the various issues that underlie the debate. For although discursive differences might, at first glance, seem to be the sole factor driving conflict in the debate, these differences can be traced (in accordance with Foucault's model) to underlying "base" discourses that not only define the "summit" differences, but tend to "demonise" them, and determine the way those differences are contested. The fact that many of the varying positions draw from the same base discourses explains why participants' views and behaviour towards opponents are often similar. In the next chapter, I want to focus on how participants come to identify with the particular orientations that I have outlined in this chapter, and how base discourses guide their involvement in the scene throughout their "career" as participants.

---

[15] Social analyst Roger Woolgar, for example, argues that New Agers have recast the "profoundly pessimistic" Eastern notions of rebirth within an optimistic Western framework of "progress" (1987:59).

Chapter 4

Becoming a
Participant

Introduction

In the previous chapter I examined the ideational positions
that participants come to occupy in the paranormal debate,
and in this chapter I want to examine the conversion processes that lead them to identify with those positions in the
first place. An understanding of the conversion process is
important not only because of the insight it provides into
the nature of people's commitment to defending particular
positions, but also to the continuity and change of those
positions over time.

I will begin by examining the reasons that participants
themselves typically give to explain their involvement in
the paranormal scene, before moving on to some of the
explanations put forward by analysts. I will then argue that,
contrary to the explanations suggested by participants and
analysts, it is largely the influence of wider societal discourses that encourage participants to become involved in
the scene and predispose them to take particular ideational
positions in the paranormal debate.

1. Involvement from an Emic Perspective

Participants themselves offer a variety of explanations to
account for their pro or anti paranormal interest, what
anthropologists refer to as "emic" (insider) perspectives
(Goode 2000:44–46). Paranormal proponents, for example,
frequently claim that their involvement was precipitated by

one or more "extraordinary" experiences that led them to question various mainstream views about the nature of reality and to seriously consider various alternative, paranormal explanations. For example, one paranormal proponent, who claims to have once seen lights doing strange manoeuvres above a field, states during an Internet discussion:

> I'll tell you something. I was once a complete skeptic about everything paranormal. Then, one evening, with five of my friends, as we were enjoying dusk after a sunny day, we all noticed something extraordinarily bizarre …

Accounts of this kind are very common. In fact, throughout my research I heard countless stories from people about their "paranormal experiences", and such stories came not only from self-confessed paranormal proponents, but also from people who would not consider themselves to be "enthusiasts" as such. These experiences tend to be cited by those who profess to having an open mind on such phenomena as pivotal events that marked their conversion from doubters to being accepting of, or at least less prone to doubt, such phenomena.

Another reason participants commonly give for their own (and others') paranormal interests is that it is part of the awakening of a latent spiritual or psychic aspect of human nature. For example, one contributor to an Internet discussion remarks:

> Most of us have this side of us de-emphasized so strongly in our upbringing that we lose touch with it. Of course, we are all learning to open up and get in touch once again.

Indeed, these participants sometimes see their initial interest in the paranormal in terms of an intuitional realisation that there is something more to reality than is acknowledged by mainstream authorities. Writes another Internet discussion participant:

> I'm sure that everyone has their own reasons, but it all starts with the suspicion that there is something out there that doesn't fit into the current scientific model of the world, and yet does not believe the more mainstream explanations (generally, religious in nature).

Yet other paranormal proponents see their interest as the outcome of their intelligence, perceptiveness or rational outlook that has given them the ability to recognise "truths" that others are unable or unwilling to perceive. Skeptics cite similar realisations and superior cognitive abilities for their scepticism, arguing that irrational impulses lead people to take up paranormal outlooks, while rational thinking underlies their own sceptical view. Writes one Skeptic in an Internet discussion: "[I]t seems likely that skeptics/critical thinkers have better critical thinking skills/reasoning abilities than true believers."[1]

Another explanation that paranormal proponents sometimes give for their interest is that it came as a result of prompting, or guidance, from "Higher Forces" — forces that exist either externally or as higher aspects of their "Inner Selves." They may, for example, see their involvement in terms of a "calling" from aliens, guiding spirits or even God. Sociologist Charles Emmons notes, for example, that many ufologists "come to be aware that they are being chosen and perhaps directed by the UFO phenomenon" (1997:68). Similarly, a self-declared witch and medium told me:

> I had a dream where the spirit of the Goddess came to me and told me the purpose of my life. This was at a major crisis in my life and became a great turning point for me. I found out that my purpose in life is to help others, and help in any way I can and that is what I've been doing ever since.

Some paranormal proponents (particularly those with New Age leanings) feel that "guiding forces" have led them in a more subtle, indirect manner to become interested in paranormal ideas. They may feel, for example, that they were guided to meet certain people, read certain books, or go to certain places — events and activities that they believe initiated and perpetuated their early paranormal-related interest. This perspective is one of the central ideas devel-

---

[1]   This explanation, which psychologist Harvey Irwin (1993:16) refers to as the "cognitive deficits hypothesis," is also favoured by some psychologists, although several studies have failed to support its validity (see Roe 1999).

oped in James Redfield's (1994) best-selling "New Age" novel, *The Celestine Prophecy*, and we can see the affinity that some paranormal proponents have with this concept in an Internet discussion where Redfield's book was brought up.[2] One participant commented: "There ARE no coincidences," to which another participant added: "It is sooooo true, I'm finding so many 'signposts' to tell me that I'm going in the right directions!! There are no 'coincidences'."

Some Christians, however, offer an alternative "guiding force" scenario, believing that paranormal interest is encouraged by the Devil, who entices people towards "dark", occult paths in an effort to lead them away from God. In contrast, Christians tend to view their own spiritual interest as a calling from God, either as a mission directly given to them by God through dreams or signs, or indirectly via their interpretation of Scripture. Skeptics, it should be said, may also refer to a "higher" force guiding them — that of Reason.

Despite the fact that many participants firmly believe that these sorts of explanations can fully account for their initial and continuing interest in the paranormal and the particular positions they come to adopt, I will argue that such subjective explanations fall short of fully accounting for their involvement. For example, not everyone who claims to have had an ostensibly paranormal experience becomes a paranormal enthusiast. Paranormal author Curt Sutherly told me that although his "UFO" encounter served to reinforce his own view that paranormal phenomena exist, it left a friend who shared the experience with him "still kind of sceptical" towards paranormal phenomena with little interest in the topic. Consequently, it must be asked of those who *do* become enthusiasts following such incidents, if it was their experience alone that led to that interest. The same question could be asked of those who believe that guidance from a Higher Intelligence prompted their interest in the paranormal, for many people dream of God, angels and the

---

[2]   This concept is referred to in Redfield's novel as "the First Insight" (1994:6).

like, but only some — such as the self-declared witch and medium quoted above — interpret it as a "Calling" that becomes the cornerstone of their outlook on life.

Given such inconsistencies, I feel that we need to look beyond the factors that participants themselves cite for their involvement. In fact, I tend to treat the explanations that participants give for their involvement with some caution, not necessarily as a matter of scepticism towards whether what they are saying is true or not, but because such perspectives can be somewhat rhetorical in nature — serving to reinforce the particular ideational position that they have taken, and applied retrospectively in an unconscious manner to reconstruct their personal histories. To fully account for their involvement, we need to consider whether other, more subtle factors are acting upon them either in lieu of or in addition to these forces.

2. Etic Perspectives

Before I discuss my own discursive perspective on the factors that underlie people's involvement in the paranormal debate, I want to briefly address other types of sociological explanations that social analysts (and some participants themselves) tend to offer for people's interest in the paranormal, namely, alleged psychological and social-structural factors. I will argue that like participants' emic (insider) perspectives, such etic (outsider) explanations also fail to fully account for people's involvement in the scene and that a more discursive explanation is required. Having said that, these etic explanations do shed some light on the basis for people's involvement in the paranormal scene that needs to be taken into account when explaining the conversion process.

2:1 – *Psychological Factors*

Social analysts often cite psychological motives as the principal factor underlying people's attraction to religious/magical belief systems. Bronsilaw Malinowski (1954), for example, argues that members of traditional societies seek out magical beliefs because they alleviate anxiety, and his functionalist explanation for magic has also been an influential perspective in accounting for Western interest in occult/paranormal subjects. Edward Moody proposes a functionalist perspective, for example, in his (1971) study of a witch's coven. Moody argues that belief in magic helps people with a low self-esteem, general anxiety and pathological traits cope with their circumstances. Sociologist and moderate Skeptic Marcello Truzzi notes:

> The various occultisms provide a great variety of need-fulfilling elements (even within one form of occultism, usually) including claims of power, love, health, knowledge, and spiritual satisfactions (1974:252).

Indeed, my own research indicates that there are sometimes very personal needs, questions and desires underlying peoples' interest in paranormal-related subjects. For example, during a conversation I had with a woman at a family social dinner, it quickly became apparent that she had more than a polite or passing interest in my research into the paranormal scene. She confided in me that a close friend of hers had died some time back — a friend whom she greatly missed — and she was eager to know about life after death. She then proceeded to ask me a series of questions about the "afterlife", but I had to explain to her that my research only looked at the sociological aspects of such topics and not the "reality" itself. She was visibly disappointed. For me, the incident underlined the intense personal factors and existential dilemmas that can lead people to become interested in paranormal ideas. However, while Skeptics might see this as a fantasy-based, therapeutic solution to the "harsh" realities of the universe we live (and die) in, proponents might see personal tragedies as a reminder or "wake up call" to the bigger mysteries that surround us all.

A psychological perspective can also explain interest in the paranormal in terms of other needs and desires. For example, we may note that, as a form of leisure, the paranormal subject can provide an outlet for people's desire to be entertained and to explore a realm of "magic and mystery." Along these lines, near-death researcher Raymond Moody observes that most paranormal proponents are: "involved with the paranormal ... as a leisure time activity" (Barbell 1993:online), and some proponents readily admit to a leisurely interest the subject—one that ignites a passion and intense curiosity to be sure. For example, in regard to paranormal-related interests, one proponent declares in an Internet posting: "This sort of thing is simply my hobby. Everyone should have one, and this has turned out to be one I'm enjoying immensely."

Another factor that may attract people to the paranormal scene is its social appeal, in terms of the many groups, social networks and communities in which people can become involved. Former Skeptic/parapsychologist Susan Blackmore provided an insight into this aspect of the scene when she told me:

> [I]f you go to a parapsychology conference, you have a great time ... You can relax, you can talk about magic and love and witchcraft, and Zen Buddhism. You know, you can have a really nice time (1996: personal interview).

Susan added that in her opinion "this is not a trivial point" when explaining the reasons why some people become involved in the scene. This sense of community is most apparent at the various meetings, lectures and conferences that are held to promote (and to oppose) paranormal ideas. An extension of this community aspect of the scene—and one that has become an increasingly popular means of sharing and opposing paranormal ideas in recent years—are the various newsgroups, mailing lists, chat-rooms and chat-channels of the Internet.

While communal and other personal motives undoubtedly have an important role to play in leading people to become involved in the paranormal scene, from a sociological perspective there are problems in simply reducing such motives to universal "psychological" traits or needs. People's perceptions of desires or needs, as I will explain later, can be seen to have a discursive basis, in the sense that anxieties and the various solutions available originate in the assumptions that bind people, rather than being inherent aspects of existence. Further, such needs cannot fully account for why participants become interested in the paranormal area over other areas. For example, the need for control over life's uncertainties can just as easily be applied to people's commitment to an orthodox Christian view of the world, or many other outlooks and philosophies. Regarding the desire for leisure and community, contemporary Western society already provides a wide variety of community groups, leisure activities and forms of entertainment that address such needs, so there would seem little need for people to seek out paranormal-related alternatives. A similar argument can be levelled at the various social structural explanations that are given to account for people's paranormal-related interests, and I will now outline those explanations and explain why I consider them to be, in and of themselves, equally inadequate in explaining paranormal-related interests.

2:2 – *Social-Structural Factors*

Some analysts argue that people can have an interest in paranormal ideas for various social structural reasons that have little or nothing to do with the attraction of the paranormal topic per se — the argument being that the paranormal subject offers solutions to various social-structural inequalities. One such view is referred to as the "deprivation theory" (Fox 1992) or the "social marginality hypothesis" (Irwin 1993, Wooffitt 2000). Robert Wuthnow (1976), the principal proponent of this perspective, links interest in astrology, for example, to "the more traditionally marginal members of society", including: "the more poorly educated, the unemployed, non-whites, females, the unmarried, the overweight, the ill, and the lonely" (1976:167). Young people might also be included in Wuthnow's list, for according to sociologist John Staude (1970), they are drawn to the occult because "they feel alienated and disillusioned with the liberal progressivist ideology of their parents and with totalistic ideologies" (1970:13, quoted by Tiryakian 1974:259). As one Proponent-turned-Skeptic told me:

> When I was in my teens, all this nonsense was very popu-
> lar, and I thought it interesting. And of course, it is one way
> to feel important and different, and there are few times in
> one's life when this is as important as in teenage [years].

Other analysts, such as Andrew Ross (1991), note that
involvement in the paranormal scene can be a form of
empowerment for people who are marginalised from the
institutionalised truth-making process (namely, that associated with orthodox science and religion). The empowerment factor was brought home to me one day when a
stranger sitting next to me on a bus in Miami told me (without any knowledge of my own interest) that he was a "parapsychologist." I asked him if he had studied this subject at
university, to which he replied that he had not — rather, he
said, his knowledge was the result of reading he had undertaken at the library.

The adoption of a label such as "parapsychologist" by a
layperson accords with Andrew Ross's contention that the
attraction of the so-called "pseudosciences" lies in "the
communitarian appeal of cultural practices in which anyone, especially the socially powerless, can join, whereas
only professional scientists 'do' science" (1991:60). The
disempowerment that some people may feel in regard to
the truth-making process of science relates to the fact that
institutional/academic science requires special qualifications and training. Although science is arguably no longer
quite the socially "elite" discipline it once was, it is still
largely restricted to those sufficiently privileged by life circumstances (financial or otherwise) and/or dedicated
enough to undergo the necessary years of study. Further,
becoming an academic requires a commitment to certain
prescribed ontological orientations such as empiricism,
which must be accepted in a way that is rather narrow and
limiting from the point of view of many lay people. Likewise, religious knowledge has traditionally been regarded
as the province of the priest, again a position that requires
long training and commitment to prescribed concepts
(varying from one denomination to another). Many paranormal proponents appear to resent being outsiders to, or

passive recipients of, this institutionalised knowledge-creation process. Rather, they tend to regard their paranormal-related interests as a quest in pursuit of the truth that is "out there", waiting for them to personally discover without the need for special qualifications or the limitations imposed by prescribed orientations.

Other analysts, however, speak of interest in the paranormal more in terms of resistance to, even a revolution against, the dominant social order — a resistance that both acknowledges and is in fact motivated by underlying social-inequalities. For example, some women's interest in the paranormal can be seen in some cases to be an ideological response to a society that oppresses women (Budapest 1989; Christ 1998).[3] A feminist orientation is quite pronounced in some aspects of the contemporary paranormal scene, such as in Wicca and neo-Paganism (which often have a strong paranormal orientation in the form of "Magick"). Nina Silver, a self-declared medium, writes:

> Neo-paganism, an Earth-centered, feminist consciousness, recognizes not only the interconnectedness and sanctity of all life, but the importance of a non-hierarchical way of dealing with relationships (1992:online).

In fact, some of the women I spoke to cite feminist interests as their main reason for becoming involved in the scene. One Wicca enthusiast, for example, told me:

> One of the main reasons I became a witch was a feminist reason. I had always been a feminist and hearing about things that were done to witches or women that were called witches [that] were terrible. A lot of it is that these were smart women who knew natural ways of healing like herbalism etc., and the doctors wanted them out of the way so they killed them off. The other reason I liked Wicca was the fact that women played such an important part, unlike in most religions where its the woman's fault for every-

---

[3]   According to some analysts, feminist-oriented involvement in the scene has a long history. For example, a number of analysts have pointed out that the female mediums of the nineteenth century were counterparts to, and in some cases participants in, the early women's suffrage movement (Goldsmith 1998; Yeager 1993).

thing bad that happens in the universe and we were created from man and should obey him, etc.

Such sentiments indicate ways in which involvement in
the paranormal scene may serve as a vehicle for addressing
social inequalities rather than simply providing therapeutic
relief or an alternative sense of power. Similarly, many scientific-oriented paranormal proponents tend to see their
involvement as a means for changing the institutionalised
truth-making process rather than being merely a
"poor-man's" version (so to speak).

There are analysts who argue, however, that people's
interest in the paranormal is not so much an attempt to participate more fully in the truth-making system as it is a subversion of the very notion of a "structured" knowledge
system altogether. Social analyst James Beckford (1992), for
example, argues that certain New Age groups are
"postmodern" in their orientation—that is, they deny the
limitations posed by "modern" notions of structure.[4] He
describes their involvement as (among other things) a "cele-
bration of spontaneity, fragmentation, superficiality, irony
and playfulness" (1992:19–20, quoted in Heelas 1993:111).

My own position on social-structural perspectives is that,
like psychological perspectives, they fail to fully account for
why people become interested in the paranormal and take
up particular ideational positions within the debate. First,
there is little that distinguishes participants from non-par-
ticipants in terms of their social-structural circumstances.
Indeed, in a study by psychologists Keely Wilson and
Michael Frank (1990), in which they compared various
"demographic" and "personality" variables between a
group of university-based believers with non-believers in
the paranormal, their conclusion was that, "we were unable

<hr />

[4] Sociologist Paul Heelas, however, has criticised such a perspective
(rightly I feel) because it ignores the "strong commitment to a form of
foundationalism" evident amongst New Agers, who tend to
emphasise an individuated or "cosmic" Self (1993:110). With regard
to other participant types (whose rationalist, even scientific,
orientation belies any postmodern categorisation), the postmodern
thesis has, I contend, even less relevance.

to find any factor which reliably predicted belief in the paranormal" (1990:946).

Even if we accept for the moment that those who are
interested in the paranormal tend to be those who are
socially marginalised (a position that, according to Harvey
Irwin (1993), is generally unsupported or rejected in
"empirical" studies on paranormal beliefs), it is difficult to
discern any unique appeal that the paranormal area offers
in terms of social-structural benefits that other areas do not
also offer. After all, there are many people who view the
social system as oppressive or unjust but who do not see
paranormal ideas as a resolution to those perceived social
ills. Many young people, for example, are highly critical of
the Establishment, but are not interested in the paranormal,
and may even be sceptical of it.[5] Rather, they may find an
outlet for their rebellion in youth subcultures such as the
punk scene.

Another problem with social-structural explanations is
that they tend to interpret factors as being social-structural
in nature when, in fact, they are cultural trends. For example, the interest many women have in the occult may relate
more to the "cultural association of women with communicative awareness or 'intuition'" (Emmons & Sobal 1981a:55)
than to a desire of female participants to empower themselves. Similarly, the interest that many young people have
in the occult may be due more to their general subcultural
preference for "trendy" or "deviant" beliefs and practices
than to any intensely felt marginalisation.

Part of the problem with these perspectives is the methodology employed to account for people's involvement, for
simply quantifying the number of paranormal proponents
in terms of specific socio-economic categories says nothing
of the reasons for their involvement, which requires a more
qualitative level of analysis that endeavours to illuminate
the subjective predispositions of individual participants.

---

[5]   By "the Establishment", I mean the conservative elements of society
      that, in many young people's eyes, promote values and norms
      consistent with those held by parents, teachers, politicians, and so on.

Such a qualitative approach also needs to take into account the actual sequence of events that leads to involvement. For example, in some cases, it is clear that people's paranormal beliefs have led them to adopt a certain socio-economic position, rather than vice versa. As one of my informants admitted, he chooses to be unemployed so that he can spend more time researching UFOs. Similarly, I know of other participants whose strong paranormal beliefs have made it difficult for them to find a compatible partner and have even caused marriage breakdowns. In such cases, Wuthnow's categories of "the unemployed" and "the unmarried" are not necessarily determinants that *lead* people to believe in the paranormal, but rather, are sometimes circumstances that *result* from their paranormal beliefs.

But even to the degree that participants themselves relate their involvement in the scene to specific social-structural factors, we still cannot assume that this involvement was determined by those factors for a number of reasons. First, I tend to treat claims of social-structural motives with caution because of the possibility that some participants develop a critical view of society only as a *result* of their involvement, either because of subcultural influences within the scene, or because of frustrations that arise from their paranormal views failing to be accepted by the wider society. Consequently, participants may retrospectively apply their current social-structural outlook to their initial reasons for becoming involved. Second, even with those who can legitimately cite social-structural motives as the main reason for their initial involvement, I think we need to be wary of attributing that involvement to social-structural conditions alone, given that not all people sharing a certain socio-economic position experience discontent or come to see the paranormal scene as a solution. Rather, I think we need to understand what influences led them to adopt such critical perspectives in the first place and what caused them to view the paranormal scene as an outlet or stage for the expression or resolution of their discontent.

In short, we need to understand how the various experiential, psychological and social-structural factors act as "primers" that can steer people towards paranormal positions when—and only when—they are legitimised by wider discourses that shape people's understandings. So, without ruling out the importance of social-structural factors (or the previously discussed psychological and experiential factors), I will now examine the discursive factors that I hold are instrumental in guiding people's involvement in the scene and their support for particular ideational positions.

3. Discursive Factors

3:1 – Discursive "Solutions"

The dominant, established discourses that circulate in Western society are generally presented as legitimate perspectives on various issues, capable of satisfying the needs and desires of those who follow the course they prescribe. According to some analysts, however, there has been a wide-scale questioning of many of these established discourses in recent decades, due to a perception that they have failed to properly address certain fundamental issues. This loss of authority is generally considered to be the result of changing societal conditions in the late modern/postmodern era (Habermas 1976).

I would see this loss of authority, however, more in terms of the emergence of new discourses that not only lead people to place importance on certain needs and desires of the Self, but also to feel that established "truths" are not addressing those needs. Overall, I see the situation more in terms of a discursively based clash between established discourses and newly emerging ones (such as feminism, democratisation and postmodern orientations) that have thrown the legitimacy of established perspectives into doubt and, in turn, have increased the legitimacy of paranormal ideas.

The fact is, the emergence of radical discourses has always been part of the Western intellectual landscape since the Renaissance and undoubtedly earlier, and occult ideas have long functioned as a vehicle for their expression. These legitimacy crises may be more pronounced in some historical epochs over others, but they have always taken place. For those who become embroiled in discursively based legitimation crises, they will turn away from the solutions offered by established institutions in favour of discourses that seem more in tune with their "new" needs.[6] Paranormal-related discourses represent one such solution and merge readily with other radical discourses in the course of people's conversion, helping to overcome "gaps" between the old and new discourses in the process, thereby minimising feelings of fragmentation. This is not a matter of occult ideas serving a functional purpose in "magically" alleviating anxiety in times of change. It is simply a matter of occult ideas appearing more valid to larger numbers of people during certain periods as a result of the legitimacy crisis, and having enough personally and existentially rich material to make these new orientations satisfying. More importantly, because occult ideas span a continuum between established discourses (existing beyond their accepted bounds), they serve as a ready bridge between the old and the new.

As an example of the manner in which an established discourse and a newly emerging discourse come to clash and then be resolved within a paranormal-related discourse, I will briefly examine the case of a magick enthusiast whom I corresponded with during my research. This lady told me: "my initial involvement [in magick] was guided by my need for answers" — a spiritual quest that she relates back to the influence of her Catholic upbringing (the established discourse in this example). She explained that she had

---

[6]   This is not to say, however, that paranormal ideas are necessarily "anti-modernist" or "anti-establishment" in nature. As sociologist Lorne Dawson (1998) points out, such labels have the tendency to neglect important continuities between "new religious movements" and the established order. But to the degree that such discourses *are* seen as alternatives to established discourses, this may be due just as much to their rejection by mainstream institutions as it is to the presence of any intrinsic alternative elements within them.

developed "a feminist outlook" (a liberal discourse), which she found difficult to reconcile with the answers offered by what she referred to as "the male dominated Catholic Church" (hence, "the clash"). So, in the end, she turned to Magick for answers.[7] She told me:

> The only feminine aspect of God ... [in the Church] was the Virgin Mary. As I learned more about Magick and the need for equilibrium between feminine and masculine energies, I began to combine the two.

The perceived compatibility that paranormal-related discourses have with the newer, "critical" ideologies is not their only attraction, for paranormal ideas have long been seen to fill perceived gaps in established discourses — particularly in regard to the religious/scientific dichotomy. As I explained in Chapter Two, many nineteenth century Spiritualists came to value paranormal ideas because they were seen to resolve a gap between their religious-inspired interest (in issues such as life-after-death) and the scientific demand for proof (which had cast doubt on the predominantly faith-based tenets of Christianity). In regard to people turning to paranormal-related ideas to resolve this science/religious dichotomy, little seems to have changed since that time. For example, one paranormal proponent told me:

> I don't place a lot of faith in religion, but if I can prove to my satisfaction that ghosts and things are real it would be kind of comforting because it would indicate some kind of existence after death.

Many times in my research, in fact, I have come across similar comments in regard to paranormal ideas — where people seeking to resolve various existential issues cite "evidence" or "provability" as the main factor determining their choice of a paranormal solution over the largely faith-based solutions offered by established religions.

---

[7]   Sociologist Adam Possamai (2000) describes a similar case, in which a man with a Catholic upbringing who was struggling to reconcile his homosexuality with Church views eventually turned to astrology to fulfil his spiritual needs.

In summary, many people come to see paranormal-related positions as legitimate because of the way such positions are seen to "make sense" of reality by resolving certain incompatibilities between disparate discursive influences. But why do some people come to accept the legitimacy of certain discourses and, hence, experience gaps while others do not? A further question is why do some people come to accept paranormal ideas as the solution while others find solutions elsewhere? In regard to this second question, for example, not all people who perceive inadequacies in a particular institution will abandon that institution altogether in favour of an outside solution — some will simply modify their existing orientation. Sociologists Karel Dobbelaere and Liliane Voyé (1990), for example, found that many Belgium Catholics who had come to "doubt or reject some traditional beliefs and ethical standards of their Church", nevertheless did not stray from the Church itself in seeking a resolution. Instead, they adopted a more individualistic approach to the Catholic faith, which included incorporating some "elements alien to their own religion" such as reincarnation (1990:S4). To understand why some people come to *completely* reject one institution or body of knowledge in favour of another and why they (and not others) come to experience difficulties in the first place, I believe we need to closely examine the type of discursive influences that they are exposed to during their lives and the manner in which they internalise those discourses — a process of socialisation and interpretive drift.[8]

3:2 – Socialisation

Many analysts consider the process of socialisation — the manner in which a person's outlook is shaped through the influences of people around them — to be one of the most

---

[8] It is important to keep in mind here that the line between participants modifying their current mode of involvement in a particular scene or institution and completely converting from one scene to another can be a fine one, due partly to the sometimes hazy nature of the boundaries between "scenes" themselves.

important in terms of why people come to accept certain ideas as legitimate and others as illegitimate. There is no doubt, for example, that the process of socialisation has a considerable impact on people's acceptance of paranormal-related ideas (Dolby 1979, Irwin 1994). Psychologist Harvey Irwin, for example, notes the importance of the process "whereby the individual absorbs paranormal beliefs through exposure to the attitudes of family members and close friends" (1994:107).[9] In fact, socialisation into paranormal-related discourses can begin at a very early age. Paranormal researcher Curt Sutherly told me:

> Ever since I've been a child I've had an interest in unexplained phenomena. I was, I guess ... ten or eleven years old, and I think my interest in this kind of thing was sparked by parents who would discuss UFO sightings and things like the abominable snowman of the Himalayas ... at the dinner table. And I would sit there as a little kid listening to this, and it was kind of like, "Wow, the world's this big mysterious place!" (1996: personal interview).

Before his UFO experience in the wilderness, then, Curt had already developed a knowledge of, and fascination for, paranormal phenomena through the influence of his parents. This knowledge would not only have helped frame the way he interpreted his later encounter (or at least, increased the range of acceptable explanations from which to draw on), but provided him with the level of comfort and motivation to move outside established canons of thinking.

Some of those who most strongly oppose the paranormal have also been socialised into their outlook from an early age. Some Skeptics I spoke with cited the influence of their family upbringing in the formation of their critical views on the paranormal and on their appreciation of the orthodox scientific approach. One Skeptic concluded: "I don't believe

---

[9]   The importance of such exposure is borne out by a recent study undertaken by sociologists Barry Markovsky and Shane Thye (2001), in which they conclude that social factors such as the number of significant others reinforcing a particular belief, the strength of their relationship and/or status to the subject, and their proximity to the subject, are important factors in the transmission of paranormal beliefs.

that skeptics are made in college—they are made at a very young age." Through the influence of Rationalist-oriented parental figures and negative encounters with unorthodox relatives and neighbours (such as one sceptical newsgroup poster who refers to his "kooky aunt" who "insists that she can sense a "presence"), the seeds of the future Skeptic are planted. Christian fundamentalists and conservatives, too, are often the product of a fundamentalist or conservative Christian upbringing. For example, Director of Cutting Edge Ministries, David Bay (who is convinced that paranormal ideas are Satanic), tells readers on his web site:

> I was born ... to a devout Christian family in Colorado ... [and] I attended a Christian college in Portland, Oregon ... In 1984, I moved to New England, where ... I soon found a Baptist Church, a fundamental, Bible teaching church that fearlessly proclaimed the "whole" of God's Word (2000:online).

Secondary socialisation processes during the teenage years can also foster interest in pro or anti paranormal ideas. In the case of pro-paranormal ideas, for example, teenagers can become socialised into a rebellious youth culture that, as I have already explained, challenges Establishment views and finds its expression in occult experimentation, even counter to the views of their parents. Students socialised into the alternative culture that is often prevalent in universities and colleges can also be drawn to paranormal-related ideas. As psychologists Jerome Tobacyk, Mark Miller and Glenda Jones speculate, the high incidence of paranormal belief amongst college students in the United States might be encouraged by the "'cognitive liberal' period of exposure to controversial ideas" (1984:258) that typically prevails in such institutions.[10] This form of socialisation seems to have encouraged the early paranormal interest of Proponent-turned-Skeptic Susan Blackmore, who attributes her initial interest in the paranormal to:

[10] Consistent with this view, studies indicate that belief in the paranormal is higher amongst students in the humanities than in the natural sciences (e.g., Gray & Mill 1990; Otis & Alcock 1982; Salter & Routledge 1971).

... my introduction to psychoactive drugs, a part of
university life in the late hippy era of the early 1970s; an
out-of-body experience I had in my first term at Oxford;
and a trip to India at the end of my first year (1986:10).

With socialisation, people tend to identify with ideas and
"truths" held by associates, such as friends and family,
school teachers, work-mates and religious authorities.
Socialisation can be considered a direct, although often subtle, means by which people can be influenced by others to
see paranormal-related discourses as legitimate. But in the
modern communication era, people can also come to accept
paranormal-related discourses as legitimate through exposure to these "truths" via mediums such as literature and
other media, and I will now examine these forms of exposure in some detail.

3:3 – Legitimacy via the Media

In her study of occult enthusiasts, anthropologist Tanya
Luhrmann notes the importance of literature to practitioners, and how: "In many cases, their enthusiasm for the literature actually led them into practice" (1989:86). Indeed, a
number of the participants I spoke to indicated that their
initial paranormal interest came from reading paranormal
literature. For example, the member of the Churches' Fellowship for Psychical and Spiritual Studies whom I introduced in the previous chapter, told me:

> I can remember [being] in the University bookshop looking
> around, browsing, and I happened to see a book on life
> after death, and I thought, gosh, that would be interest-
> ing—I wonder what that's all about! So I bought it, and
> that, I suppose, was one of the first indicators of my real
> interest.

A number of factors contribute to the persuasive impact
that written and visual literature can have on people. First,
an overwhelming proportion of books, television documentaries and other forms of media that address various
paranormal topics treat those topics as legitimate phenomena worthy of further investigation. When people are consistently being told through the media that paranormal

phenomena are real, or at least possible, and that their existence is of great significance to them, then it is not surprising that some will begin to take such matters seriously.[11] Second, the fact that there is so much media coverage of the paranormal (in bookshops and newsagents, in film and on television) can itself be a legitimising factor. In other words, its high visibility can create something of a "band-wagon" effect, where people may be attracted simply because of its perceived popularity or widespread acceptance. Third, a number of the authors, media personalities and others promoting paranormal perspectives command respect by virtue of their perceived authority. For example, actor Leonard Nimnoy, famous for his role as the super-scientist Dr. Spock in the science fiction television series *Star Trek* (1966-69), narrated a number of UFO documentaries and paranormal-oriented shows such as *In Search Of* (1976-82).

In summary, the media appear to play an important role in legitimising paranormal-related discourses and thereby encouraging the interest of the general public, even if their positions regarding its reality may be somewhat ambivalent. Given the widespread legitimacy that the media can bestow on paranormal-related discourses, it is little wonder that competition to influence media coverage of the paranormal has become an important aspect of the politics surrounding the paranormal debate, as I shall examine in detail later.

4. The Internalisation Process

Once discourses and various "significant others" have legitimised paranormal-related perspectives for participants, further processes then work to integrate those perspectives within their worldview. I wish to examine these processes of integration in some detail, for it is the key to understanding the manner in which participants become fervent defenders of pro- or anti- paranormal views.

---

[11] Skeptics often lament the media's role in popularising the paranormal, as I will explain in a later chapter.

4:1 – *Discursive Reinforcement*

One of the reasons that paranormal-related discourses can have such a powerful influence on people is because the processes that lead people to internalise these perspectives tend to be self-reinforcing. Pre-existing, discursively based needs and desires (including various experiential, psychological and social-structural perceptions that I have discussed) tend to be framed by, and in turn reinforce, the paranormal-related discourses that people turn to.

We can see how the process of reinforcement works in the example of Curt Sutherly, which involved a combination of socialisation, psychological and experiential factors. In summing up the effect that his UFO encounter (described at the start of the book) had on him, Sutherly told me:

> … [T]hat was something that kind of precipitated, or I should say, perpetuated my interest in the UFO phenomenon. I guess it kind of put me on the track, on a track that sent me more down that direction than any other direction (1996: personal interview).

Sutherly's upbringing led to a predisposition (or "openness" as he might prefer to term it) towards accepting the paranormal as a possible explanation. It also led to an inquiring, adventurous spirit that for Sutherly required (psychological) fulfilment in some way (and in this respect, his career in the Air Force and as a journalist might be considered in keeping with this). In contrast to his friend, who remained sceptical and disinterested in paranormal matters even after the event, the sighting crystalised in Sutherly a commitment to a paranormal path of discovery that he had already been exposed to through his parents and possessed the enthusiasm to explore. While it is possible that Sutherly may have pursued an interest in such matters irrespective of the experience, the event certainly confirmed the possible legitimacy of such phenomena and his desire to learn more about it. In this case, the experience could be said to have reinforced, in a sense, the very perspective that framed it.

Such a circular reinforcement process has been noted by anthropologist Tanya Luhrmann (1989), who argues that occult practitioners tend to confirm their occult perspec-

tives by drawing on various experiences and rationalisations that such perspectives themselves frame.[12] While
Luhrmann tends to present her theory in a way that suggests that such experiences and rationalisations are without
empirical merit, no such assumption need accompany her
thesis, for what is at issue is the way reality is interpreted,
not the status of that reality itself. To put it another way, the
theory can just as easily be used to explain how someone
comes to perceive something that others, in their blindness,
have failed to perceive, as it can to explain someone who
imagines something that is not really there. The important
point to note is that discourses serve to situate experiences
(objective or imaginary) and realisations (logical or illogi-
cal) within a framework of understanding that serves to add
further legitimacy to that framework.

The reinforcement process often takes place over an
extended period of time, tending to make the acceptance of
paranormal-related solutions a more gradual process than a
sudden conversion. Luhrmann has devised a theory to
account for this process, which she labels "interpretive
drift." She defines "interpretive drift" as "the slow shift in
someone's manner of interpreting events, making sense of
experiences, and responding to the world" (1989:12). So
gradual has this shift been for many of the people in my own
study, in fact, that very often they have been unable to pinpoint the precise moment or pivotal event that led to their
interest in the paranormal. For example, the member of the
Churches' Fellowship for Psychical and Spiritual Studies
told me: "I became interested in matters concerning psychical experience ... [but] I don't think I can say why. It's one of
those things." Similarly, many Skeptics do not know precisely what events led them to become opposed to paranormal ideas. One Skeptic told me, for example: "What leads
someone to become a skeptic? What made me question? It's
hard to pinpoint one exact point." Another Skeptic remarks:
"I don't know exactly why I started questioning the validity
of these fairy tales, but I did."

---

[12]   Also see D. Snow & R. Machalek (1982).

The reason for such vagueness, I contend, is that very often the process that leads to major shifts in an individual's worldview involve small, incremental changes in their outlook over time, each change in itself often being minor, and therefore fairly imperceptible to the individual. Because each step in this process is only marginally different from the previous one, the individual tends to have little difficulty assimilating it with the views he/she has already come to accept, and hence the individual often does not experience a profound "paradigm conflict" or monumental transformation at all.

This facet of interpretive drift is particularly important in regard to the legitimacy process discussed earlier, where the value that people place on paranormal-related discourses to resolve various issues and fulfil certain "needs" is very much dependant on the degree to which those discourses accord with people's pre-existing discursive affiliations. The sense of continuity between pre-existing and new ideas that interpretive drift can foster can also play an important role in the socialisation into paranormal-related discourses beyond the formative childhood years — what Peter Berger and Thomas Luckmann refer to as "secondary socialisation" (1967:150). As social analysts Robert Balch and David Taylor (1977) note in their study of a "UFO cult", successful recruitment of "cult" members depended more on individuals finding a link between cult beliefs and their own pre-existing beliefs than it did on the cult establishing "affective ties" with potential new members (1977:846).[13] I would argue, in fact, that the successful internalisation of *any* ideational position depends on the establishment of such continuity. Indeed, Balch and Taylor see such a potential for subtle shifts between discourses (with people possessing what they describe as a "protean identity") that they

[13]   The cult in question here was led by "Bo" and "Peep" – "Bo" being the individual who later led 39 people to their death in the Heaven's Gate tragedy.

de-emphasise the notion of sharp conversions altogether.[14] They write:

> Whenever one identity grows naturally out of another, causing little disruption in the lives of those involved, the term "conversion" is inappropriate (1977:857).

Similarly, sociologist Adam Possamai (2000), in his "profile" of New Agers, prefers sociologist Richard Travisano's (1970) term "alternation" to conversion. Travisano defines "alternations" as:

> ... relatively easily accomplished changes of life which do not involve a radical change in the universe of discourse and informing aspect, but are a part of or grow out of existing programs of behaviour (1970:601).

Although I agree with Possamai's preference for the notion of "alternations" over "conversions", nevertheless I do not want to understate the impact of the changes that an individual may face during the course of their burgeoning interest in the paranormal topic, which terms such as "drift" or "alternation" might imply. It must be said that many people do experience profound "paradigm" disruption, even conflict, at various stages of their involvement, particularly if they experience supposedly unexplainable experiences. When considering the concept of interpretive drift, then, the links between discourses that can ease a transition should not be privileged over discontinuities that can make for a "bumpy ride." However, by understanding how continuity is established in regard to paranormal-related discourses, it is possible to gain an insight into one of the main reasons why people involved in the paranormal debate promote and defend their positions with such passion. They do so, I maintain, because they see those positions as logical or natural extensions of their evolving worldview and taken-for-granted assumptions about reality. My task in the remainder of this chapter is to identify how those extensions or links are made.

---

[14] The concept of "protean identity" is one that Balch and Taylor borrow from Robert Lifton (1970).

4:2 – Continuity of Life Pathways

One way in which continuity is established between ideational positions is through the roles that people associate with those positions. For example, people may see two positions as quite distinct, but if they identify with a particular role that they see as applicable to both positions, then a sense of continuity between those positions is established. An example of continuity via role identification can be seen in Balch and Taylor's study of the Bo and Peep group mentioned above. In their study, the analysts make the point that participants had, prior to joining the groups, "organised their lives around the quest for truth" – what Balch and Taylor refer to as the "role of the seeker". They note that this particular role is also common to other UFO-related "cults", and more generally, to scenes such as the New Age movement and the paranormal scene. Consequently, new recruits to the Bo and Peep group coming from those other scenes found the transition particularly easy – it was, according to Balch and Taylor, "a logical extension of their spiritual quest" (1977:856). It was the similar narrative schema of the "quest" that I alluded to in my discussion of Sutherly's interest, even though his mode of involvement is undoubtedly quite distinct from that of the devotees of Bo and Peep.

We can, in fact, identify a number of other roles that can allow people to bridge scenes with a similar ease. A role that could be called that of the "Goddess Worshipper", for example, seems to have enabled the self-declared witch/medium quoted earlier to bridge the divide between her early Catholic upbringing and her current paranormal-related involvement as a self-declared "witch", "medium", and "feminist." She told me that, for her, the connection between the two paths was the element of the Goddess in both Catholicism (which stresses the importance of the Virgin Mary) and neo-paganism (which emphasises the Earth Goddess). She explained:

> I have been Goddess oriented all my life, though I was brought up a Catholic. Convenient still, since Catholicism has the Virgin Mary. When I was 15 I actively started turn-

ing more and more towards the Virgin Mary, and peripher-
ally also the female saints.

So meaningful was the goddess element that she perceived in both paths, that it seems to have enabled her to
successfully make the transition from Catholicism to
neo-paganism despite the fact that Catholicism itself
denounces pagan beliefs and practices and also does not
lend itself well to feminist ideals.

The role of "investigator" is another that has helped people make a relatively smooth transition to paranormal-related interests. I am referring here to those
participants who view themselves as researchers of the
paranormal — a role that they tend to regard as an extension
of orthodox rational/scientific inquiry. Indeed, a number of
academics (for example, psychiatrist John Mack of Harvard
University and astrophysicist/computer scientist Jacques
Vallee) have made what seems to have been a relatively
easy transition from conventional academic research to
paranormal research. I would also point to the area of overlap in the speculative aspect of knowledge construction
common to both paranormal-related research and certain
"frontier" areas of science such as theoretical physics. As
science writer David Peat and the late theoretical physicist
David Bohm (who had a strong interest in spiritual and
paranormal areas) argue, "creative play is an essential element in forming new hypotheses and ideas" (Bohm & Peat
1989:48). Hence, to some participants, speculation regarding the paranormal may seem little different from the speculation that takes place in orthodox science. Indeed, social
analysts Ingo Grabner and Wolfgang Reiter ask:

> How come … frontier scientists claim for themselves all the
> advantages of the "anything goes" slogan and at the same
> time, with a self-confidence that amounts to precognition,
> reject pseudoscience as rubbish? (1979:80).

Many paranormal proponents would ask the same question, and have little difficulty in seeing a link between frontier scientific speculation and paranormal-related
speculation.

Another factor that can establish continuity between discourses is the overlap that people perceive between various discourses. For example, psychologists L. Zusne and W. Jones (1982) contend that paranormal beliefs tend to go hand-in-hand with other beliefs that share a "subjective" and "esoteric" orientation.[15] Such overlap can, as sociologists Colin Campbell and Shirley McIver point out, serve as "cultural paths" along which "individuals might travel in making the transition from a conventional to an occult commitment" (1987:41). To take a specific example, an interest in fantasy literature (such as science fiction) — which for most people serves as merely one aspect of the socially acceptable escapist practice of leisure and entertainment — may, for others, serve as the catalyst for an interest in paranormal and occult-related topics (Campbell & McIver 1987). It is interesting in this respect that there has been a great deal of controversy in recent years over books that might encourage children's interest in the occult/paranormal. For example, "occult themes" were cited as a common factor with four of the books on the American Library Association's (ALA) list of "Ten Most Challenged Books of 2000" (see "Harry Potter series again tops list of most challenged books" 2001:online). The popular "Harry Potter" children's series by J.K. Rowling has been attacked by Christian groups because of its "themes of witchcraft and wizardry" (see "Harry Potter on list of controversial books" 2000:online).

Even opposition to paranormal ideas, expressed in the delineation of boundaries (such as those between fact and fantasy, science and pseudoscience, and religion and the occult), can serve as an unintentional bridge between discourses. As anthropologist Lissant Bolton explains:

> It is also important to recognise that a boundary is in fact a link — by separating two or more things a boundary connects them. A boundary constitutes a link even where that link is a rejection (1999:3).

---

[15]   Zusne and Jones' perspective has been labelled the "worldview hypothesis" (Irwin 1993:12).

Setting such boundaries can accentuate the possibility of associations that people might not otherwise have considered, and what might seem a clear distinction to some people might be regarded as a "fine line" that can easily be bridged to others. Hence, there are many cases of proponents becoming Skeptics (such as Susan Blackmore), and vice versa. The walls that demonisers construct between positions can, for some people, be doorways that are easily traversed.

A point worth emphasising about linking (and which is particularly pertinent to the somewhat arbitrary nature of boundaries just discussed) is that overlaps need not *actually* exist between two discourses for effective bridging to take place. All that is really required is that there is a *perception* that commonalities exist. Such a perception is itself often the product of an individual's exposure to certain linking discourses — what I refer to as pan-narratives — which I will now explain.

4:3 — *The Power of Pan-narratives*

It is my contention that links often tend to be defined by pan-narratives, which are orientational discourses that relate two or more discourses to one another. The power of pan-narratives is that they outline a well-trodden "pathway" of established links between discourses, the legitimacy of which people therefore tend to take for granted and so can move readily between.

Pan-narratives can be found in many scenes including the paranormal. For example, Wicca, Magick and neo-paganism contain a pan-narrative that emphasises a connection between spirituality and feminism. As one male Wicca enthusiast told me: "I think it is the way of [a] Wiccan, at least partially, [to be] feminist." This spiritual-feminist connection is one that, earlier in this chapter, I explained served as a way for one magick enthusiast to reconcile her pre-existing feminist and spiritual interests. As she explains, it was as she "learned more about Magick and the need for equilibrium between feminine and masculine energies", that she began to "combine" her Catholic-based interest in spirituality with her feminism. We should note that she would not have needed to personally make a connection between her two existing interests, for the pan-narrative element within Magick that links spirituality and feminism had already made it for her. It was just a matter of her discovering this pan-narrative and internalising it.

The discursive linking effect from pan-narratives can be so compelling that participants can be drawn to the linked discourses that are being promoted, even when they had no particular interest in them previously. For example, the self declared witch/medium told me that she developed a feminist outlook *after* she became involved as a witch and medium:

> I would say I have a strong feminist orientation in my spirituality. The feminist part didn't develop until I had started developing my powers as a witch and a medium though.

A person might eventually shift to such a degree that they leave the pan-narrative behind. For example, one Pagan enthusiast told me that although she "first got into Paganism through feminist Goddess worship", she does not "currently identify as a feminist pagan" at all. She explained:

> I suppose when I first started it really was a political [i.e. feminist] thing. I chose witchcraft because of its image of divinity and its compatibility with my political outlook. But somewhere along the way, it ceased being a political decision. I started really getting something out of it spiritually. Part of that spiritual search was to seek balance.

Her current view is that: "The two beliefs [feminism and paganism] are separate in my practice."

The manner in which individuals shift between positions during the course of their involvement results in changes to the way that individuals conceptualise opponents and participate in the debates that take place. A person's defense of the occult might initially be a matter of challenging the subordination of women, but as a more spiritual orientation takes hold, it becomes a defense of cosmic harmony against disruptive forces. The manner of the demonisation changes as a person's position in the discursive matrix changes.

4:4 – *Discursive Customisation*

The interconnected nature of discourses also means that participants can customise their position to suit their own idiosyncratic preferences. Often when participants first become involved in the paranormal scene, they identify with one of the established positions in a quite generalised way. Over time, through the exercise of preferences and the process of interpretive drift, the participant will often find themselves integrating that position within their identity and ontology in a much more specific, personally meaningful way as they find their particular "niche" in the scene. This is made possible by the array of positions and sub-fields available.

A UFO enthusiast, for example, may drift towards an interest in alien abductions as opposed to the more general topic of sightings as they read widely on the topic. They might take a New Age leaning on the topic, and view the abductions as a positive experience involving the spiritual enrichment of abductees. This may lead them to an interest in other spiritual areas such as channelling and psychic abilities – perhaps even into other fields, such as crop circles. Alternatively, they might lean towards a negative view that sees abductions as part of a plot by aliens to steal human genes. They may eventually become something of a conspiracy theorist, with a suspicious view of their own government and of extraterrestrial designs on planet Earth. A conspiratorial view may lead them to an interest in other conspiratorial topics, such as secret underground alien bases and cover-ups by high-level government officials collaborating with menacing aliens. They may, of course, come to an interest in alien abductions from a conspiracy theory background to start with – the shifts being bi-directional.

As participants immerse themselves deeper into the scene, an increasing array of positions appear which serve as potential pathways for involvement. Prior orientations undoubtedly play an important role in determining which position a person leans towards, as do the particular fellow participants that an individual comes into contact with, and also other factors that influence their exposure to the flow of information in the scene. But the effect of interpretive drift in causing a position to increasingly appear more logical and valid cannot be underestimated, and gradually it can reach a point where a person's outlook has become fundamentally transformed by the particular sets of truths that characterise that position and to which they now fully subscribe.

The net effect of this shift is that participants come to hold a sense of duty to promote and defend their positions to detractors. What may have been initially viewed as a mere intellectual disagreement over the existence of paranormal phenomena is now seen as a fundamental challenge to the proper order of things with potentially dire consequences. From their point of view, people must "wake up", or else aliens will destroy us (so say some UFO proponents), Satan will consume us (the view of Christian fundamentalists), or society will degenerate from the tide of nonsense beliefs (as many Skeptics hold).

Some may seek ways of resisting this positional hardening. One rather unorthodox strategy for resisting such radicalisation was undertaken by former parapsychologist Susan Blackmore, which is instructive for understanding the powerful effect of the discursive forces that operate on participants. A reading of her (1986) autobiography reveals that Blackmore had long forged her own rather unique position, adapting certain established positions to suit her own particular outlook and proclivities. For example, when I interviewed her in 1996, she was in the unique position of being a member of the executive councils of both the pro-paranormal Society for Psychical Research and the Skeptic organisation CSICOP (she has since resigned from both). She told me at the time:

> It definitely has given me a great freedom ... And in a way, I'd rather not be in any organisation and that's perhaps what I'm heading for now ... and the best next thing is to belong to competing ones, because it does give you a freedom ... There would always be a temptation if you're in some organisation to feel an obligation to stand up for whatever it is they stand up for, and I don't know whether I would succumb to that. You know, there's a part of me that

says, I will not succumb to such pressure! But it's much easier not to succumb if you are simultaneously a member of
an organisation that seems to have a totally different kind
of view on the world (1996: personal interview).

Such individual choice making enabled Blackmore to
bridge or combine positions that others might regard as
mutually exclusive, but which Blackmore saw as, in principle at least, complementary. In a recent follow-up interview, Blackmore pointed out:

> [T]hese are two organisations that say they are doing the
> same thing ... (SPR — to critically examine, without preju-
> dice ... etc. and CSICOP "investigate claims of the paranor-
> mal") ... It was more that I was fighting for the declared
> aims of both sides (2006: personal interview).

For Blackmore, such simultaneous affiliation enabled her
to feel personally dissociated from the diametrical-opposed
orientations of Belief and Skepticism, even though outwardly she had to contend with colleagues on both sides
(more so the psychic researchers whom she had less conceptual agreement with) who were more deeply entrenched in
their respective positions. In keeping with the interpretive
drift process I have outlined, however, she explained in our
1996 interview that she never "deliberately sought freedom" when making her choices, and it was only in retro-
spect that she came to the conclusion that the notion of
freedom was a major factor in her decision-making (1996:
personal interview). I would argue that people almost
imperceptibly drift away from their particular positions in
much the same way they tend to drift into the scene in the
first place. For Blackmore, the scepticism inherent in her
academic involvement undermined the validity of the psychic paradigm, and the effect of this was an interpretive
drift away from a paraphysical view of consciousness to a
materialist view that was better suited to empirical demonstration. Her simultaneous membership of SPR and
CSICOP was the mid-point of this transition, and in this
ambivalent position she temporarily found a certain
"freedom" from the opposing discursive forces that pitted
each side against the other.

An important question that is raised by the preceding analysis is to what degree discourses in the paranormal debate function to lock individuals into specified positions. There are several factors that come in to play in terms of determining the strength of the binding effect of positions in the scene. First, each participant is subject to a somewhat unique set of discursive influences due to the multiplicity of discourses that they are positioned within, which means that they are pushed and pulled in different directions. Blackmore started off as a psychic proponent, but she was also encapsulated within an academic discourse that does not accord readily with a paraphysical view of reality. Blackmore's course of involvement in the paranormal scene was determined in many respects by the struggle between the two discourses within her own personal outlook, which meant that the naturalisation and radicalisation of positions inherent in the interpretive drift process never achieved a lasting effect. Second, most positions lack specificity, which allows participants a degree of interpretive flexibility in how they apply discursive truths. This is both a strength and a weakness, for individuals can stick with positions even though their orientations may vary somewhat, but it may eventually reach a point where an individual no longer feels enough affinity with a position to identify with it. Blackmore, for example, was able to decide what it meant to be a "psychic researcher" in her own unique, somewhat rebellious, way. Although the forces of conformity were certainly powerful, Blackmore did not feel chained to a particular mode of involvement. Such "freedom", however, was only felt to a certain point, and her lack of commitment to the pro-paranormal position eventually led her to de-identify with that position, and eventually from the scene altogether. Finally, discourses themselves often endow participants with a degree of manoeuvrability in terms of how their truths should be applied (which is the factor that, I contend, enables discourses to be adaptive to changing circumstances). One might argue that Blackmore's straddling of diametrically opposed positions is a natural—albeit uncommon—outcome of a common discursive base beneath paranormal research and Skepticism that values free-thinking and the empirical search for knowledge. As I will contend later, such flexibility provides a glimmer of hope that the current intransigency in paranormal discussions between Skeptics and Proponents can be overcome under certain circumstances.

Conclusion

In this chapter I have identified various processes that lead people to become interested in paranormal-related subjects, and that shape their perspectives over time. I argued that many enthusiasts perceive gaps between various discourses — between science and religion, for example, and between newly emerging "liberal" discourses and established discourses — and that some find in paranormal-related discourses a resolution to those gaps. I then examined how enthusiasts first come to be exposed to paranormal-related discourses through processes such as socialisation and media exposure, and finally, how they integrate these perspectives into their pre-existing outlook through various internalisation processes. Integration, I argued, is greatly facilitated by discursive processes such as interpretive drift, role identification and pan-narrative link-making, which provide a sense of continuity between new and pre-existing perspectives.

In my analysis, I have not only resisted taking participants' own explanations for their involvement at face value, but have also resisted a common analytical tendency to portray peoples' ideational positions as being the result of psychological or social-structural conditions. I have also avoided an overly simplistic intersubjective perspective that sees individuals as coming to share the outlooks of their "consociates" through common experience or socialisation. Rather, I see the process as a somewhat lengthy, often very subtle one, whereby people gradually learn the discourse or "language of truths" that others subscribe to, and then come to identify with such truths, but in their own unique ways. I have also resisted portraying individuals as freely choosing their own discursive orientations. Instead, my emphasis has been on the subtle effect of discourses that, I have argued, influence people to take up certain positions within the debate through a gradual process.[16]

My contention is that the manner in which individuals are influenced by these discursive processes, and the extent of that influence, largely determines the ideational position they initially take in the paranormal debate, the strength of their commitment to that position, and the changing nature of their involvement over time. In terms of the strength of their commitment, for example, the associations, or links, that participants make between various wider discourses and their paranormal-related position, can lead them to attach a much greater significance to that position than their paranormal ideas alone might seem to warrant. Discourses, then, tend to situate the paranormal debate within a wider matrix of ideas and influences, bringing all sorts of non-paranormal related issues (such as the basis of knowledge and awareness, social equality and personal identity) to bear on the debate. In this respect, a discursive approach allows us to incorporate various emic and etic explanations within a single, overall framework, thereby offering a much more comprehensive explanation of people's involvement than explanations that rely on one or two processes alone. It also enables us to see how particular ideational positions in the debate link up with wider discursive formations, and in so doing, turns the paranormal debate into a struggle of global, even cosmic, proportions.

Of course, many participants in the debate would oppose the discursive perspective that I have presented in this chapter — at least as it applies to their own involvement. For

---

[16] In this respect, my perspective is more in keeping with a passive, deterministic view of converts than a view that characterises them as active agents (see Kilbourne & Richardson 1989 for an overview of these different perspectives). However, in accord more with the latter view, I accept the importance of individuality, seekership, multiple conversions, negotiation and gradual change. It is simply that I do not attribute the individual with a pivotal role in effecting such outcomes.

them, the "truth" of their position is reason enough for their initial and ongoing attraction (or resistance) to the paranormal, and it is by virtue of their special abilities, experiences and insights that they have come to see the "truth", not because of the influence of various truth-defining discursive formations. On the other hand, they often see their opponents as being drawn to their positions due to the sort of simplistic psychological, social-structural or socialisation factors that I have cited in this chapter. It is the manner in which participants see wider issues as factors that contribute to their opponent's positions that I will examine in the next chapter, for these too, I contend, are fundamentally discursively based.

Chapter 5

The Discursive Basis of Conflict

Introduction

As we know from the history of religious wars and ideological conflicts, people's beliefs can invoke passionate advocacy and defence, and this is also true of the outlooks found in the paranormal debate. My aim in this chapter is to examine the issues that participants believe lie at the heart of disagreements about the paranormal and that motivate them to promote and defend their adopted positions with such passion. I will show how the concerns that participants see as underlying the debate often relate to the perceived wider interests, biases and ulterior motives of their opponents. These are factors that, from the perspective of many participants, make fair and rational dialogue with those of opposing points of view a difficult, if not impossible, task. I will argue, however, that while there may be some substance to these concerns, at the heart of the discord in the paranormal debate lies more fundamental, discursively driven factors. It is these factors, I contend, that hinder a more positive dialogue from taking place and frequently turn the debate into a passionate dispute that struggles to find resolution.

1. Clashes Between Opponents

It should be noted up front that not all paranormal proponents and Skeptics view each other as enemies. Some participants even feel that their opponents have a rightful place in the scene. For example, paranormal author Brad Steiger told me: "I think the Skeptics and debunkers have their place—they keep us sharp." He likens the relationship between paranormal proponents and Skeptics to the "symbiotic relationships we see in nature".[1] Former parapsychologist Susan Blackmore (1986) and anthropologist David Hess (1993) go so far as to suggest that paranormal proponents and Skeptics are dependent on one another for their very identity—each side sustaining their ideational position largely via the perceived incongruity between Self and Other.

But just as tensions and territorial rivalries exist between symbiotically related animals in nature, so too are relationships in the paranormal scene often characterised by tension and rivalry. I have already noted, for example, that many Skeptics seem very antagonistic towards paranormal proponents, and vice versa, and argumentative clashes between paranormal proponents and Skeptics are a normal aspect of dialogue in forums where the two sides come together. I will present an example of such a clash drawn from my fieldwork research in order to illustrate the typical nature of these confrontations.

1.1 – An Example of a Proponent-Skeptic Dispute

The following exchange took place on an Internet newsgroup and begins with a posting by a Skeptic, whom I shall refer to as Richard.[2] Richard begins by arguing that paranormal-related claims have no basis in objective reality, and to support this position he cites the example of belief in angels—stating that: "just wishing real hard, fervently *believing* that angels exist is not enough to bring them into being." Richard, sounding like an amateur psychologist, attributes such wishful thinking to functional tendencies. He writes: "We live in an unstable, constantly shifting

[1] Sociologist Trevor Pinch makes a similar observation, noting the way that parapsychologists and their critics are "locked into a symbiotic relationship" (1987:604).
[2] All participants in this Internet discussion have been given pseudonyms in order to protect their privacy.

and complex world ... and there are lots of things that would be nice and comforting to believe in ..." To further support his sceptical position he cites two personal experiences. In one, an astrologer drew up what he considered was an inaccurate and overpriced horoscope. In another, he attended a séance where "no spirits showed up." The medium, he adds, expected to be paid regardless, and blamed the failure on the presence of scorn and disbelief, which Richard felt was a "convenient dodge".

Scott, a paranormal proponent, defends the "paranormal sciences" against Richard's criticisms. He counters Richard's statement that fervent belief will not bring angels into existence by arguing that: "By the same token ... fervently believing that human beings don't exist is not enough to bring them out of being." He also challenges Richard's scepticism of the field of astrology, by stating that one negative experience is "hardly enough on which to base an opinion which tends to condemn it." In response to Richard's criticism of the psychic he visited (and her demand for payment), he states that "real ones do not (in fact cannot) do it for profit." Finally, with regard to Skeptics' general demand for proof, he remarks: "The real master does not feel compelled to prove anything to the uninitiated. What matters is that they know they can do it and in fact use it to help others more so than even themselves."

The Proponent-Skeptic dispute gathers momentum as another Skeptic, who I shall refer to Travis, responds — in a manner he describes in a follow-up post as intentionally "sarcastic" — to Scott's remarks about the "selfless" attitude of the psychic "master." He asks:

> Is this why psychics regularly break the banks at Las Vegas, Monte Carlo, and Atlantic City ... and give the proceeds to charity? Either they can't do this, or they are all *very* selfish ... (emphasis his).

Brian, a psychic proponent, then responds to Travis by criticising what he considers the materialist tone of his remarks. Specifically, he quotes psychic Edgar Cayce's view that: "... Material success ... may become the very stumbling block for soul development." In another post he directs his attention to the original poster Richard, beginning with a pointed reference to the "sarcasm" in Richard's post. Like Scott, Brian is critical of Skeptics' demand for proof, stating that: "Absence of evidence is not evidence of absence — it may be a difference in root assumptions." He also appears to be essentially in agreement with Scott regarding the perceived bias of Skeptics (or "cynics" as he refers to them at one point), citing Thomas Kuhn's notion of the paradigmatic basis of thinking to support his point that beliefs "can affect perception". His suggestion here is that Skeptics are predisposed toward certain biased views that preclude the possibility of a paranormal reality.

In response to Brian's post, the original poster Richard declares that he is "prepared — and inclined — to trade insults well into the next century." He then refers to paranormal phenomena as "new age metaphysical psycho-babblistic nonsense."

Finally, another paranormal proponent, Aaron, joins in the fray, in one post calling Richard a "fool" for making "sarcastic remarks about things you don't understand", and in another post responding to what he calls Richard's "psychobabblistic" labelling. He refers to Richard as a "cultist bigot" who "look[s] down upon such people for their beliefs." He also tells Richard that he is "deluded" for thinking that he is "'engaged' in battle" with Brian, adding in a follow-up post that: "you are fighting yourself, not him, and not me." Regarding his own opposition to Richard, Aaron declares: "I have the sword of truth, and will swing it at you ... ".

While this particular debate perhaps reveals as much about the process of Internet dialogue as it does about the politics of paranormal disputes, it highlights several issues that I believe are fairly typical of paranormal debates in general, and I will next examine the main issues in some detail. What I am most interested in here is not so much the outward issues that are being disputed (such as whether mediums are con-artists or not), but what participants see as *really* being at issue in these disputes — that is, the factors that they believe are motivating their opponents' "misguided" positions.

1.2 — *Fundamental Issues Raised*

The central issue of concern in the discussion was the degree to which beliefs and biases shape the positions taken by Skeptics and paranormal proponents in regards to the paranormal subject. The sceptical position presented was typical of the view of Skeptics generally, namely, that acceptance of paranormal ideas has more to do with unfounded belief than any critical examination of the evidence or the employment of rational thought processes. Richard, for example, felt that the available evidence did not support the validity of such ideas, and the functionalist argument he uses (regarding the comfort of certain beliefs) is, again, typical of the sceptical position generally — namely, that those who accept the validity of paranormal claims have a "will to believe", even when such claims contradict a rational perspective on reality.

On the other hand, the paranormal proponents in the Internet debate seemed to be of the general opinion that the position of Skeptics is based on its own preconceptions and biases. This perspective is evident in Brian's criticism of Skeptics, and, in fact, he at one point quoted psychologists Gerald Davison and John Neale's view that:

> [S]cience is *not* a completely objective and certain enterprise. Rather, as we can infer by the comment from Kuhn, subjective factors, as well as limitations in our perspective on the universe, enter into the conduct of scientific enquiry (their emphasis) (1994:24).

In a similar vein, Scott, a paranormal proponent, countered Richard's criticism of astrology by arguing that one experience is insufficient to make such a general condemnation. One often hears paranormal proponents levelling such criticism at Skeptics — the general idea being that Skeptics do not examine paranormal-related phenomena in a fair-minded manner. In other words, they simply have a "will to *disbelieve*" in such phenomena.

The typical Skeptic counter-argument to this is that, given the extraordinary nature of paranormal claims, the burden of proof falls on paranormal proponents. Further, Skeptics argue that it is near impossible to disprove paranormal claims, because the evidence is generally presented in a manner that is both unverifiable *and* unfalsifiable (Popper 1972:269). For example, other Skeptics would almost certainly agree with Richard's assessment of his séance experience, because the medium's explanation for the séance's failure (namely the presence of his "disbelief") could neither be proven nor disproven. From a Skeptic's perspective, acceptance of such claims as valid is simply "blind belief."

It can be seen from the Internet debate, then, how both paranormal proponents and Skeptics see the other's position as being biased towards belief or disbelief respectively, and how such mutually negative perceptions tend to undermine the paranormal debate's potential to resolve differences and achieve rational agreement. A Skeptic's perspective on these types of impasses can be seen in the comments of the President of the Australian Skeptics, Barry Williams, who writes in regard to an exchange of emails between a UFO proponent and himself:

> It demonstrates the difficulties that can be experienced in conducting a rational dialogue with someone whose mind is fully and irrevocably made up" (1999:40).

It is interesting to note, however, that both paranormal proponents and Skeptics can exhibit a certain degree of selective relativism in their assessment of their opponent's bias, with both tending to apply constructivist-type formulations to their opponents' ideas but not their own.

Another issue that concerned participants in the Internet debate was the question of who has the authority to speak on paranormal matters. This issue is, in fact, one of the more hotly contested ones in the paranormal debate as a whole, which is not surprising when one considers that paranormal-related inquiry is one of the few knowledge-construction areas where people can, if they so desire, become their own self-appointed "authority." Essentially, the issue concerns who is, and who is not, in a position to provide an informed and reliable opinion on matters concerning the nature of reality.

Paranormal proponents, for example, often question the right of Skeptics to speak with authority on paranormal subjects, a point that was challenged by Richard in his initial post to the Internet debate outlined earlier. Richard asks:

> [W]hy do astrologers insist that skeptics learn as much about astrology as they do, when any perceptive person can observe that astrology usually fails to deliver on its claims?

On the other hand, Skeptics generally claim that paranormal proponents have no authority to associate paranormal ideas with science such as Scott did in the Internet debate when he referred to paranormal study as the "paranormal sciences." In this respect, Skeptics are fond of referring to paranormal inquiry as "pseudo science", a view that is implied in a distinction that Richard makes in one post between paranormal interest and "real science." Aaron's response to this remark was to refer to Richard's skeptical views as "not real science" but a "religion" that Richard only "perceives" as being scientific. This comment is indicative of the way that many paranormal proponents question the authority of Skeptics, and even scientists themselves, to speak in the name of "real" science when what they espouse is perceived to be anti-paranormal dogma.

Psychological dispositions are another factor that participants in the paranormal debate often see as influencing the position taken by their opponents. Roswell researcher Karl Pflock, for example, blames much of the disagreement that takes place between fellow UFO researchers on "ego." He says simply, "there's a lot of ego at stake!" (1996:online). When participants accuse their opponents of possessing such personality traits, the suggestion usually is that such dispositions are clouding their opponent's judgements, causing them to behave in an irrational and confrontational manner, or leading them to make outrageous claims. Indeed, participants in the exchange described above tended to attribute negative personality traits to their opponents. For example, I noted how the Skeptic Richard argued that paranormal proponents were prone to accepting the reality of such ideas because they are "comforting" in our uncertain world. As can be seen from the responses from paranormal proponents such as Brian and Aaron, on the other hand, paranormal proponents tend to have their own psychological assessment of Skeptics — for example, seeing them as, by nature, "cynical", "bigoted" or "sarcastic."

A final issue that participants saw as an underlying factor to the dispute was that of morality. While a range of moral issues can be of concern to participants, one of their main concerns is opponents' tendency to distort the truth in pursuit of their own self-interests. Moral concerns were clearly evident in the Internet debate. For example, the morality of psychics who charge for their services was of particular concern to Skeptics Richard and Travis, and also to the paranormal proponent Scott. A fear that many participants have in this respect is that fee charging may involve deception for financial gain.

2. An Etic Perspective on Issues Underlying Conflict

The general concern that participants in the debate described above seem to be expressing is that opponents are not participating in the paranormal debate with the appropriate degree of impartiality and integrity. Moreover, by portraying opponents in a negative light, participants are indirectly (by virtue of a dichotomic comparison) portraying their own position as the factual, natural, authoritative, neutral, objective and responsible one. Is it the case that the issues raised by participants are to some degree serving a rhetorical purpose, or is there some sociological support for the basis of these charges? Let's examine some sociological explanations for the conflict over paranormal ideas.

2:1 – Ontological Incommensurability

As I noted earlier, one of the participants in the Internet debate, Brian, suggested that disputes over evidence are fundamentally a question of differences in "root assumptions", which is a somewhat more relativist perspective on the matter than the simple charge of "close-mindedness" that participants usually make. Some social analysts relate such differences to "incommensurability" — a condition that is said to prevail when people are unable to comprehend the rationale of another's point of view because that view is so fundamentally different from their own. Under such circumstances, an opponent's position will always appear to be irrational in comparison with one's own.

The notion that incommensurability is the basis for paranormal-related conflicts has become very popular with some analysts (see, for example, Goffman 1974; Zusne 1981; and Collins & Pinch 1982).[3] Like Brian's view noted above, the view of these analysts is generally based on Thomas Kuhn's "incommensurability" model of scientific disputes. Kuhn characterises incommensurability in scientific disputes as follows:

> To the extent ... that two scientific schools disagree about what is a problem and what [is] a solution, they will inevitably talk through each other when debating the relative merits of their respective paradigms. In the partially circular arguments that regularly result, each paradigm will be shown to satisfy more or less the criteria that it dictates for itself and to fall short of a few of those dictated by its opponent (1970:109–110).

Although Kuhn later distanced himself from the suggestion that incommensurability necessarily implies disagreement or a "communication breakdown" (1970:198ff), some analysts (such as Collins & Pinch 1982) apply a more radical interpretation of Kuhn's incommensurability thesis to the paranormal debate.[4] They argue that in certain types of debate it is not possible to reach a consensus, and that, in such cases, controversies can only be settled by "some

[3]   Sociologist Erving Goffman (1974:322ff) refers to conflicts that are characterised by incommensurability as "frame disputes", while other analysts adhere to Kuhn's terminology and label them "paradigm disputes."

[4]   Kuhn's modification of the incommensurability thesis can be found in a postscript to his original (1962) discussion, which was included in his (1970) Second Edition of *The Structure of Scientific Revolutions*.

means not usually thought of as strictly scientific" (Collins 1983:99), such as "rhetorical presentational and institutional devices" (Collins 1983:95–96).

The incommensurability thesis, applied in this manner, gives the impression that the particular gripes that participants have with one another are simply failings to understand each other's position due to ontological differences. But the problem with such an argument is that it presupposes that participants on opposing sides differ greatly in their ontological outlooks, while those on the same side presumably share a similar paradigmatic outlook—a perspective that, I contend, is questionable when applied to the paranormal debate. For example, one informant, who told me that she was president of a Canadian-based Skeptic society, differs from the majority of Skeptics in that, as she confessed to me, she has "a strong mystical streak" and "very personal religious views that are not at all conventional."

The incommensurability thesis has come under scrutiny by other social analysts, who have pointed to a similar lack of ontological commonality in the scientific community, despite the level of agreement that often seems to exist between scientists (Dolby 1979; Myers 1990). Social analyst Greg Myers, for example, notes that there is a "striking" level of agreement between members of the scientific community *despite* deep ontological and epistemological divisions that exist (1990:x). He concludes that, rather than being the outcome of any shared paradigms or methodology, scientific agreement is largely a rhetorical construct. He explains:

> Scientific discourse creates the consensus of the scientific community; it turns tensions, challenges, and even bitter controversies into sources of strength and continuity. Scientific texts help create the selectivity, communality, and cumulativeness that both scientists and nonscientists attribute to scientific thought (1990:x).

Perhaps the best-known critic of the incommensurability perspective is social theorist Jurgen Habermas. Habermas argues that participants in most debates, despite their claimed differences, already share some taken-for-granted assumptions that could provide the basis for a positive dialogue and agreement. On the subject of "alternative life-styles", for example, he remarks:

> One thing you must not forget in any case: for every ele-ment of the most explored, well-worn and well-tried life-world that is changed or even consciously accepted, there are untold masses of elements that, even in the course of the most radical weighing of alternatives, never even crossed the threshold of thematization (1992[1981]:109).

Habermas' argument is that there always exists some level of agreed-upon premises that participants can, if they want to, fall back on to find common ground.

Although I am reluctant to essentialise "base" common-alities between participants any more than I wish to essentialise "base" differences, I do believe that participants are just as capable of finding and emphasising various com-monalities as they are of finding and emphasising differ-ences, or, at least, of acknowledging the merit of opposition viewpoints, even if they do not agree with them. As social analyst Rita Felski notes:

> Both the construction of commonality among subjects and the assertion of difference between subjects are rhetorical and political acts, gestures of affiliation and disaffiliation that emphasize some properties and obscure others. It is only in such contingent terms that their value can be assessed (1997:17).

Which "properties" participants do choose to emphasise, however, will, I contend, depend on the kind of relationship with their fellow participants they are interested in promot-ing. This raises the question of the degree to which conflict within the paranormal scene is actually the result of a lack of *desire* to seek mutual understanding rather than a basic *inability* to achieve such understanding (a question I will take up in more detail later).[5]

---

[5]   Sociologists Barry Barnes and Donald MacKenzie, for example, contend that paradigm disagreements tend to be due to competing instrumental and social interests rather than incommensurability. "[T]echnical problems of communication and mutual under-

I would suggest, in fact, that paranormal disagreements are perpetuated, not so much because participants are incapable of understanding their opponent's position (although this certainly can play some part, particularly in the rationales used by different sides in defining their standards of evidence), but rather, because one or both parties refuse to consider the merits of their opponent's position. After all, incommensurability can hardly be blamed if participants are not willing to make a sincere attempt to understand the position of their opponents (or, perhaps more precisely, to understand the nature of their own positions that "blind" them to the merits of alternative viewpoints). Also, it has to be asked why paranormal-related ideas in particular invoke such *heated* opposition — more so, in fact, than many other ideas that could be perceived as being equally, if not more, incommensurable with orthodox science and religion. As social analyst Brian Wynne remarks:

> Why is it that divergence, or an attempt at it, is treated in some cases as a major threat and calls forth violent reaction, whilst in other situations an apparently roughly equivalent degree of divergence is accepted routinely, perhaps hardly even recognised as such (1979:68)?

In my opinion, then, factors other than, or in addition to, incommensurability underlie conflict within the scene, and I shall now explore some of these other factors in some detail.

2:2 — Rivalry

One factor that seems to cause a great deal of division in paranormal-related discussions is that of rivalry, particularly in regard to the issue of authority that I examined earlier. My own experience has been that at almost every level of the paranormal debate — from disputes between individuals to group and field disputes — there is competition over who is the foremost authority on various paranormal-related subjects. At the organisational level, for

---

standing," they argue, can be overcome "given only a minimum of incentive" (1979:51).

example, rivalry manifests in disputes over who is doing the most serious research, who is being the most scientific, who is maintaining the most loyalty to spiritual ideals, or who is on the right track in terms of their theories. In the last chapter, I quoted Susan Blackmore's comment on the pressure to represent one's organisation against rival organisations. At an individual level, rivalry manifests in the quest of many paranormal researchers to be the leading authority on a particular topic. At a more general level, there is the rivalry between Skeptics and paranormal proponents, and between Christian conservatives and proponents, over who has the authority to define "invisible reality" (Tiryakian 1974:10). As sociologist Edward Tiryakian remarks:

> The magician, the priest, the scientist, and the prophet/charismatic leader ... can perform "miracles" whose common denominator is the transformation of the world of appearances. They share in common an extraordinary consciousness of reality, a vision of a dimension of reality other than that experienced by the ordinary sense; each is a sort of visionary who does not operate under the constraints of the "natural attitude" (1974:8).[6]

As I indicated in my historical examination, rivalry over who has the authority to speak on the "hidden" aspects of reality has long been an ingrained aspect of Western civilisation, with competition between the priest and the magician, for example, being a prominent aspect of Judaeo-Christian traditions. The issue of competitive authority owes much of its more recent significance, however, to the "rational" authority structures that govern modern social organisation (see Weber 1947). For example, the concept of the "expert" and his/her "field of expertise" — which are important elements in most paranormal discussions — are modern notions associated with the specialisation of knowledge.

Such concepts not only derive from a compartmentalised view of how groups and individuals should be organised to investigate reality (namely, the modern notion of a "divi-

---

[6]   See anthropologist Paul Riesman (1980:213) for a similar comparison.

sion of labour" between experts), but also from a compartmentalised view of reality itself. Indeed, in the atomistic ontology that has come to dominate Western thinking, reality is seen to be comprised of discrete types of phenomena (e.g., astronomical bodies, weather conditions, rocks, and lifeforms), each phenomenon being able to be studied as a separate field (e.g., astronomy, meteorology, geology and biology). In keeping with this compartmentalised view of reality, people dedicate themselves to an in-depth study of a certain area, and come to be regarded by others (and view themselves) as experts in that area, with greater entitlement to speak on matters related to that area than outsiders or others considered to be less qualified in that field.

The main point to note about rivalry is that it is not necessarily a product of incommensurability between positions. In fact, it is often the case that the more parties share a similar outlook, the more intense the rivalry is between them. For example, analysts often note how some of the most intense conflicts that have occurred down through history have been between groups who are closely aligned ontologically and ideologically. Interdenominational disputes between Christians are a case in point, and social analysts Raymond Eve and Francis Harrold note in regard to this that: "the closer theologically two religious factions are, the more proponents of each side seem upset by minor departures from doctrine by the other" (1987:142). A similar observation could be made about many debates among academics and scientists.

The fact that even "minor departures from doctrine" can "upset" participants points to another important aspect of rivalry in regard to authority—namely, that often such rivalry is not for the sake of authority alone, but is a means of protecting cherished ideals or views of reality—a point that I made earlier with respect to hegemonic interpretations of historical struggles. Moreover, rivals are often seen to pose a real threat to social, even "cosmic", well being—whether that threat is perceived to come from promoting "corrupt" governments or church institutions, or alleged "evil forces" such as irrationalism, Satan or malevolent aliens.

Hence, rivalry for the sake of power alone is not an adequate explanation for the tensions that exist within the paranormal debate. This position is in contrast to the view presented by some social analysts of the paranormal scene. For example, Ingo Grabner and Wolfgang Reiter (1979) and John Fiske (1993) argue that the attempt by proponents of institutional science to demarcate differences between themselves and paranormal proponents is motivated by the desire to maintain a monopoly on the "truth." Fiske writes:

> Scientific rationalism does not provide the only way of knowing and representing the world, although it claims to. Despite these monopolist ambitions it has to recognize, however reluctantly, that other knowledges exist and contradict it, so part of its strategy of control is to define the realities known by those other knowledges as "unreal" and therefore not worth knowing (1993:181).

According to Fiske, competing social groups inherit conflicting knowledge-paradigms as part of their own struggles — struggles that are often unrelated to the issues central to those paradigm conflicts. In particular, society's marginalised "masses" tend to converge on counter-Establishment ideologies such as the paranormal in order to mount a challenge to the Establishment. Fiske writes:

> Popular knowledges often deal with the paranormal, not because the people are essentially "superstitious" (to use the term by which scientific rationalism delegitimates such knowledges) but because the relationship of superstition to science, of paranormality to normality, reproduces that of the people to the power-bloc (1993:188).

But we need to understand the discursive processes that underlie the rivalries. For example, participants may feel that the most effective way to establish and preserve particular ontological, social and moral ideals is to contest power in a social-structural sense. This perspective is similar to that of philosopher Rom Harré, who criticises the notion that scientific elites set up "institutions of rationality" in order to preserve their own power. Harré remarks:

> [I]t would be a gross example of the naturalistic fallacy to identify grounds for belief with social pressure ... because it might be that the scientific community maintains by

social pressure, just those criteria for theory choice that best embody the practices that experience has shown are the best ways of judging theories for their truth (1981:vii).

In line with Harré's remarks, I hold that it would be both an exaggeration and a somewhat superficial treatment of the facts to regard rival tendencies as simply an expression of power-hungry motives. Rather, we need to consider discursive factors that lead participants to initiate rival behaviour to protect various ideals. This is true, I contend, even with participants such as some feminists and militia enthusiasts whose primary reason for becoming involved in the debate may be because it presents (to borrow a phrase from social analyst Wendy Brown 1998:37) a "stage of political possibility".[7] For they, too, often have secondary interests of a spiritual or paranormal nature that accord with their primary interests — believing, for example, that the spiritual/paranormal is being suppressed by the "patriarchal" (according to feminists) or "conspiratorial" (according to militia enthusiasts) authorities. In such cases, their ontological, paranormal-related ideals tend to be inseparable from their broader social movement objectives.

It is easy to understand, however, why participants come to view the campaigns of truth-dissemination carried out by opponents as being guided solely by hegemonic motives. Participants' views in this respect are often influenced by various discourses (such as Marxism, feminism and various conspiratorial theories) that encourage participants to attribute power-interests to their opponents' positions and to defend their own positions and "rights" passionately.[8] Hence, the notion of difference can be an artefact of rivalries between participants, which are fundamentally discursively based.

---

[7]   Wendy Brown remarks: "Openings along fault lines, and incitements from destabilized (because denaturalised) configurations of the present comprise the stage of political possibility" (1998:37).

[8]   In terms of my discussion in Chapter Two regarding the relationship of academics to the politics of the debate, we can note the influence of academic ideas in encouraging some of these hegemonic interpretations, in much the same way that Kuhnian ideas regarding incommensurability have become part of the politics of the scene.

2:3 – Identity factors

Some social analysts regard conflict over paranormal ideas as a consequence of participants trying to preserve distinct identities or groups vis-à-vis others. Anthropologist Frederick Barth (1969) has argued that one of the main strategies employed to define and maintain a group or community is to promote differences, or boundaries, between it and "the Other" in terms of acceptable norms and values. Indeed, both sociologist Ben-Yehuda (1985) and anthropologist David Hess (1993) view such "boundary-work" (Gieryn 1983) as an integral aspect of relations within the paranormal scene, where "identity is constituted not by essential characteristics but instead by a set of relationships to the Other, or whatever is not the Self" (Hess 1993:43). Hess adds:

> Skeptics, for example, could not really exist—or would certainly be fundamentally different—if they were not situated oppositionally in an ideological arena of parapsychologists, New Agers, fundamental Christians, and others who hold what skeptics view to be pseudoscientific beliefs (1993:43).

But counter to Barth's thesis, Ben-Yehuda and Hess do not seem to view such boundary-work in the paranormal debate as being primarily motivated by a desire to promote a subcultural identity or sense of community for the sake of that identity or sense of community alone. It seems to be more the case that boundary-work functions as part of an effort to reaffirm what Ben-Yehuda refers to as "moral boundaries", that is, the lines between deviant and non-deviant groups (such as between "pseudoscientists" and "proper" scientists, or between "wayward" Christians and "righteous" Christians). Such boundary-work is, I contend, ultimately directed toward wider ideological and ontological ends, where the maintenance of the moral order is seen as essential to the preservation of social and cosmic order generally.

So the prime motivation in group allegiances (as in the case of rivalry) is to serve and protect the social and cosmic order as various discourses have led participants to define them. When boundary-work *is* undertaken to reaffirm a sense of "Self" and community, the ultimate aim is to promote and defend the group's *ideals* rather than the promotion and defence of the group entity itself. To the extent that the group entity becomes important to protect, it is for the sake of maintaining a united force against opposing participant types, and hence, against the violation of one's cherished ideals. In the next chapter I will have more to say about the various strategies that are employed to promote group integration as part of broader discursive objectives. The point I wish to emphasise here, however, is that it is the discourses that are associated with various participant types, rather than any sense of communal belonging or identity, that are primarily driving group affiliations and loyalty.

2:4 – Psychological Factors

Antagonism between participants is also fueled by psychological predispositions towards conflict. My views here should not be confused with psychological theories concerning "personality types." A number of psychologists, such as James Alcock (1981) and Tom Randall (1991), have explored the relationship between paranormal-related beliefs and various personality traits (such as authoritarian, dogmatic, credulous or fantasy-prone tendencies).[9] However, I question such "personality" perspectives on two counts: first, I question the criteria by which various "personality" characteristics are judged to be "positive" or "negative"; and second, I question whether characteristics that might appear to be personality-based should really be treated as psychological traits at all. I contend that personality factors can be better understood as *discursive* constructs.

In regard to the first point – the criteria by which various personality characteristics are judged – I would argue that, from another perspective, so-called "negative" personality traits could be regarded as "positive" traits. Suppose, for example, that a paranormal proponent labels a Skeptic

---

[9] See psychologist Harvey Irwin (1993:21ff) for a comprehensive overview of such studies.

"arrogant" or "dogmatic." From the perspective of a fellow Skeptic, however, this same person might be described as having a "serious", "passionate" and "responsible" disposition — attributes that are generally considered to be positive in nature. By the same token, a paranormal proponent who is labelled by a Skeptic as "gullible" and "ridiculous" may well be viewed by a fellow paranormal proponent as open-minded and even-handed. Characteristics that are viewed as villainous from one perspective tend to be viewed as virtuous from another.

In regard to the second point — whether individual characteristics can properly be understood as being personality-based at all — from a sociological perspective (and, indeed, from the perspective of many social psychologists) those same traits could be seen to have a social, cultural or discursive basis. For example, an individual who is "responsibly" promoting and defending a position may be acting out of a sense of moral duty to uphold socially instilled values that are discursive in origin. Bluntness is another ostensibly personality-based characteristic that can have a discursive basis. David Hess, for example, notes that Western culture (American culture in particular) encourages its citizens to be outspoken and direct in communication, in contrast to, say, Brazil where, "the culture of personalism and the political history of repressive authoritarianism have resulted in much less of a tendency to engage in blunt disagreement" (Hess 1993:179). In fact, I would suggest that many participants in the debate see it as their *right* to strongly voice their opinion, and that they are generally contemptuous of those who might violate that right. This brings me to the final factor that, I contend, is at the heart of the paranormal debate — the moral dimension.

2:5 — Moral Factors

I mentioned earlier that morality is an issue that participants see as in important factor in the disputes that take place. Indeed, it is clear that many participants believe they are promoting or protecting important ideals against what they perceive as damaging forces. The moral importance that participants attach to their actions within the paranormal debate can be traced to the influence of a number of wider discourses. In particular, participants are influenced by discourses that define a demonised "Other" who is seen to pose a threat to the proper order of things (however they might define such order).

An important aspect of preserving the "order of things" is that of protecting the ideals that they believe underpin that order, and here, too, we can see the influence of various discourses at work. For example, we can note the influence on participants of the discursive notion that ideals should be kept "pure" from erroneous ideas—a view that treats knowledge much like a precious resource such as water that can become murky or impure if not protected from contaminants. There is a notion, for example, that science is a pure form of inquiry that should not be infected by pseudoscientific "rubbish", or that Christianity constitutes a pure path that should not be polluted by occult ideas.

Other discourses encourage participants to feel a moral responsibility to preserve their ideals from discrimination and persecution. Such notions are enshrined within Revolutionary and Crusade traditions, which have, historically, encouraged the ideal of fighting for one's beliefs in the face of tyranny or infidels. We have seen how some Skeptics associate paranormal ideas with despotism. Paranormal proponents view Skeptics and Christian opponents as agents of hegemonic institutions, while some Christians view the occult as a weapon of Satan.

But the imposition of one's ideals upon another can also be regarded as a morally responsible act. Some participants may even feel a humanitarian responsibility (as enshrined in Humanist and Christian-missionary ideals) to educate others in terms of understanding the truth (as they see it). For example, the Skeptic Kendrick Frazier writes:

> [I]f an informed and rational citizenry is indeed important
> to a democracy (as I believe it is), then scientists have an
> obligation to help the public understand the difference

between sense and nonsense, good science and bad science, scientific speculation and outright fantasy (1986:xii).

As one Skeptic told me in a somewhat wry manner, "some skeptics can't resist explaining the facts of life to the lesser-educated."

While the discourses examined so far are largely those that tend to encourage confrontational behaviour with regard to other ideational positions, I would also note the influence of discourses that make the alleviation of tension part of a participant's moral duty. For example, an important ideal for many New Age participants is to achieve "universal harmony", and the means of achieving this include tolerating differences and overcoming tensions that might undermine such harmony. As one New Age-oriented crop circle researcher told me: "Everyone has their own ideas, their own theories, and we don't push for any particular one." Having said that, one wonders how far these same crop circle researchers would tolerate a vocal sceptic in their midst?

What most interests me about all these discourses is the often subtle way they encourage participants to see it as their moral duty to serve particular discursive objectives and carry out their adopted roles based largely on their own initiative. The reason for such dutiful service, I contend, relates not only to the benefits seen in performing such action (or the consequences if one does not), but also to the fact that for many participants this is an "instinctive" response, based on taken-for-granted differences and demonisations that underlie their views of opponents. It is the processes by which participants incorporate such characterisations of the "Other" into their individual outlooks that I shall now examine in some detail.

3. The Doxa of Conflict

As I suggested in my critique of the incommensurability perspective, there is, in my opinion, no significant, *objectively-based* differences between participants in the paranormal debate that should lead them to set themselves so strongly against opponents in the manner that they often do. However, participants themselves seem largely unable, or unwilling, to recognise any commonalities between themselves and their opponents, and their failure to do so can, I contend, be attributed to two main factors. First, participants may not see it in their best interests to acknowledge that they have anything in common with their opponents. On the contrary, for rhetorical reasons, there is a tendency for participants to want to divorce themselves as much as possible from opponents as part of a strategy of demonisation. The second factor that can obscure common discursive forces is the way that discourses themselves promote differences — differences that can become so internalised and naturalised within participants' outlooks that they do not even think to question their validity and look for common ground with opponents.

In the paranormal debate, participants are primed to see their opponents as irrational and immoral. Once a fellow participant has been identified as subscribing to a certain ideological camp, the content of what they actually say becomes immaterial, because their overall point of view — or their motivation for presenting it — is seen as contrary to their own, and everything they do and say is framed by this politicised context.

Take for example a UFO researcher and a Skeptic who reject a particular UFO sighting on much the same grounds (say, insufficient evidence), and may well find agreement on a whole range of cases, methods and notions. Regardless of the common position, the UFO researcher and the Skeptic are felt to differ regarding their general optimism towards the possibility of alien visitors, and it is this point of difference — above any commonalities — that is regarded as pivotal to defining the nature of their relationship and their interaction. Hence, the UFO researcher would see the Skeptic as rejecting the sighting because they don't want any UFO cases to be proven as extraterrestrial, and consequently would feel very little affinity with them. The Skeptic is seen to be discrediting the field as a means to reinforcing a human-centric view of the cosmos that is contrary to open-minded inquiry—an assumption that is felt to be inscribed into the very heart of Skepticism and contrary to the principles of true scientific inquiry. It never enters the mind of either the UFO researcher or the Skeptic to intelligently address the intrinsic conservatism of mainstream academic inquiry that discourages radical departures from established findings without strong evidence to the contrary. The two sides are simply too entrenched in their demonised conceptions of one another to enter into such a risky reflexive dialogue. The differences between them are seen to be too fundamental, too natural, and such fundamental differences present a threat to rational inquiry and the cosmological and social order on which it depends.

Pierre Bourdieu is perhaps the main social theorist to explore the naturalisation process of ideas, and he characterises it as follows:

> [T]he established cosmological and political order is perceived not as arbitrary, i.e. as one possible order among others, but as a self-evident and natural order which goes without saying and therefore goes unquestioned (1977:166).

Bourdieu refers to this unquestioned aspect of knowledge as "doxa", which he contrasts with disputed knowledge (which consists of "orthodox" and "heterodox" ideas) that, because it is not taken-for-granted, belongs to what he refers to as the "field of opinion" or the "universe of ... argument." Bourdieu argues that doxa is reproduced habitually, unless some disruptive event, such as "culture contact" or "political and economic crises correlative with class division" (1977:168), results in a legitimacy crisis and "brings the undiscussed into discussion" (*ibid*).

At first sight, the paranormal debate—where so many taken-for-granted truths are openly contested—might seem to be a "field of opinion" that operates outside the influence of doxa. In this respect, it might be argued that participants have separated or "bracketed" normally doxic elements, and have subjected them to intense scrutiny. However, the possibility that *any* discussion can take place above and beyond the influence of doxic assumptions is naïve. This is because doxic assumptions are subtly influencing so many aspects of people's outlooks that their effect can never be completely negated.

I would go so far as to argue, in fact, that the very debate itself is constituted by unquestioned doxic assumptions, such as the distinction between matter and spirit, between apprehension and imagination, and between rationality and irrationality. Doxic truths are largely responsible for motivating participants to debate their ideas in the first place, and they also play a role in determining which ideas are open to question and even the way those ideas are debated. Participants often cite "doxic" assumptions as lying at the heart of their opponents' (although seldom their own) positions. Skeptics, for example, frequently criticise paranormal proponents for basing their ideas on (what is to Skeptics at least) the false assumption that there is a magical/spiritual dimension to reality. Likewise, paranormal proponents often challenge the views of Skeptics because they see them as being based on unquestioned materialist assumptions. Neither of them, however, question the possibility that the material-spiritual dichotomy could be a spurious one to start with, or that such concepts might be mere artefacts of language. This is not to elevate the point of view of philosophy, but simply to point out that participants in the debate are guided by sets of assumptions that are not normally interrogated.

Some social analysts argue that debate over matters such as "spiritual existence" actually have the effect of reinforcing the doxic assumptions underlying their conception (Latour, 1993:123–124). Social analyst Richard Harvey Brown argues, in fact, that the concealment of the arbitrary nature of these concepts and the distinctions made between them is essential to the functioning of the social order (1994:236). Brown remarks:

> [T]he processes of definition and exclusion are not only logical properties of discourse; they also are preconditions of intelligibility, sociation, social order, and social control. To make reality mutually comprehensible in an intersubjective group and to regularize symbolically

> guided social behavior, some versions of reality must be
> legitimised at the expense of their competitors
> (1994:234–35).

Doxic assumptions, then, are part of the overall framework for understanding the world around us, and cannot be readily subjected to scrutiny as isolated elements. Brown's formulation helps us to understand how difficult it is for participants to bracket any perceived differences between themselves and their opponents. Foucault gives us an indication where the problem with bracketing lies when he writes:

> ... there is no statement in general, no free, neutral, inde-
> pendent statement; but a statement always belongs to a
> series or a whole, always plays a role among other state-
> ments, deriving support from them and distinguishing
> itself from them: it is always part of a network of state-
> ments, in which it has a role, however minimal it may be, to
> play (1972:99).

The general idea here is that each statement or truth claim is reinforced by other statements or truth claims, and so on *ad infinitum* in a process of circular reinforcement. Consequently, to properly bracket the claims in dispute, participants would need to follow the trail of assumptions right back through the network of interdependent truth claims.[10] Further, such an inquiry would require a high degree of commitment to, and skill at, the practice of reflexivity in order to expose all the underlying doxa—and there are a number of obstacles that would have to be overcome in this respect. A commitment to reflexivity, for example, tends to be undermined by the various discursive forces (such as the demonisation of the Other and notions of ideological, moral and cosmic dangers) that make such critical reflection a risky endeavour.

---

[10] This is a process that might be viewed more one of deconstruction than reflexivity. Deconstruction can be defined as "a strategy for revealing the underlayers of meanings 'in' a text that were suppressed or assumed in order for it to take its actual form" (Appignanesi & Garratt 1995:80).

Indeed, assumptions about the differences between concepts such as "matter" and "spirit" are not what drive the disagreements between participants. It is the way those differences are invalidated and their proponents demonised that is at issue. The problem begins when differences are cast in terms of "judgemental" hierarchical distinctions such as those of good/evil or moral/immoral. It is through such associations, themselves doxic, that a distinction such as the normal/paranormal one plays a role in a greater social or cosmic drama than the paranormal debate itself.

Conclusion

My main objective in this chapter has been to examine the issues that underlie conflict within the paranormal debate. I first presented a critique of the incommensurability thesis, which has been a popular explanation amongst analysts to explain conflict within the debate. Contrary to this theory, which proposes that differences emerge and cannot be resolved because opposing positions are too divergent, I indicated that difference is largely a discursively based perception that is encouraged by a number of factors (themselves discursive) such as rivalry, psychological "drives" and communitarian "needs." But the factor that I identified as contributing most to the perception of difference in the debate was the influence of various discourses that motivate participants to oppose (often on moral grounds) those who are seen to threaten the social and cosmic order. It is because these discourses are so taken-for-granted that participants fail to realise the arbitrary nature of the differences that they believe separate them from their opponents.

The conclusion that can be drawn from this chapter is that the paranormal debate, although held by participants to *ideally* be a rational dialogue over the nature of reality, is in fact a *dispute* that is primarily discursive in nature. In particular, I have argued that the dispute appears to centre on underlying discursive structures that have produced (or at least exaggerated) certain paradigmatic dichotomies as a means of defining a noble "Self" against a demonised "Other."

This "otherness", I argued, is not simply a means of defining in-group identity, but is a distinction that is deeply discursive in nature — centering on epistemological, ideological and ontological notions concerning the value and place of virtues such as discipline, spirituality and dutifulness in the proper functioning of society and the cosmos as a whole. In the next chapter, I want to explore the different strategies that participants employ to deal with such perceived transgression and deviance, and how these efforts themselves have the effect of reinforcing the demonised views that participants have of one another.

Chapter 6

Strategic Action Within the Debate

Introduction

I argued in the last chapter that the main motive of those who participate in paranormal debate is to promote and defend various positions that encapsulate their particular view of reality and their place within it. In this chapter I want to examine the strategies that participants employ to achieve this end. I will argue that most strategies take a form that tends to reflect the wider discursive-based ideals that I have outlined in previous chapters, and are aimed more at enforcing those ideals than at reaching any mutual understanding or agreement with opponents. It is in this chapter that I will reveal the strategic manoeuvring that takes place within the paranormal debate to serve and protect those ideals, and where we will see the politics of truth in its most transparent and intense form.

1. Understanding Strategic Action

When analysts talk of a strategy, they are generally referring to a plan of action aimed at achieving a particular end or objective. In practice, however, the distinction between a strategy and an objective is not all that clear-cut, because a particular objective may itself be one of a number of intermediate steps, which are themselves strategies for achieving larger objectives. For example, the strategies that participants in the paranormal debate employ against their opponents usually have one of the following objectives:

eliciting a confession, degrading an opponent's status, or silencing them. But these objectives, in turn, are often strategies aimed at achieving more general objectives — such as discrediting opponent positions or persuading opponents to accept a particular point of view. The situation is further complicated by the fact that even the more general objectives can themselves be strategic devices aimed at larger objectives — for example, discrediting opponents can indirectly serve to protect one's own cherished ideals, which in turn participants might see as protecting the social or cosmic order. I have listed some of the main strategies and objectives that I will be examining in this chapter in the following table:

Primary Strategies	Intermediate Strategies/ Objectives	Ultimate Objectives
Labelling		
Ridicule	Silencing	Protect Ideals
Ostracism	} Confession }	Defeat opponents
Legal action	Degradation	Force a dialogue
Controlling sites		

Table 1: Types of Strategies/Objectives in the Paranormal Debate

I will now briefly examine the various intermediate strategies/objectives that participants tend to employ in the paranormal debate before examining the more primary strategies.

1:1 – Eliciting a Confession

It could be argued that a central objective in the Internet debate examined in Chapter Five was participants' desire to elicit a confession from their opponents that their position is in some way misguided. The Skeptic Richard seems to have been seeking an admission from his pro-paranormal opponents that mediumship and astrology are flawed. Richard's opponents, however, not only failed to "confess" to any possible error, but they themselves seemed to have been seeking a confession from Richard that his Skepticism was misguided.

The art of persuading people to confess the "error" of their ways has become an important strategy not only in the paranormal debate but in Western discourse generally. Foucault notes:

> Since the Middle Ages at least, Western societies have established the confession as one of the main rituals we rely on for the production of truth (1980[1978]:58).

Foucault adds: "The truthful confession was inscribed at the heart of the procedures of individualization by power" (1980[1978]:58–59). What he means by this is that the practice of confession has historically formed an important component of strategies that aim to encourage individuals to monitor their thoughts and behaviour and to correct any "errors" that may be present, thereby reinforcing their conformity to discursive-based norms. But confession, in its more dramatised form, serves a more public function by demonstrating to others what are and are not acceptable modes of thought. For example, the witch-hunts in the sixteenth and seventeenth centuries attached great importance to eliciting a public confession from the accused (typically by torture), which had a demonstrative effect on the public generally. The effect was to reaffirm the moral order of the day and the authority of the Church as the guardians of that order. As French philosopher Jean-Francois Lyotard remarks:

> At confession, Satan speaks the language of God ... Whether the criminal pays or not is beside the point. What matters is that integrity and uniqueness have been restored to the language of communication by his confession and public declaration, even if they have been fabricated (1992:109).

While physical torture is no longer legally sanctioned within Western society as a strategy to elicit such confessions with respect to occult claims, participants in the paranormal debate employ a range of more "civilised" strategies to elicit this confession of error, as will be seen from the strategies I examine throughout this chapter.

1:2 – *Degradation*

Another intermediate objective that participants in the paranormal debate frequently seek is to degrade their opponent's position. Participants often attempt to do this by employing various forms of "character assassination", and the Internet debate examined in Chapter Five was replete with acrimonious name-calling and put-downs (as is perhaps common in public Internet forums, but also common in dialogue between protagonists in the paranormal debate regardless of the arena). Such strategies are directed towards both psychological and public objectives. In psychological terms, degradation aims to lower an opponent's self-esteem, with the more general objective of silencing them or possibly converting them to one's own position. In terms of its public objective, degradation serves to strip opponents of their status – what Harold Garfinkel (1956) refers to as a "status degradation ceremony". The status I refer to is that of the authority to speak on what is and is not real in the universe. Degradation also has a demonstrative effect in terms of serving as a warning to others of the consequences of deviating from the ideals that one is promoting. In this latter sense, degradation acts as a deterrent.

1:3 – *Silencing/Isolating Opponents*

A third objective pursued by participants is to silence opponents. A whole range of strategies are employed in paranormal disputes to silence one's opponents – some threaten punishment if opponents should speak out, others attempt to disrupt an opponent's means of communication (such as preventing access to the media, educational institutions, and so on). In the next section, I will examine such strategies in some detail, as well as those used to achieve the other intermediate objectives discussed above.

2. Strategic Devices

Participants in the paranormal debate employ a range of strategies to achieve their various intermediate objectives, although this choice is determined in part by certain limitations inherent within the paranormal debate itself. For example, social analysts have long realised that the strategies available for social control partly depend on the degree of social integration within a community, with tight social integration allowing the employment of more judicial means of control, and loose integration requiring more "diffusive", coercive measures (Beattie 1964:167,172). As I have pointed out, the paranormal scene is best described as a loosely integrated network of participants characterised by a multiplicity of ideational boundaries.

Further contributing to the problem is the lack of overarching organisational structure and social control mechanisms that might aid integration. For example, with the exception of a small number of highly integrated "cult" communities, most paranormal interest groups and organisations are generally weak in terms of control over their membership, and certainly do not form a united body in terms of policing the various fields or the scene as a whole. Moreover, there is little in the way of a peer-review process or reward system that could foster conformity and compliance, such as one finds, say, within the academic community (Myers 1990:16; Nowotny 1979:10). Nor is there a strong internal hierarchy of authority such as one finds in Church organisations. But a more significant obstacle to integration than the lack of control mechanisms is the individualistic ethos that prevails amongst many participants — namely, the "privatised" element that sociologist Thomas Luckmann (1991) has drawn attention to.[1] In short, paranormal proponents largely view their pursuit as a personal journey, in which formulating their individual out-

---

[1]   This spirit of individualism is, however, tempered to some extent by many participants' desire to be part of a collective social movement in order to wield greater influence in the "public sphere."

look amongst the array of possibilities is seen to be intrinsic to framing their mode of involvement.

With participants in the paranormal scene lacking a strong commitment to integration, and not being subject to an overarching authority or much in the way of institutional control mechanisms, it is not surprising that they tend to employ a range of more diffuse, coercive strategic devices to achieve their various objectives. I will now examine these strategies in some detail.

2:1 – Rational Critique

In the Internet debate described earlier, participants were clearly seeking to establish their position as being the most rational vis-à-vis that of their opponents. Indeed, the notion of debate in the form of reasoned argument has long been an important tool in Western culture for discrediting opposing positions by demonstrating their irrationality. This is a tradition that has come down to us from Greek philosophy, where debating one's position in a rational manner was considered an important means for establishing "truth". The questioning of positions that is so prevalent in paranormal-related debates can be seen as a reflection of this "noble" tradition, and consequently, debating paranormal-related issues is a highly valued mode of interaction for nearly all participants. As Michael Corbin, Director of ParaNet Information Service, puts it simply: "It is our philosophy to encourage debate on paranormal issues" (1992:online), and in many respects, the debates that take place seem little different from debates among academics, at least in terms of their form (although certainly not their content).

The general impression that one gets from the sociological literature, however, is that rational debate is strictly a non-strategic form of interaction. According to Habermas (1979), for example, "argumentative speech" involving rational debate between participants is where the "force" of the better argument prevails in a "democratic" spirit. Habermas contrasts this with "strategic action", which consists of persuasive strategies ranging from subtle techniques such as rhetoric, to more blatant coercive measures such as verbal or physical violence. However, it is my contention that even in its purest form, argumentative speech can be a useful strategy to subordinate opposing positions. In fact, argumentative speech seems to be one of the most popular strategies employed in the debate to promote one's position and undermine that of one's opponent, whether this objective is achieved through "rationally" eliciting a confession of error, degrading one's opponents by demonstrating their "irrationality", or discouraging them from voicing their views for fear of being rationally critiqued. Employed as a strategy in this manner, rational criticism is not so much intended to discover truth, as it is to persuasively maintain the truth that one has already come to accept.

But it is in its less-than-ideal form that argumentative speech reveals its true potential as a strategic device. At this level, demonstrating that one's opponent is being irrational can take a highly rhetorical form, where participants seek to establish no more than the *appearance* that an opponent's position is irrational (and, consequently, that their own position is rational).[2] Apart from the "rational" style of language rhetorically employed to achieve a "mantle" of rationalism (Ross 1991:17), there are a range of other rhetorical devices that participants employ, such as "straw-man" arguments and *ad hominem* attacks (such as those I described in the previous chapter, where the Internet debate eventually degenerated into personal attacks on opponents).[3]

---

[2]   It might be argued, however, that if there is no universal foundation to judgements of rationality, then all claims of rationality are ultimately rhetorical in nature. But even if this is the case, it is still possible to make a distinction between those claims that tend to be genuinely made in accordance with certain prescribed "rational" ideals, and those that falsely or "rhetorically" claim to be of this form.

[3]   In a "straw man" argument, the weakest version of an opponent's position is presented and then knocked down, with their entire position subsequently declared (or implied) to have been

Even when employed internally (i.e. amongst those who
support one's position) or reflexively (i.e. as a self-critique
of one's own perspective), rational argument can serve the
political and therapeutic function of reaffirming the validity of one's own position. As social analyst Jodi Dean notes
with regard to UFO proponents: "The reflexivity of the UFO
discourse, its critical and self-critical practices, helps
ufology reassure itself of its own rationality" (1998:56).

2:2 – *Labelling Strategies*

Social analysts such as Howard Becker (1963) view the
employment of labels as important devices of social control
in Western society generally, so it is not surprising that
labelling has become an important strategic device in the
paranormal debate as well.[4] For example, a form of labelling
was used in the Internet debate, when Aaron, a paranormal
proponent, referred to the Skeptic Richard in a series of
posts as a "bigot", a "fool" and a "cynic." Often, however,
labelling is applied in a subtler manner, using what appear
to be relatively innocuous labels. It is these labels that I shall
focus on here.

Most of the labels (or schemas) employed in the debate
tend to revolve around a common set of cultural dichotomies that have pejorative connotations, and Hess (1993) lists
some of the main dichotomies employed by participants
when he remarks:

> [T]hey rely on a shared set of cultural categories such as
> disinterested/commercial, spiritual/material, holistic/
> mechanistic, mind/body, rational/irrational, scien-
> tific/religious, future-oriented/past-oriented, and fron-
> tier/backwater (1993:69).

---

invalidated. *Ad hominem* arguments attack the credibility of the
claimant rather than the claim itself.

[4]   In using the term "labelling," however, I am not implying (as Becker
does) that "the person becomes the thing he is described as being"
(Gove 1980:13–14). Rather, my usage refers only to the strategy
employed to achieve such an effect, while the success of this strategy
is an issue that I will deal with separately later in this chapter.

Hess notes how these categories draw on shared understandings that are embedded within the wider culture, and I
will now discuss how such labelling reveals, yet again, the
influence of wider discourses on participants.

Beginning with the future-oriented/past-oriented label,
Hess observes that, in paranormal debates, "the Other is frequently located in a space and time of "there and then", as
opposed to the "here and now" of the Self" (1993:44). The
basis for most characterisations of this type is the favourable
manner in which, in this technological, progress-oriented
society of ours, the present and future are valued over the
past. Hence, Skeptics hold that paranormal ideas are remnants of the Dark Ages (when, so it is argued, the true workings of reality were largely unknown), and consequently
such ideas have become synonymous with ignorance. Similarly, paranormal proponents locate Skeptics within a conservative, inflexible Establishment that clings to an
old-fashioned, Victorian-type rationality, while they see
their own activities as being at the forefront of a for-
ward-looking "scientific revolution" (Hess 1993:78ff).

The frontier/backwater schema is another labelling
device that is popular in the debate, and which again draws
on a common Western discursive tradition — in this case,
that of colonisation. The frontier schema is a very positive
label in Western discourse generally, where explorers are
regarded as heroes — brave people who risk dangers and
fight the odds in the noble pursuit of discovering what is
"out there", and ultimately conquering the unknown. Skeptics, for example, regard the orthodox science that they generally uphold as a frontier exploration of the wider
universe, while they see paranormal proponents as being at
the "fringe paranormal ghetto" (as Richard puts it in one of
his Internet newsgroup posts) of territory already covered
and dismissed by science long ago. The Skeptic Kendrick
Frazier writes:

> If the frontiers of science are a newly discovered ocean for
> exploration, the borderlands of science are a murky,
> backwatery swamp right here on land. If science is an
> advancing, forward progression of the frontiers of knowl-

edge, the pseudosciences are a much-trodden farmed-out field at the rear flanks (1981:viii).

Paranormal proponents, on the other hand, locate themselves firmly at the frontier of exploration, and locate Skeptics, not so much at the fringes, but in the conservative heartlands far away from the real challenges and most important discoveries waiting to be made at the frontier.[5]

Another popular Western label that emerges in paranormal disputes centres on an open/closed-minded dichotomy. For example, in reference to the general public's growing acceptance of paranormal phenomena, one crop circle researcher told me, "People are becoming more open-minded about things." Paranormal proponents generally regard Skeptics, on the other hand, as being close-minded to the possibility that there are mysterious phenomena for which orthodox science does not have adequate explanations. But Skeptics tend to regard such characterisations as quite hollow. For example, according to a newsgroup post by one Skeptic:

> This "open-mindedness" is really a rhetorical device. For the psychics, being "open minded" does not mean looking at their claims and being willing to accept them if they show evidence for it, which skeptics are willing to do ... It means, "accept all I say as true without evidence, or else I will call you close-minded!!!

Skeptics have their own definition of what properly constitutes an "open-mind". They equate open-mindedness with a questioning, critical approach—qualities that are the essence, they contend, of rational scepticism. Some see those who hold paranormal/religious type convictions as being too open-minded in fact, and are fond of the adage that "one's mind should not be so open that one's brain falls out!" Generally, however, Skeptics view paranormal pro-

---

[5]   Not all participants, however, identify with the frontier schema. Conservative and fundamentalist Christians, for example, tend to believe that both paranormal and scientific frontiers are off-track—leading people away from the age-old, well-established path to God.

ponents as close-minded to the facts of reality (as they see them), clinging irrationally to gullible beliefs.

Skeptics, it seems, take pride in their cautious approach to intellectual inquiry, and such caution, which is generally viewed as a positive attribute in scientific enquiry, has become enshrined within the "sceptic" label. It is not uncommon, however, to come across paranormal proponents who also claim to be sceptical in their outlook. For example, Australian UFO researcher Simon Harvey-Wilson told me:

> I'm a real sceptic. For example, if President Clinton got up
> on television tomorrow and told us UFOs are real, I would
> listen very carefully to what he said, but if you asked me
> now whether I'd believe him, my guess is probably not. So
> am I sceptical? Yes. But I mean, I'm even sceptical of people
> who claim to channel information from aliens. I'm sceptical
> of quite a lot of the New Age gurus (1996: personal
> interview).

Hess makes a similar observation about how New Agers "see themselves as skeptics in their own right" (1993:14). Christian conservatives and fundamentalists, too, emphasise their own brand of scepticism, which centres on an ethos of questioning the atheistic values of Western society and being alert to the possible "Satanic" content of contemporary trends, especially paranormal ideas. This again points to the same discursive notions being applied in countervailing ways.

Another popular label derived from the wider discursive environment centres on the moral/immoral dichotomy. For example, many Skeptics regard paranormal proponents who take high-profile roles within the scene as being motivated by the "immoral" incentives of power and profit. With regard to the profit motive, for example, Richard made pointed references in the Internet debate to both the astrologer's and the medium's fees. At the same time, Skeptics generally overlook the safe income-generating aspect of the orthodox academic and scientific professions that they support, seeing them as noble career paths that are oriented towards the advancement of society (with their own Skepti-

cal position seen as an important aspect of this progress).
Hess writes:

> In locating skepticism on a place above this-worldly values
> such as social prestige and material success, skeptics por-
> tray themselves as motivated by the loftier values of mind
> and reason rather than material interest and emotional
> needs (1993:63).

But, as Hess also points out, psychical researchers and
New Agers, too, see themselves as being motivated by
"purer motives" (1993:63). Many paranormal proponents,
for example, see themselves as being willing to sacrifice the
safe, comfortable position of orthodox science in order to
nobly pursue the truth, and many justify any income-generating aspects of participation as a necessity, caused by the
lack of financial support for paranormal-related activities
from the Establishment. In contrast, they tend to see
sceptical academics as people who are toeing the orthodox
line because of the ignoble motive of wanting to preserve
their careers and the financial and psychological security
that established knowledge and "safe" careers are seen to
provide. New Agers are even more prone to regard Skeptics
as being supporters of an Establishment (which includes
the government and other mainstream institutions)
founded on greed and materialism, in contrast to their own
role as the spiritual ambassadors of a more loving, harmoni-
ous order. This ideal of action guided by pure motives is
one that, in Western society, is largely derived from
Judaic-Christian traditions that have, down through
history, tried to set religious/spiritual pursuits apart from
worldly, merchant-oriented activities.[6]

Another popular label that participants in the paranormal debate tend to employ is that of the "underdog" — in
that they see themselves as having to fight against seemingly overwhelming odds to gain acceptance for their ideas.
Paranormal proponents, for example, often represent their

---

[6]   In Christianity, this principle can be traced back to the biblical story
of Jesus admonishing the moneylenders in the temple (*Matthew*
21:12–13).

situation in terms of a small minority fighting a powerful, tyrannical establishment (Ben-Yehuda 1985:216). As parapsychologist Caroline Watt told me about her field: "... it's like David and Goliath at the moment. I think we're David, sort of throwing a little pebble at Goliath" (1996: personal interview). She later pointed out to me that this was no "representational strategy":

> It is a fact in terms of simple numbers — parapsychologists ARE hugely outnumbered by mainstream scientists and as a consequence have relatively tiny resources, e.g., in terms of grant income and 'manpower' — it's just arithmetic, not a rhetorical strategy ... Sybo Schouten (1993) once calculated that the entire resources devoted to psychical research and parapsychology since 1882 was equivalent to less than two months of American psychology. This helps to put things into perspective (2006: personal interview).

However, it needs to be kept in mind that parapsychology is a sub-field in the discipline of psychology along with many others — some well resourced, others not. The basis for talking of parapsychology as being up against the discipline as a whole or against mainstream science as a monolithic entity only makes sense from an "underdog" schema. In other words, the representation precedes the "arithmetic".

The underdog representation is also evident in the following remark made by a speaker at an Australasian Society for Psychical Research meeting I attended:

> I think that for all of us here ... we are a tiny minority, a very small minority, and the fact is that it is not easy for us to keep going with the distortion, the lies, the ridicule, the hostility around us.

Interestingly, Skeptics also tend to see themselves as a small, yet dedicated minority — one fighting against an overwhelming tide of irrationalism. Hess observes:

> In this social drama between the skeptical Self and the paranormal Other, the skeptic is cast in the role of the underdog. Skeptics who oppose the paranormal do so against great odds: both against the media, which over-whelmingly favors the paranormal, and against wide-spread popular support of supernatural belief ... (1993:63).

Meanwhile, many Christians (particularly Fundamentalists) also employ this label—representing themselves as a small but loyal band of "God's servants" fighting against a worldwide tide of spiritual ignorance and sin.

Despite the popularity of the underdog schema, however, all sides of the paranormal debate are quick to draw on notions of wide support when it suits them. Paranormal proponents, for example, often claim widespread support from the general public for their position (justifiably so, if we are to accept the Gallup poll statistics tabled in the Appendix). Skeptics, on the other hand, tend to claim strong backing from the scientific community and other Rationalists to support their position as the dominant one in Western society, while conservative and fundamentalist Christians claim to have the powerful support of millions of other Christians, of Scripture and of an omnipotent God.[7]

Another label widely employed by participants is the "subversive" schema. For example, the term "occult", which tends to be applied to paranormal ideas by some opponents, can have pejorative connotations of veiled deception and deviancy. Indeed, the word "occult" itself means hidden or esoteric, and has long been employed as a derogative label by the Church. Skeptics also tend to portray paranormal proponents as somewhat shadowy figures who need to be "exposed." Some paranormal proponents employ a similar strategy of portraying the Establishment (including the government, military, scientific community and the Church) as being the secretive ones in terms of their alleged involvement in conspiracies and cover-ups. This whole discourse that surrounds secretive, subversive activities is one that is derived from Western traditions. Foucault, for example, contends that modern Rationalist discourse generally has sought to,

> ... demolish the unlit chambers where arbitrary political
> acts, monarchical caprice, religious superstitions, tyranni-

---

[7]   Writes Christian fundamentalist, Ken Ham: "We know that even though we are a minority in this world, with the Creator God on our side, we become a majority" (1992:online).

cal and priestly plots, epidemics and the illusions of ignorance were fomented (1980[1977]:153).

As evidence of the wide-ranging influence of such discourses within society generally, we might note that conspiratorial accusations are also a common aspect of
inter-denominational conflict within religious circles and
disputes between parties in the political arena.

The labelling of groups in the scene as "cults" is another
manifestation of the discourse of subversion, as cults are
one of the main paranormal-related groups often associated
with deviant, secretive practices. Cults have variously been
associated with brainwashing, mass suicides and other
"extremist" activities and beliefs, and paranormal proponents are particularly susceptible to being negatively associated with such ideas and practices. For example, after the
1997 "Heaven's Gate" cult-suicide tragedy, some Skeptics
and the media made associations between the cult's
UFO-related ideas and those of UFO proponents generally.[8]
In response, a number of UFO proponents went into damage control by distancing themselves from cult-like beliefs
and activities. For example, UFO proponent Anne Ramsey
Cuvelier wrote:

> I would like to correct the misguided notion being
> expressed in the media that the suicides are in some way
> connected to serious research of UFO phenomena. The
> activities of this bizarre cult had about as much to do with
> the study of UFOs as the Jim Jones group had to the teach-
> ings of Christianity (1997: A25).

But Skeptics do not have a monopoly on the strategic use of
the "cult" label. Some paranormal proponents refer to Skepticism as a cult. Aaron, a participant in the Internet debate
described in Chapter Five, referred to Skeptics on one occa-
sion as a "Skepti-cult."

---

[8]   The Heaven's Gate cult's UFO-related beliefs are stated on the cult's
      website (http://www.heavensgate.com) where, prior to their
      suicide, it was announced: "Hale-Bopp's approach is the 'marker'
      we've been waiting for—the time for the arrival of the spacecraft
      from the Level Above Human to take us home to 'Their World' "
      (online, 1998).

Other labels that are sometimes used against opponents in paranormal disputes are the "fundamentalist and "religious" labels. Participants on all sides of the paranormal debate tend to apply the fundamentalist label to indicate that their opponent's position is extreme and dogmatic in nature, while the religious label carries the connotation bestowed upon it by Humanism—namely, that of a close-minded commitment to an outdated belief system. Skeptics, for example, often portray paranormal interests as a religious-like faith. Conversely, a crop circle researcher I spoke to described Skeptics as part of "the most powerful religious orthodoxy in the world—Scientism." In another example (again drawn from the Internet debate), Aaron at one stage referred to the belief system of the Skeptic Richard as a "religion." Aaron writes:

> The problem with *ORTHODOX* science is that even common sense is thrown by the wayside in favor of doctrines of an old, decaying religion, orthodox science.

By associating orthodox science with religion, science is being characterised as a system based on doctrines and faith, rather than on an objective search for "facts."

The notion that religion itself is "unscientific" is derived from the historical struggle between Humanism and Christianity, in which Christianity was eventually assigned the status of a faith-based belief system. In fact, most of the labels that I have discussed here derive their power from historical struggles that have become part of modern Western consciousness. The concept of "frontier", for example, derives its power from the expansionist programs of colonial powers and the conflicts (such as the American War of Independence) that emerged between the pioneers of the "New World" and those who remained in the "Old World." Although such schemas originated in political disputes and struggles that, in most cases, are totally unrelated to the paranormal dispute, they have become so romanticised within our Western culture and embedded in our common discourse that they have carried over into the paranormal debate, where they are employed as rhetorical devices against opponents.

Collectively, these labels serve as metaphors that conjure up a dramatised and emotionally charged perspective on reality and society that participants can identify with and employ to frame their interaction with others. It is interesting to note in this respect how the future/frontier-oriented, open-minded, sceptical, pure-minded and underdog labels are all closely related to one another in a conceptual sense. Collectively they conjure up an image of an unexplored territory (i.e. the "frontier") which awaits discovery (i.e. a "future- oriented" realm) and into which participants who are prepared to adapt to the "new" (i.e. are "open-minded"), yet who exercise a degree of caution (i.e. are "sceptical") and have good moral judgement (i.e. are "pure-minded"), bravely venture without the support or the consent of the masses (i.e. as underdogs and rebels). Their opponents, on the other hand, are characterised as "close-minded" individuals who cling to the safe auspices of an "outdated" belief system.

Each label uniquely emphasises a certain quality (such as a psychological, temporal or spatial aspect) that the other labels do not on their own fully address. Cognitive and linguistic theorists George Lakoff and Mark Johnson point out:

> … we need two metaphors … because there is no one metaphor that will do the job … The various metaphorical structurings of a concept serve different purposes by highlighting different aspects of the concept (1980:95).

However, such labels are not used merely as rhetorical devices to portray oneself in a positive light and one's opponent in an unfavourable light, for participants can be quite sincere in the labels they apply to themselves and their opponents and perceive them to be factually based, as I will discuss in more detail later in this chapter. Rather, I would emphasise the influence of discourses in encouraging such perceptions as part of the "political" construction of identity and ontology in the paranormal scene — namely, that of heroic selves and demonised others engaged in high-stake cosmic struggles, which is inscribed into the outlooks of participants as taken-for-granted truths.

2:3 – Ridicule

Another popular strategic device that participants employ against their opponents in paranormal disputes is that of ridicule. For example, ridicule has long been a favourite device employed by Skeptics against paranormal proponents. Writes prominent Skeptic Martin Gardner:

> People are not persuaded by arguments to give up childish beliefs; either they never give them up or they outgrow them ... For these reasons, when writing about extreme eccentricities of science, I have adopted H.L. Mencken's sage advice: one horse-laugh is worth a thousand syllogisms (1981:xv–xvi).

Paranormal proponents seem to almost expect at some stage to be called a "loony", "kook", "weirdo", or to be made the butt of jokes that bring into question their mental stability. The use of ridicule is intended to have a degrading or silencing effect. With regard to its silencing effect, many experiencess cite the fear of ridicule as the main reason for their reluctance to go public with their experiences. For example, one woman who claims to have seen a UFO explains: "I hesitated to ever speak out about this because I feared criticism and ridicule" ("Music that's out of this World!" 1990:online). The aim of ridicule is to reduce paranormal proponents to the status of a spectacle or joke—people whose views should not be taken seriously. Similarly, both paranormal proponents and Skeptics are inclined to ridicule Christian fundamentalists, and even Skeptics are increasingly complaining of being subject to ridicule from paranormal proponents, the media and the general public (see, for example, Sutcliffe 1996).

Social analysts have long understood the way that ridicule can be an important weapon employed by just about anyone (including the socially downtrodden).[9] Even when not employed directly as a weapon, ridiculing another can

[9]   Youth subcultural theorists such as Paul Willis (1977) argue that youths employ ridicule as a way of resisting the authority of teachers and other authoritative figures in their society, while anthropologist

have a therapeutic effect in terms of boosting one's own self-esteem. For example, derision of opponents, even when they are not present, plays an important role at many of the Skeptic and pro-paranormal meetings and conferences I attended, where it seemed to serve the purpose of reinforcing the superiority of the attending members vis-à-vis their detractors.

2:4 – Legal Strategies

Another strategy employed by participants to gain the upper hand in paranormal-related disputes is the threat, and occasional carrying out, of legal action against opponents. This strategy – which typically involves accusing opponents of slander or defamation of character – while not widely used by participants, has become an important strategic device for some (notably Skeptics and "psychics"). The threat to use the legal system to address grievances is sometimes regarded as the only recourse available to some participants, given the absence of any institutionalised form of redress within the paranormal scene itself.

One of the most publicised examples of legal action employed in the paranormal scene was the 1991 attempt by "spoon-bender" Uri Geller to prosecute prominent CSICOP member James Randi, for (amongst other things) defamation, after Randi had accused Geller in a newspaper interview of using "tricks" rather than psychic powers to perform his feats (something he had been accusing Geller of for many years, in fact).[10] A desire to discourage Randi from this ongoing crusade to discredit him would seem to be the most obvious motive for Geller's lawsuit.[11]

Keith Basso (1979) notes its use amongst American natives seeking to resist the authority of colonial powers.

[10] Geller lost the case and was fined US$150,000 for initiating a "frivolous complaint" against CSICOP (Karr 1995).

[11] Paul Kurtz characterized Geller's legal action as the "kind of suit being used as a means of silencing debate on significant scientific issues" (Karr 1995:4).

Certainly, the ideological dimension of legal action—namely, the courts' role as an important institution for defining societal norms—has long seen the courts play a significant role in the politics surrounding the paranormal issue generally. For example, in Chapter Three I showed how the Church employed the legal apparatus of the day as a tool to wage war on suspected witches during the "witch craze" era of the sixteenth and seventeenth centuries. Later, the legal system supported the new Rationalist perspective and the ideological concerns that Rationalists had with occult beliefs. For example, legislation was introduced in England during the reign of George IV in the form of the fortune telling act, under which mediums who were accused of fraud, imposition or intent to deceive were liable to three months imprisonment (Fodor 1966).[12] Similar laws prohibiting certain psychic practices have since been introduced in the United States and other Western nations. These laws have been challenged many times over the years. For example, one high profile challenge to the English law mentioned above was made in 1930 by Sir Arthur Conan-Doyle, President of the London Spiritualist Alliance (and the renowned fiction author who created the character Sherlock Holmes).

Despite the legal system's long history of involvement in paranormal disputes, it has in recent decades gradually shifted its position to one where "official" ideologies do not enjoy, to the same degree they once did, a favoured position in the eyes of the courts. For example, Michael Argello of Lincoln, Nebraska, was charged in 1997 with operating a fortune-telling service, but Magistrate Thomas Thalken ruled that although trying to look into the future was "inherently ridiculous", fortune-telling was protected under the First Amendment that guarantees freedom of speech (and he consequently acquitted the accused). Chief Judge Richard S. Arnold spoke out in support of the judge's decision, stating that:

---

[12] Act 5, c. 83, in the general category of rogues and vagabonds (Fodor 1966:online).

> Government is not free to declare certain beliefs—for
> example, that someone can see into the future—forbidden.
> ... In short, government may not prohibit a certain kind of
> speech simply because it disagrees with it ("Appeals
> Court: Nebraska city can't ban fortune-telling" 1998:
> online).

Given the reluctance of modern-day courts to intervene in
paranormal-related disputes, the role of the courts in the
paranormal debate has been increasingly reduced to one of
simply limiting the strategies that competing sides can
employ against opponents (such as deterring the use of
physical violence) rather than being a strategic player with
the power to intervene and silence opponents or rule certain
views invalid.[13]

2:5 – *Ostracism and Isolation*

Another strategy commonly employed in the paranormal
debate is that of ostracism and isolation. UFO researcher
Simon Harvey-Wilson told me of an experience he had with
members of a local Christian group that illustrates this
strategy:

> I had actually spoken to one of these ladies without know-
> ing that she belonged to this group. And she'd spoken
> about people being possessed or exorcisms and the para-
> normal and UFOs, and I had no more than a five, maybe
> ten, minute conversation with her before she had to leave.
> But that was enough for the information to filter through ...
> [I] was told that they thought I was dancing with the devil
> and wasn't particularly welcome at their house ... (1996:
> personal interview).

Both ostracism and isolation have long been considered
an effective means of maintaining social norms in Western
society generally. Foucault notes, for example, how the

---

[13] The view that the legal system remains neutral to metaphysical
claims is advanced by political and legal analyst Leo Pfeffer (1974).
Religion analyst John Burkholder (1974), however, is sceptical of the
legal system's avowed neutrality, pointing out that, at the very least,
the legal system is required to demarcate religion from secular affairs
for juridical purposes, and that such a demarcation will of necessity
favour some metaphysical definitions over others.

emergence of the prison system as a form of isolation was very much associated with normative control. He writes:

> ... through the reflection that it gives rise to and the remorse that cannot fail to follow, solitude must be a positive instrument of reform ... (1979:237).

Within the paranormal debate, some participants employ isolation strategies to achieve the same end — that is, they encourage the marginalisation of opponents as a strategic means of coercing them to reflect on their views and to seriously consider a more "acceptable" position. In this respect, the Skeptics' marginalisation campaign against paranormal proponents was, until recent times (when the popularity of paranormal-related ideas seemed to increase considerably), particularly effective, to the point where paranormal proponents often experienced feelings of abnormality for holding their particular beliefs.

As a means of promoting or resisting such marginalisation, participants sometimes strive to set aside their differences in order to form a united front against opponents.[14] For example, in my 1996 interview with parapsychologist Caroline Watt, when I asked whether women tended to be marginalised in the predominantly male field of parapsychology, she told me:

> [I]n a sense, you are already in a minority if you are a parapsychologist ... It's already us and them, it's us against the rest of the scientific community if you like. And it's better in that case to sort of work together. I'm not saying that as a mission statement, I just think that is the way that it's happened (1996: personal interview).

This tendency for participants to present a united front against opposition was evident in many of the Proponent-Skeptic debates I witnessed, where participants would often put aside their differences and "gang up" on common adversaries. In the absence of common adversaries, how-

---

[14] The process of fostering a strong group identity in order to fight opponents is the reverse of the one outlined by Evans-Pritchard (1940), who saw feuding with an external enemy as part of a strategy to achieve a strong in-group identity.

ever, they tended to fall back into their old habits of arguing amongst themselves.

2:6 – Controlling Sites of Knowledge Dissemination

In addition to the strategies I have outlined above, which are directed primarily at individuals, there are a range of more impersonal strategies that target general knowledge dissemination sites. The sites in question are those that are important to the distribution of paranormal-related information and views, such as the media, schools, colleges, churches and the government. All factions in the paranormal debate endeavour to monitor and control these main knowledge production sites through a variety of strategies, thereby subjecting these sites to a great deal of contestation.

In regard to how knowledge production/consumption sites can be contested in ongoing struggles between various interest groups in general, cultural theorists Peter Stallybrass and Allon White note:

> An utterance is legitimated or disregarded according to its place of production and so, in large part, the history of political struggle has been the history of the attempts made to control significant sites of assembly and spaces of discourse (1986:80).

In the process of such contestation, particular groups may come to exercise greater influence over certain sites than opposing groups, who may then try to undermine that influence. Such contestation has become an important form of strategic action in the paranormal debate, and I will now examine how participants contest some of the more important knowledge dissemination sites in this manner.

2:6(i) – Influencing Media Representation

One important knowledge production site is the popular media. In fact, many participants see the media as the primary site for disseminating paranormal-related ideas to the general public.[15] Paul Kurtz, founder of CSICOP, remarks:

> The media have now virtually replaced the schools, colleges, and universities as the main source of information for the general public ("CSICOP announces the *Council for Media Integrity*" 1996:8).

At some of the bigger paranormal-related conferences I attended in the United States, paranormal authorities seemed generally keen to be interviewed by journalists and television crews. While the ego satisfaction and promotional value of such media attention cannot be ruled out, it seemed to me that these authorities regarded media exposure as an important aspect of their role as spokespeople for the paranormal. Brad Steiger, for example, who when I interviewed him in 1996 had just begun work on a television series in America called *Could It Be A Miracle?* (1996–1997), talked of the importance of using the media "as a force for good".

For its part, the media have become increasingly receptive to paranormal ideas — a development that has alarmed some Skeptics. Writes Barry Williams, President of Australian Skeptics:

> Popular magazines and TV stations produce more and more items which deal uncritically with paranormal and pseudoscientific nonsense (1994:3).

To counter the media's promotion of paranormal ideas, CSICOP announced in 1996 the creation of a media watchdog committee called the "Council for Media Integrity." CSICOP maintained that in doing this it was not trying to silence the media's paranormal coverage, but was only concerned with making it more "responsible." CSICOP co-founder Paul Kurtz remarks:

> The new Council will monitor such programs, and attempt to persuade producers, directors, writers, and the general public to leave room for the appreciation of scientific methods of inquiry ("CSICOP announces the *Council for Media Integrity*" 1996:8).

---

[15] See, for example, Ron Westrum's (1977) discussion on the importance of the media as a source of knowledge on UFOs.

The main objective of CSICOP's watchdog committee seems to be to encourage the media to present television shows, movies, newspaper articles and magazine stories on the paranormal subject in a sceptical, critical manner – or, at the very least, in a balanced manner.

Regardless of the efforts made by participants to influence the popular media, it is important to note that the media itself has a considerable degree of autonomy in the way that it selects and treats its material. Lacking the means to profoundly influence the media's treatment of paranormal topics at the site of production, participants tend to fall back on influencing the public's reception of media representations at the site of consumption. Taking the popular TV series *The X-Files* (1993–2002) as a case in point, we can note the manner in which different sides of the paranormal debate encouraged particular interpretations of the show's paranormal content.[16] Skeptics, for example, encouraged people to view the series as fantasy-based. Barry Karr (well known for his scepticism towards the paranormal) says that although many Skeptics "would have problems with *The X-Files*, since it presents the paranormal as a given", that he personally enjoys the show. He declares: "It's fiction; it's labelled as fiction. Our culture loves horror stories, and this series is entertaining" (Bischoff 1994:47). In the way Karr phrases these remarks, there seems to be a subtle urging of people to view *The X-Files* in the same fictional manner that he does.

Paranormal proponents, in their efforts to influence the way the audience interprets paranormal material in the media, tend to employ a strategy similar to that of Skeptics. Again, using *The X-Files* as an example, a speaker told an audience at one Australasian Society for Psychical Research meeting I attended that *The X-Files* was "so accurate" and, at the same time, "so anti-government", that it is "a wonder

---

[16]   In fact, a familiar theme in *X-Files*' episodes themselves is the politics played out between belief, skepticism and Christian conservatism, although Mark Wildermuth (1999) has argued that later episodes blur the boundaries between these positions.

the producers were even allowed to make the show." He urged members to watch the show if they did not already.

Some Christian conservatives and fundamentalists employ a similar strategy to counteract perceived media misrepresentation of paranormal topics, and I will draw on a personal experience to illustrate this point. During a chat with an acquaintance at a function once, he mentioned to me that he was a regular viewer of *The X-Files*, but during the course of our discussion, his boss (a devout Christian) joined us and voiced his disapproval of the show, saying that he did not like its paranormal content. He added that he much preferred a "science fiction show like *Star Trek*." My acquaintance (who is also a Christian) then hastily qualified his interest as being only in the show's science-fictional aspects, such as UFOs, rather than the paranormal aspects of the show — a qualification that seemed to me to have been influenced by his boss's remarks. The view expressed by my acquaintance's boss in this incident highlights, I believe, a widespread concern among Christian fundamentalists and conservatives that fictional shows such as *The X-Files* may be a bad influence on viewers. Writes David Bay, Director of the Christian organisation Cutting Edge Ministries:

> There may not be a more Satanic TV show on the air right now than *The X-Files*. It is full of Satanism, and occult practices ... An entire generation is getting very comfortable with the practices of the occult, which is a necessary ingredient in conditioning people to accept the occult world of Antichrist (1997:online).

Educating people on the perceived dangers of such shows is one of the strategies used by Cutting Edge Ministries to stem what it sees as the growing influence of the "AntiChrist."

Influencing how the public interprets paranormal-related material, however, has become much more difficult with the introduction of new mediums such as the Internet. The absence of authoritative control over the way information is presented in such a medium makes petitioning for responsible journalism largely ineffective, and efforts to encourage distinctions between fact and fiction very difficult. But the inability to carry out surveillance on a medium such as the Internet does provide a strategic advantage for more marginalised participants in the paranormal debate — namely paranormal proponents — in that it can give them an anonymity and inaccessibility that limits censorship by adversaries.

But no doubt the greatest advantage that the Internet offers more marginalised participants is that it allows them to promote and share views in ways that would not otherwise be possible. For example, social analyst Jodi Dean remarks that new developments in communication networks are enabling UFO proponents to "get their message out" and to "reclaim their rationality on their own terms" (1998:9). Former UFO researcher Michael Lindemann, who at the time of our interview in 1996 ran an Internet information service on UFOs called CNI News (Contact with Non-human Intelligence) but has since moved away from the UFO research area, echoed these sentiments when he told me:

> [There is] much more information flowing today than ever before, raw information, unfiltered by the news media, it's a very democratising influence on the information stream as you undoubtedly know (1996: personal interview).

Given that so many paranormal-related interest groups and individuals seem to be recognising the opportunities offered by the new information mediums such as the Internet and other broadcast mediums that are becoming more available to participants (such as community radio and community television), we should expect that participants will increasingly see such new media as important sites to target in their efforts to influence the course of the paranormal debate.

The Internet is complementing traditional mediums that are directly utilised (as opposed to merely influenced) by participants for the purpose of disseminating information to the general public. The array of paranormal magazines available at newsagencies, such as *Fate*, *UFO Magazine*, and *Nexus*, together with innumerable newsletters distributed by paranormal organisations to subscribers, constitute a direct media outlet for paranormal proponents to inform enthusiasts about the latest developments in their field. The magazines are filled with glossy pictures, entertaining articles and the latest news on sightings and events. Skeptics have their own magazines, such as *The Skeptical Inquirer* and *Skeptic*, which similarly contain glossy photographs and entertaining articles aimed at a general readership.

There is a general perception by postmodern analysts (such as Jean Baudrillard) that the public is susceptible to consumer-oriented strategies in which the power of a particular claim rests largely on its appeal as a glitzy "product" sold through clever marketing, and these populist magazines can certainly be understood in this light. Within this consumer-oriented environment, paranormal-related ideas, with what some might call their "trendy" or "sensational" appeal, are in some respects better positioned than their conservative, and some might say lacklustre, scientific and religious competitors. The established scientific and religious ideologies, which were previously secure within a framework of disciplinary power, have now been thrown into a consumer-driven discursive environment where they must compete with paranormal ideas and other forms of knowledge on a much more equal footing. The general showmanship of tele-evangelists is one example of how some religious leaders are adapting to the changed environment by using traditional mass media to promote their evangelical ideas to the general public in an entertaining manner.[17] Skeptics, too, must nowadays compete alongside paranormal proponents to promote their ideas to the general public in a popularist fashion. As evidence of this, CSICOP includes cartoons and illustrations in its flagship publication, *The Skeptical Inquirer*, and shies away from technical academic discussions that might alienate a general readership.

2:6(ii) — Influencing Academic and Church Institutions

---

[17] See R. Laurence Moore (1994) for an examination of the "commodification" of religion in the United States.

Other sites of knowledge dissemination targeted by participants are academic and religious institutions, which are
largely controlled by the groups who oppose paranormal
proponents — namely, orthodox Rationalists and conserva-
tive/fundamentalist Christians. Contestation over these
sites typically involves paranormal proponents trying to
gain support from these institutions (particularly academia), while Skeptics and Christian conservatives/funda-
mentalists try to keep paranormal proponents out. I will
first examine the contestations that take place in regard to
academic establishments such as colleges and universities.

Both pro-paranormal and Skeptical participants pride
themselves on having a rational view of the reality they
espouse and believing that their view is based on empirical
support. Therefore it is not surprising that many have been
eager to gain support for their ideas from academia — the
"bastion" of rationality and empirical science. However, as
I pointed out earlier, while academics generally are ambivalent in their attitudes towards the paranormal, the "gatekeepers" of these institutions have tended to be rather
intolerant of paranormal ideas. This is true no only of the
physical sciences, but of the social sciences as well. With
regard to the field of anthropology, for example, James Lett
remarks: "The kind of thinking that leads to paranormal
beliefs is all too common outside anthropology; we need
less of it within our own ranks" (1991:325). As pro-paranormal sociologist Andrew Greely notes in his tongue-in-cheek
summing up of the stance of many Rationalists within
academia:

> It is bad enough if the superstitious — particularly the
> bizarrely superstitious — remains anywhere in advanced
> industrial society, but for it to break out in the supposed
> bastion of secularity — the great university — is clearly an
> affront to all decent, pious, agnostic men (1974:296–297).

In fact, the academic system itself has been structured in
such a way (in terms of the monitoring and culling process
of the examination and peer-reviewsystem) that the "bastion of secularity" is largely insulated from the many "deviant" ideas that circulate in our society. As social analyst

Stanley Aronowitz notes with regard to the supervision of post-graduate students, for example:

> The graduate student is often completely under the domination of faculty, which not only approves the results, but intervenes at every step of the research to ensure that the intellectual canons of the scientific community are observed (1988:325).

Generally, academics wanting to protect academia from the "incursion" of paranormal-related ideas employ a largely ideological strategy, needing only to promote the view that such ideas are pseudoscientific and consequently have no place in academia. The aspiring graduate, keen to impress their supervisor, other faculty members and the all-important thesis examiners, is readily amenable to internalising this point of view and, later, promoting it to others. This perspective, to be sure, is largely tacit in nature, rather than one that it is directly communicated. Students develop a sense of the kinds of formulations that are acceptable in their field and of those that are not, by virtue of taking note of the prevailing perspectives that are recognised as authoritative. This results in an inter-generational cycle of Skeptical ideological reproduction in academia, which is normally sufficient to keep paranormal ideas at bay.

On the occasions when paranormal ideas have infiltrated academia, particularly its "upper rungs" (such as when faculty members themselves start promoting unorthodox paranormal-related ideas), more direct action has resulted. Perhaps the incident that gained the most international publicity in terms of academia's concern about staff members holding unorthodox, paranormal-related views was the review of late Harvard Professor of Psychiatry, John Mack, by his own department, the Harvard Medical School. The review of Mack's professional academic activities followed the publishing of his book, *Abduction: Human Encounters with Aliens* (1994). In that book, Mack presents a number of case studies of people claiming to have been abducted by aliens, and contends that their experiences do not appear to be hallucinatory or delusional. While many people felt during this review that Mack's university career was on the line (see Beam 1995:85), the committee's review of Mack did not ultimately result in any punitive action being taken against him—for much the same reason that Chief Judge Richard S. Arnold explained that people could not be prosecuted for being involved in fortune telling— namely, a different perspective on reality was not grounds for misconduct. But Mack was veiledly warned by the Dean of Harvard Medical School (both personally and publicly) that,

> [I]n his enthusiasm to care for and study this group of individuals, he should be careful not, in any way, to violate the high standards for the conduct of clinical practice and clinical investigation that have been the hallmark of this Faculty (Emery, 1995).

Mack (2002) later remarked that the Dean "left it up to me to determine what these were." So while Mack retained his University tenure and also continued in his public role as an authority on alien abduction research, the University's initial decision to officially investigate the matter and its veiled warning to not stray from the University's standards for conduct is a clear indication of how academia, when threatened with intrusion from paranormal-related ideas, can respond very sharply.

One academic who has publicly spoken out about the difficulties that academics can face in this respect is alien abduction researcher and Temple University historian David Jacobs, author of *The UFO Controversy in America* (1975). Jacobs remarked in a conference held on the Internet:

> I have been in academia all of my adult life. Academics do not like this phenomenon ... Suffice it to say that this has not helped my career ... The university has not been happy with my work. I won't go into my personal situation, but there is a "situation" (Compuserve, UFO forum, 17 September 1996, file no. s6091796).

Jacob's "situation" does not appear to be an isolated case. For example, sociologist Paul Allison reports that 53 members of the Parapsychology Association claim to have suffered discrimination because of their interest in parapsychology. He writes:

> Of 183 instances of discrimination claimed, 25 per cent had
> to do with publications, 26 per cent occurred in the area of
> hiring and promotions, and 29 per cent centred on funding
> or facilities (1979:279).

The high incidence of such treatment is confirmed by Hess
who notes:

> I have gathered many horror stories from parapsycholo-
> gists, psychologists, and other scientists who have
> attempted to do ESP research in academic settings and, as a
> result, have had their careers ruined by skeptical col-
> leagues ... (1993:160).

Given the high incidence of censure noted by Allison and
Hess, it is not surprising to find that even when paranormal-related research such as experimental parapsychology
does manage to establish a presence in academia, its position is nevertheless a somewhat tenuous one. Of the few
parapsychology departments that do exist (namely, Duke
University and Edinburgh University), each struggles for
acceptance by their peers (Moore, R. 1977:210ff).

There is also an immense challenge faced by academics
advocating pro-paranormal ideas in terms of having their
work published in academic journals. The peer review process ensures that papers with what are perceived to be questionable arguments do not make their way into journal
publications, and while parapsychologists have had a rea-
sonable hearing in certain psychology journals (for example, *Psychological Bulletin* and a special issue of *Behavioral
and Brain Sciences*), other paranormal fields have not been so
fortunate. Even those journal editors willing to take the bold
step of including pro-paranormal papers face an up-hill
challenge. In an introduction to a special issue on psi in the
Journal of Consciousness Studies (Volume 10, Issue Numbers
6–7), Anthony Freeman (2003) describes the difficulties
experienced in putting together the collection of papers.
Freeman writes:

> The underlying problem was to find a way of including psi
> papers in the journal without appearing to accept uncriti-
> cally the claims for paranormal or anomalous phenomena
> that such submissions regularly contained. The obvious
> solution was to publish a balance of sceptical and para-

psychological papers, but that was easier said than done (2003:2).

Freeman reports that many of the pro-psi submissions were held off for several years until the editors could work out a way of presenting the issue in a balanced, fair-minded manner.

As a result of the difficulty in having their research published in mainstream academic outlets, many paranormal researchers have been forced to restrict their publications to self-published journals in their respective fields which, unlike the glossy paranormal magazines available in newsagents and the numerous organisational newsletters distributed online or by post, take a rather formal academic approach. These journals include titles such as *The Journal of Scientific Exploration, Journal of Parapsychology,* and *Journal of UFO Studies.* Writing about the field of Ufology, David Jacobs contends that this "turn inward" has "not solved the problem of 'building bridges" between them and the scientific community", with mainstream academics lacking ready access to these journals and experiencing ridicule when they do seek out such access (2000a:3). According to psychologist and editor of the *Journal of UFO Studies,* Stuart Appelle (2000:10), the outcome of this is a self-perpetuating marginalisation of the field within academia — the lack of mainstream scientific attention to the area gives the impression that the field lacks credibility, and the perceived lack of credibility in turn discourages mainstream scientific investigation of the area.

A sceptical treatment of the paranormal subject, on the other hand, has generally been welcomed by academia. For example, Suzanne Engler describes her success in introducing a unit that critically addresses "pseudoscientific" beliefs, and expresses her wish that "one day we will see general education classes in debunking pseudoscience as a regular part of college curricula" (1987:97). Introductory academic text books in the fields of archaeology, astronomy and psychology (the fields most impacted by public interest in paranormal ideas) routinely reject paranormal claims. Astronomy textbooks generally target astrology, but occasionally attack beliefs in UFOs as well.[18] Archaeology text-books are fond of discrediting the alien hypothesis of Erich Von Daniken, which is variously referred to as "nonsense" (Renfrew & Bahn, 1991:484), "fanciful" (Sharer & Ashmore, 1987:551–556), "goofy" and "outlandish" (Thomas, 1998: 66-67).[19] Psychology textbooks tend to take principal aim at parapsychology, generally describing it as questionable or misguided inquiry.[20] It is introductory textbooks such as these that ground students in the principles of their fields of study, and so they are a prime means of disseminating gate-keeper perspectives.

Contestations over the paranormal subject also take place in Church establishments. The strategies employed by Christian conservatives and fundamentalists to exclude paranormal ideas from such establishments can range from the delivery of sermons containing ideological reminders of the taboo nature of occult topics, to the ostracisation — even ejection — of members who express paranormal sentiments. Evangelist Pastor Dale A. Robbins lists "participation in occult practices" as one of the seven sins that warrant a per-son to be "removed from the fellowship" in order to "pre-vent sin from spreading, and to impress upon them their need for repentance" (1997:online). Some Christian para-normal proponents have endeavoured to overcome such rejection by presenting their paranormal ideas in a more mainstream Christian manner (much as scientific-oriented paranormal proponents try to present their ideas in a more scientific manner in order to gain academic acceptance). For

[18] Examples of astronomy textbooks that reject astrology include Abell (1982:28–29), Seeds (1986:20–21) and Snow (1993:8). UFOs are discredited in the introductory astronomy textbook by Pasachoff (1978:299–304) and Pasachoff & Kutner (1978:553–561).

[19] Examples of other sceptical treatments of "pseudo-archaeology" in introductory archaeological textbooks are Hayden (1993:30–32) and Rahtz (1991:123–135).

[20] Examples of psychology textbooks taking a sceptical stance towards parapsychology include Atkinson et al (1983:158–161), Buss (1978:296–298), Dempsey & Zimbardo (1978:128–131), McNeil & Rubin (1977:31–35), Marx (1976:236–242), Price et al (1982:122–123) and Wallace et al (1990:134–135).

example, a member of the Churches Fellowship for Psychical and Spiritual Studies in England told me:

> I think the fact that the Fellowship have taken a fairly strong orthodox Christian line as its central emphasis, I think has won respect from various areas of the Church.

Because of their efforts to accommodate mainstream Church concerns and ideas, many members of the Churches' Fellowship for Psychical and Spiritual Studies believe it is only a matter of time before psychic-related ideas are accepted by Church organisations generally.

While many paranormal proponents wait for acceptance by academic and Church establishments, some pro-paranormal groups have sought an unofficial presence in such establishments. For example, the Australasian Society for Psychical Research meetings I attended here in Perth were held at Murdoch University, and while the university itself has no connection with the society or their meetings, such a venue could be seen as an important symbolic link with academia. Similarly, a "spiritual awareness" program I attended in London — which featured talks on subjects such as channelling, psychic healing, life after death, and earth energy — held its meetings in a traditional inner city Church. It can also be argued that the organisation of paranormal-related societies, conferences and journals is a means for paranormal proponents to establish their own independent "academic" community.

2:6(iii) — Influencing the Political Arena

The political arena is another site that is contested by both the pro- and anti-paranormal sides of the paranormal debate, with paranormal proponents interested in fields such as ufology and cerealogy being particularly active in pressing for official government investigation into paranormal-related matters. The support of politicians is valued for both ideological and practical reasons. Politicians' ideological value lies in their role as definers of "official" positions on various issues (much the same as the legal system's role that I discussed earlier). In a practical sense they are valued

because they have influence over various forms of legislation, policies and institutions that are considered by some
participants to be important in terms of resolving certain
paranormal-related issues.

According to former UFO researcher Michael Lindemann,
however, governments in general and politicians in particular are reluctant to involve themselves in paranormal-
related issues, because, he says, they are by nature "conservative and risk aversive" (1996: personal interview). Such
criticism of politicians by paranormal proponents range
from accusations that politicians do not make enough effort
to officially investigate paranormal subjects, to allegations
that they are part of conspiracies to deceive the public by
concealing evidence of paranormal phenomena.[21] Given
this perceived reluctance, and also the inaccessibility of
most politicians to the general public, strategies to gain government support generally follow the same path that most
minority groups who are trying to influence (what they see
as) a recalcitrant government tend to follow — namely, that
of petitioning politicians and staging public protests. For
example, ORTK (Operation Right To Know), which was a
small Internet based organisation whose objective was to
bring an end to alleged government secrecy concerning
UFOs, organised demonstrations at key government loca-
tions, including the White House, the Pentagon, the United
Nations, and the British Parliament. They also encouraged
people to write to their political representatives to urge
them to investigate alleged UFO and conspiratorial activities.

Despite the efforts of participants to influence the political arena, however, the level of support that politicians have
shown in regard to paranormal-related matters has
remained low. When I asked Michael Lindemann if he
thought government support in relation to UFOs, for example, was likely to change in the future, he replied, "When

[21] Some conspiracy enthusiasts argue that the government is
meanwhile quietly and subtly promoting interest in the paranormal
through the popular media, in order to prepare the world for a
forthcoming "disclosure" (Bloomberg 1993:online).

and only when it absolutely has to" (1996: personal interview). He believes, however, that if public demand for information on UFOs continues to grow, and if it were in the government's best interests to do so, then "it could very quickly become a political issue where votes would count."

3. The Expressive Aspect of Strategic Action

It is important to understand that strategic action by participants is not always the outcome of reasoned calculation. There is a strong "expressive" aspect to strategic action within the scene, which reflects the way in which ontological views are intertwined with the strategic objectives sought by participants. For example, attempts by UFO proponents to persuade politicians to acknowledge the existence of UFOs are not so much based on an "instrumental" attempt to use the political arena to further their cause, but from a genuine frustration that politicians "know something" that they are not revealing to the general public. Actions directed at politicians are based on paranormal proponents' view that UFOs are so evidently "real", that governments would be misguided or crazy if they did not take them seriously (and most UFO proponents do not believe the governments to be misguided or crazy).

In fact, the expressive aspect can be so overriding and doxic that often participants are not aware that they are acting strategically at all. From their perspective, they are simply expressing genuinely felt sentiments, based on their particular ideals and ontological perceptions of their opponents. For example, what might appear to be a conscious strategy of ridicule might instead be a genuine expression of amusement at what is seen to be the gross error of one's opponents' views. Similarly, what might appear to be a conscious strategy of marginalisation or isolation might instead be an expression of an instinctive aversion to people who hold beliefs that are seen to be akin to a form of madness (the view of Skeptics) or Satanism (the view of Christian fundamentalists/ conservatives).

Further complicating the matter is the fact that participants' assertions and behaviour can be simultaneously both expressive and instrumental. For example, participants might genuinely believe that their opponent's position is ridiculous, but then proceed in a strategic manner to ridicule that position so that others will also come to share this view. But while the identification of participants' assertions and behaviour as consciously manipulative or merely expressive may need to be assessed on a case-by-case basis, it is nevertheless possible to say more generally that strategic action is an inextricable aspect of the expression of idealised views of self and demonised views of Other, that can, on occasions, be employed in a more consciously strategic manner.

Conclusion

In this chapter I have shown how participants in the paranormal debate employ a variety of strategies to achieve particular ideological objectives. The strategies I covered included rational persuasion, labelling, ridicule, isolation, legal action, and influencing the main sites of knowledge production. I argued that these strategies are largely designed to degrade, silence or elicit a confession from opponents so that one's own ideational position can prevail within the paranormal debate. Consequently, I see these strategies as being a key part of the political manoeuvring that makes the debate more a discursive struggle than a "rational" negotiation or exchange of ideas.

An essential aspect of my examination was the wider discursive basis of strategic action, and in this respect, it could be seen from the various strategies examined that there are, in fact, multiple discursive influences that act upon the paranormal debate. Moreover, I not only demonstrated how various strategies are fundamentally discursive in their make-up, but also how the choice of strategies itself is influenced by wider discursive factors. In fact, as I argued, so ingrained are the discursive formations that underlie strategic behaviour, that often participants do not regard their actions as strategic at all. Rather, they are seen as a natural and logical response to perceived threats.

Given the deeply embedded nature of the expressive sentiments that underlie participants' strategic behaviour within the paranormal debate, and the apparent deadlock that has resulted, it might be wondered if the current state of the debate is likely to improve in the foreseeable future. Indeed, it is the possibility of a more positive dialogue emerging amongst participants that will be the focus of the next and final chapter.

Chapter 7

Conclusion

The Possibility of a Positive Dialogue

In this book I have primarily been concerned with the way participants in the paranormal debate are caught within a complex web of discursive-based interests and preconceptions, which govern both their orientations and their behaviour, and often take precedence over efforts towards mutual understanding and the fair-minded resolution of differences. The "politics of truth" that such a discursively motivated mode of involvement produces, severely limits, I have argued, the potential for a "positive" dialogue taking place over the paranormal subject between those with differing views on its validity. Instead, the result is what James Alcock (2003:30) describes as "a dialogue of the deaf."

In brief, the argument I have made in this book can be summarised as follows: the history of ideas in Western society (Chapter Two) has led to the formation of various ideational positions with regard to the paranormal issue (Chapter Three), which participants internalise (Chapter Four) and promote rhetorically as "rational", "scientific", "moral" and so on with respect to other positions (Chapter Five). They employ a variety of strategies (Chapter Six) in order to affirm their position as the correct one and that of their opponents as misguided. A key point throughout my discussion has been how demonised conceptions of the "Other" guide the way participants distinguish themselves from opponents and interact with them, and I argued that the perception participants have of the differences between their own position and others is fundamentally discursively based, as is their mode of interaction with other participants. I would like to refer to the remarks by late alien abduction researcher and Harvard psychiatrist, John Mack, regarding public reactions to his own work, in order to encapsulate my thesis:

> Language traditionally applied to political betrayal and religious heresy … has sometimes greeted my writings, suggesting that something more than scientific discourse is taking place. These reactions have of course been mild compared with the fate of Renaissance figures whose observations challenged the prevailing authority of their time, but their seeming emotionality has made me appreciate that the way we construct reality is politically as well as scientifically determined (2000:246).

In this final chapter I want to examine whether there is any potential for the debate to serve as a site for a more positive dialogue, given the deeply "political" nature of the barriers that exist. In particular, I am interested in how the paranormal debate, which addresses so many diverse religious, scientific, moral and social issues, might serve as an indicator of the potential and likelihood of a more positive dialogue (that is, a productive, civil and democratic dialogue) taking place in society more generally. This is especially relevant in light of contemporary social trends of globalisation and multiculturalism that are bringing many diverse "truths" into contact and, in many cases, into direct competition with each other. I will argue that such an improvement may be possible *if* certain discursive changes were to occur—changes that might not only improve dialogue in the paranormal debate itself, but in society at large.

1. Conducting a Positive Dialogue

Before I explore the possibility and likelihood of an improved dialogue taking place in the paranormal debate, I should specify exactly what I mean by a "positive dialogue". I define a positive dialogue as one that is "productive", "civil" and "democratic" in nature, although the meanings of these terms are themselves in need of some clarification. For example, some participants might feel that their dialogue with opponents is more "productive" if they engage them in an aggressive manner—a "tribalised" perspective that sees dialogue in terms of one faction trying to gain an advantage over another faction. The definition of a "productive" dialogue that I have in mind, however, is a more communitarian one, in which all participating factions negotiate their various points of view in a cooperative manner. To the degree that inter-factional competition is an aspect of such dialogue, it is situated within the overall objective of working towards a collective understanding rather than a vanquishing of one's opponents.

By a "civil" dialogue, I mean a dialogue that is undertaken in a respectful and polite manner. While such a dialogue need not require participants to express profound respect or appreciation of their opponent's views, it does, nevertheless, entail more than an outward expression (that is, a feigning) of "good manners" towards opponents (Gurstein 1998). I have, for example, witnessed a number of disputes between participants where an outwardly displayed "civility" has disguised an underlying contempt towards opponents, creating an atmosphere of hostility rather than one of mutual respect. By "civil", then, I mean a dialogue characterised by what might be termed a sense of "fair play", where participants are courteous, gracious and attentive to the assertions made by other participants, even if they do not agree with them.

Finally, by a "democratic" dialogue I mean a participatory form of dialogue where *everyone* can voice their ideas in a free and open manner, in contrast to the more representational form of democracy where only certain *selected* individuals have the opportunity to speak on behalf of others. In some respects, the two forms of democracy are not compatible, for the push by factions for a representational form of dialogue with decision-making bodies in the public sphere (such as with the government, academia, the media and churches), can be at the cost of a participatory dialogue in the micro-public sphere. In such cases, dissenting voices within and without one's own ranks may be seen to undermine a strong representation at the public sphere level, leading to an exclusion of those voices at the level of the micro-public sphere.

As a final point of clarification, I would emphasise that my definition of a "productive", "civil" and "democratic" dialogue will not depend on whether consensus or mutual understanding results from such dialogue. I am more interested in the way a positive dialogue might be conducted, and the intentions of participants in undertaking such a dialogue, than I am in a consensual outcome. Neither will my definition of such forms of dialogue depend on the presence of qualities such as "reason", "intersubjective understanding" or "empirical awareness" — qualities that are, in my opinion, under-determined at best, and perhaps essentially more rhetorical constructs than objective ones. In short, I do not assume (although would not rule out) that a positive dialogue has the universal potential that theorists such as Jurgen Habermas hold. Rather, I see such a dialogue as minimally a discursive construct, involving the application and perceived fulfilment of certain forms and ideals that are part of Western "Enlightenment" discourse, even if their inalienability as universal conditions might be questioned.

Having explained what I mean by a "productive", "civil" and "democratic" dialogue, I now want to briefly address the relationship between these different forms of dialogue. For example, although the conditions required for a productive dialogue can be related to the more general conditions required for a "civil" or even a "democratic" dialogue, a dialogue can still be productive even in the absence of these other ideals. In fact, one paranormal researcher told me that, in his opinion, paranormal discussions would be more productive if *less* people (particularly those who are "uninformed") were allowed to participate. Also, we should not assume that a "democratic" dialogue is necessarily going to be a "civil" one.[1] For example, after a member criticised the Australasian Society for Psychical Research meetings for being monopolised by the Committee, the Committee decided to turn one meeting into an open forum, which featured a number of somewhat "uncivil" exchanges. This was in contrast to the predominantly congenial (albeit less participational) mood at the other Australasian Society for Psychical Research meetings I attended. Consequently, it will be necessary in the examination that follows to maintain a distinction between notions of a productive, civil and democratic dialogue, even if, in many cases, these forms of dialogue tend to coincide.

2. The Possibility of a Positive Dialogue

Beginning with the possibility of conducting a more *productive* dialogue on the paranormal, there are a number of obstacles that would need to be removed for this to occur. For example, in my 1996 interview with Proponent-turned-Skeptic, former parapsychologist Susan Blackmore, I asked whether she thought the dialogue between parapsychologists and Skeptics was "constructive" or not, to which she replied, "mostly not." She then described to me the barriers that have prevented such a dialogue from taking place. Blackmore explained that the two sides have drifted apart in terms of their perspectives— so far apart, in fact, that "they're actually not addressing the same issues" (1996: personal interview). One particular problem she noted is the preconceptions that each side has of the other. She explained that Skeptics, for example, have committed themselves to the view that: "We think science is good, and we think everything to do with the paranormal is anti-science." In these remarks, Blackmore has more or less summed up the perspective that I have presented in this book, where demonised views

[1]   On this point, I disagree with social analyst Stephen Carter (1998) who argues that civility is a precondition for a democratic dialogue.

of the "Other" have created seemingly irresolvable barriers to a more productive dialogue.

In our interview, Blackmore added that it had reached the point where Skeptics were "no longer prepared to put in the work to follow what's going on in the claims of the paranormal." In a paper titled, "Why I have given up", Blackmore (2001:92) admits that much effort is involved in learning the intricacies of experimental research in the field of parapsychology so that a proper critical assessment of claims can be made. She remarks that it is "hard work" and "emotionally taxing" to "make a reasonably fair and unbiased assessment of any paranormal claim", and that this was partly why she had ceased her involvement in the scene, as well as a loss of faith in the fruitfulness of psychical research. More recently, Blackmore summed up her personal quest to encourage a dialogue between psychical researchers and Skeptics as follows: "I tried to bridge the gap and get each talking to the other. It was exhausting ... " (2006: personal interview).

Despite this seemingly negative view on the productive value of dialogue between paranormal proponents and Skeptics, Blackmore also admitted that such an attempt at dialogue had been "possibly useful". Indeed, there are three factors that lead me to believe that a productive dialogue between participants is possible, despite the intransigency of the positions of participants that I have outlined in this book. First, we should not have an over-simplistic view of the constraining effect of discourse, for discourse is probably not only flexible to some degree, but it tends to produce the conditions for its own "growth", including the potential to take account of and, to some extent, incorporate, other points of view (the inclusive nature of New Age discourse is a case in point). The history of ideas surrounding the occult and preternatural (see Chapter Two) is evidence enough of the way that discourses, such as those that underlie Christianity, can radically shift position on such matters when certain discursive conditions prevail. Second, because participants are bound by so many competing discourses — some that may overlap with opponent positions—there is always the possibility that opponents may be able to recognise sufficient common ground or, more importantly, compatible objectives, to productively negotiate their differences. Finally, there are precedents for such productive dialogues already in the debate. Susan Blackmore brought one such case to my attention—the Hyman-Honorton exchange that took place in the mid-1980s between Ray Hyman (a prominent CSICOP committee member and a professor of psychology at the University of Oregon) and Charles Honorton (a leading parapsychologist). I wish to examine this case in a little more detail, in order to identify the factors that led to its measured "success."

3. The Auto-Ganzfeld Debate

During our interview, I asked Susan Blackmore if she knew of an instance of a constructive dialogue between paranormal proponents and Skeptics. Susan responded:

> The one that everyone would think about is the Hyman-Honorton debate over Ganzfeld. And that was in a way very productive … [T]he good thing about this debate … was one of the questions going through it was parapsychologists saying, "Okay you Skeptics, you say this is not good enough, well how good has it got to be? If you lay down how good it has got to be, and then we do that, and then we get results, will you then say, Now you believe it." … He [Honorton] successfully pushed them into that corner. What happened was that Honorton came up with the auto-Ganzfeld (1996: personal interview).[2]

The invention of the auto-Ganzfeld device was widely hailed as a productive result of the Hyman-Honorton debate, because it was based on a mutually agreed-upon set of conditions aimed at producing a reliable experimental outcome (Hyman & Honorton 1986). However, despite the success of the experiments in producing results that were, as Hyman himself later admitted, "highly significant" (1994:19), Skeptics (including Hyman) did not believe that

---

[2]   The auto-Ganzfeld device automatically generates random images in remote viewing experiments.

the results necessarily demonstrated the existence of psi. As Blackmore remarked to me: "the auto-Ganzfeld got good results, and the Skeptics still didn't believe it. So you could say that it wasn't productive in the end" (1996: personal interview). However, the Hyman-Honorton case does illustrate the way in which opposing sides of the paranormal debate can come together and, without necessarily putting aside their ontological biases and ideological concerns, still participate in a relatively productive dialogue.

There are several possible explanations for why Hyman and Honorton were able to conduct what I consider to have been such a productive dialogue. For example, Hyman and Honorton were undoubtedly committed to the epistemological discourses of academic rationalism and the experimental rationale of empiricism, which would have provided them with a sense of common mission and, hence, the motivation to seek merit in the other's position. On the surface, this perspective might seem to support analysts who promote the commensurability thesis that some common ground (at least in terms of an agreed set of rules for adjudicating a satisfactory outcome) is the important factor in any productive dialogue. However, many similar debates in parapsychology have failed to produce *any* agreement at all, nor have they been productive in any significant manner (see Collins & Pinch 1982). What I feel set the Hyman- Honorton exchange apart from these other debates was the preparedness of both participants to attempt a "cooperative search for truth" as Habermas puts it (1976:108), despite any doubts they may have had regarding each other's ontological and epistemological conceptions. Many analysts have long held that such cooperation is the key to successful dialogue (see, for example, Thompson 1944:289; Nuernberg 1973), and it is this "spirit" (or perhaps I should say, "discourse") of cooperation that often seems to contribute more to a productive dialogue than any common ground that may actually be present.

This leads me to consider another important aspect of the Hyman-Honorton debate, which was, I contend, its civil or "fair-minded" nature, in that both parties seemed to be committed to a respectful, inclusive dialogue, rather than one that ignored or excluded opposing viewpoints. Fair-mindedness appears to be an important principle to Hyman, as he indicated in an article concerning the value of extending the "principle of charity" to paranormal proponents. He wrote:

> I know that many of my fellow critics will find this principle to be unpalatable. To some, paranormalists are the "enemy", and it seems inconsistent to lean over backward to give them the benefit of the doubt, but being charitable to paranormal claims is simply the other side of being honest and fair (1993:online).

Calls for participants of opposing positions to take part in a civil exchange of ideas are common in the paranormal debate, but such requests are often more rhetorical than genuine, in that they are accompanied by (either tacit or explicit) accusations that one's opponents are intentionally working *against* a fair-minded dialogue. Consequently, such calls tend to be counter-productive, doing little more than reinforcing participants' demonised views of the other as "untrustworthy." In this respect, the Hyman-Honorton exchange may owe much of its success to the willingness of the two participants to set aside the demonised views of the Other that commonly prevail in psi debates, and to see each other more as colleagues than as enemies. In this respect, there may have been a willingness to simply trust one another regardless of the consequences.[3]

Most effective in terms of bringing about a lasting improvement in the quality of dialogue, I contend, are those interests that encourage a *genuine* commitment to the ideals of civility and inclusiveness. Such ideals tend to be already enshrined within the ontologies and ideologies of most of the debate's participant types. A New Age enthusiast may, for example, hold the ideal of "spiritual enlightenment" in high regard, and this interest might encourage him/her to conduct a more "civil" or "inclusive" dialogue than might

[3]   This willingness conforms to Seligman's (1997) "risk-based" notion of trust.

otherwise be the case. Indeed, sociologists Colin Campbell and Shirley McIver contend that occult interests are often founded on "several of the most fundamental values of modern democratic, industrial societies" such as "free inquiry" and "tolerance" (1987:57). Similarly, Skeptics generally value Humanitarian ideals such as the "freedom of speech", a toleration of difference, democracy and a civil and reasoned approach to resolving disputes. The only problem is that most participants tend to make an exception when it comes to applying such ideals to opponents, because they are not seen to be amenable to such ideal forms of dialogue and are often seen as a threat to those principles more generally. Nevertheless, we can see that the ideals required for a more positive dialogue are already largely present within the paranormal debate, and can, under certain circumstances, foster a genuine commitment to undertake such a dialogue, as I hold was the case in the Hyman-Honorton exchange.

There is still the question, however, of what changes might be required to encourage such a commitment in participants more generally, where demonised conceptions of opponents may be much stronger than those held by individuals like Hyman and Honorton. It is this issue, then, that I will address next.

4. The Conditions for a Positive Dialogue

Before I discuss the changes that I believe could produce a more positive dialogue, I first want to critically examine some perspectives put forward by other theorists on this matter. In particular, I want to take issue with those theorists who tend to view a positive dialogue as a universal potential — even *tendency* — that only requires the removal of certain obstacles in order to be realised.

Jurgen Habermas (e.g. 1974, 1976, 1979) is one theorist who takes this perspective, arguing that a commitment to a democratic and productive dialogue is an inherent characteristic of linguistic communication — a potential that has been largely unrealised in contemporary Western society because "rationalised" and "technocratic" social structures have taken the process of truth deliberation out of the hands of lay people. Habermas argues that, given this state of affairs, certain social-structural changes will have to occur before a more positive dialogue can take place. Specifically, Habermas argues that, in contemporary Western society, technocratic institutional bodies must give way to liberal consensus forums, where participants can negotiate their differences in a rational and free manner. In fact, Habermas contends that these changes are already underway, in the form of new social movements that are challenging technocracy and forging a new, democratised "public sphere."

In accord with Habermas' perspective, the paranormal debate might be seen as an attempt to reclaim the deliberative process from the institutional truth-making bodies, particularly in regard to the "democratised" challenge mounted by paranormal proponents against the Establishment. In such a scenario, Skeptics could be seen as the "border-guards" who strive to protect the norms and institutions of the technocratic system from such challenges.

I suspect, however, that Habermas himself would see the situation somewhat differently, with Skeptics being cast as the liberators of the new public sphere, seeking to arrest the "palpable regression into new forms of paganism" (Habermas 1992[1977]:60) that paranormal proponents have, in a rather dysfunctional manner, fallen back on as a result of the fragmentation of their world-views by the rationalisation process. But regardless of which scenario might be the more accurate, it is nevertheless the case that an "ideal speech situation" is still lacking in the paranormal debate—a failure that Habermas might attribute to either the incompletion of the liberation process, or (in regard to the second scenario) the failure of some participants to exercise the rational principles of reflexivity required for such a dialogue.

My assessment of the failure to produce an "ideal speech situation" in the paranormal debate is that, while the elitist/hegemonic behaviour and sentiments exhibited by participants can certainly obstruct such a dialogue, these elitist tendencies are not adequately explained by any sort of "technocratic" rationale. Rather, I maintain that these elitist/hegemonic tendencies are based on discourses (many of them doxic in nature) that define the necessity of protecting certain institutions and hierarchies in order to preserve the social and cosmic order generally. Hence, I do not feel that the type of changes in technocratic-based social structures that Habermas proposes will resolve the problem.

In Habermasian terms, then, I would attribute the debate's failure to produce an "ideal speech situation" to participants' failure to question the largely doxic "traditions" that dominate their "lifeworld" and that prevent them from exercising the kind of "discourse ethics" that would be *acceptable* to all parties involved in the debate. However, in emphasising "acceptable", I am suggesting that there are no universal conditions that are required for a positive dialogue. Rather, it is participants themselves, discursively guided, who determine the set of conditions (i.e. the "discourse ethics") that need to be met before a dialogue can be labelled a "positive" one. Also note that by "traditions" here I not only mean the assumptions that underlie the religious and "magical" ideas held by paranormal proponents and by Christian critics of the paranormal, but also the precepts that underlie much of so-called "rational" science and Skepticism—with particular emphasis on the doxic assumptions that underlie the demonised views that participants have of each other.[4] It is these unquestioned assumptions, and the divisions and demonisations that they give rise to, that I have argued are primarily responsible for the elitist and uncivil aspects of the contemporary paranormal debate. To produce a more positive dialogue, then, I contend that it is the doxic assumptions themselves

[4]   I should note here that, as Peter Dews (1992:17) observes, Habermas has in more recent works come to acknowledge the role that "traditions" continue to play in defining the content of contemporary Western ideas. In fact, some analysts have gone further and even begun to question the tradition/modern dichotomy itself (see, for example, Luke 1996), which, since the days of Comte and Durkheim, has dominated sociological thinking.

that would need to undergo change, not primarily the social structures that advantage one side over the other.

Habermas' formulations on the way that traditions are subject to critical examination in the course of dialogue offers one perspective on the type of changes to doxa that might lead the debate in a more positive direction. Habermas, like Bourdieu, argues that through the exercise of reflexivity, unquestioned doxic elements can be exposed and, through bracketing, their influence negated.[5] More specifically, Habermas talks of a "hypothetical approach to phenomena and experiences", which are "isolated from the complexity of their life-world contexts and analysed under experimentally varied conditions" (1984b:240, quoted in White 1988:147). It is this "reflective attitude", he explains, that is typically associated with rationality (Habermas 1984a:20).

But there are two reasons why reflexivity alone is unlikely to lead to a more positive dialogue. First, reflexivity will inevitably be susceptible to at least some degree of discursive bias, because we can never fully bracket the assumptions that underlie our perspectives on reality. Second, it appears that even when a degree of reflexivity does expose doxic elements that are causing division, a more positive dialogue does not necessarily result. For example, although German intellectual Carl Schmitt (1996[1932]) insightfully recognised the "friend and enemy" dichotomy as being largely responsible for international tensions, he encouraged the heightening of "friend/enemy" distinctions at a national and domestic level, because he believed the alternative was a weakened State, susceptible to external domination and internal anarchy by unidentified threats.[6] Such views supported the rationale (if one was

[5]   The notion of reflexivity that Habermas has in mind here is one that is intersubjectively produced through mutual critique, in contrast to the Kantian notion of self-reflection exercised by the individual (see Habermas 1974:144–5).

[6]   I should note here that Schmitt did not view such a division as an ideal, but as an expedient measure taken in the modern political

even needed) for the aggressive foreign policies and internal persecutions carried out by the Nazi party in the lead up to the Second World War. So while reflexivity can be of value in helping identify barriers to a positive dialogue (as I will explain later in this chapter), it is not the most important factor in producing the dialogue itself. Again, as I indicated in the last section, the most crucial factor in this respect is a firm *commitment* to such a dialogue.

It is not altogether clear from Habermas' writings, however, why participants would choose to commit themselves to a positive dialogue (what Habermas labels "argumentative speech") instead of pursuing the type of coercive, strategic action that I described in the previous chapter. Habermas simply states that "action aimed at reaching understanding" (what I have termed a productive dialogue) is an instinctive tendency inherent within communication, while strategic action is a derivative of such a tendency (1979:1), employed to achieve certain self-interests. But rather than settling on the notion that there is something instinctive or universal about the desire for a positive dialogue, I would emphasise the need for discursive factors that encourage a commitment to such a dialogue and, in particular, those that encourage participants to see some benefit in pursuing this end. I would equally emphasise the discursive factors that discourage such a commitment — namely, the demonised views that I have outlined in this book. Indeed, given that most participants in the paranormal debate already tend to subscribe to such ideals, the question is what might prompt them to overcome the discourses that discourage them from applying these ideals for productive dialogue to their opponents?

One change that might be considered likely to improve the quality of dialogue in this respect — at least between Skeptics and paranormal proponents — would be if a definitive, empirical demonstration of the existence of paranormal phenomena occurred that resulted in paranormal ideas

arena to ensure the stability of the State and the preservation of a society's way of life.

no longer being seen as a "pseudoscientific" threat to conventional science. If such evidence were to manifest, then perhaps many Skeptics would come to view a dialogue on paranormal ideas as potentially productive and in the interests of science. However, I would argue that even in such circumstances, there is no guarantee that Skeptics or scientists would want to conduct such a dialogue with "lay" enthusiasts (which is where technocracy becomes relevant). Nor, for that matter, is there any guarantee that paranormal proponents would want to talk to Skeptics and scientists, who would likely attach a completely different significance to such findings (such was the case with Mesmer's discovery of hypnosis, which — when finally accepted by mainstream academia as a legitimate effect — was reduced to the phenomenon of an altered mind-state, contrary to Mesmer's claim of occult causation). At any rate, the precondition that alleged paranormal phenomena conform to standard criteria for empirical demonstration before a productive dialogue is possible is rather limiting, particularly if those paranormal proponents who claim that such phenomena are not amenable to normal laws are correct.

Alternatively, we might see a more positive dialogue emerge if there is less condemnation by both paranormal proponents and Skeptics of opposing ideas *per se* and of those who propose such ideas. Instead, the emphasis could be on the manner in which such ideas are formulated and presented. As Skeptic/academic Frank Trocco explains: "The question is not *what* you study, but *how* you study it" (emphasis his) (2000:631).[7] In fact, Trocco himself actually encourages his students (some of whom he claims are supportive of paranormal ideas) to study what he calls "weird things", because, he believes, it encourages them to reason intelligently, regardless of the conclusion they come to (*ibid*). The Skeptic Ray Hyman also seems to have employed

[7]   Such an emphasis is reminiscent of Francis Bacon's objections to preternatural ideas — an objection that was not based on the impossibility of such ideas, but on the way in which evidence for them was presented (see Chapter Two).

this rationale when he directed his criticisms at the way past ganzfeld experiments were conducted rather than the "psychical" hypotheses that motivated them. This approach is getting close to the kind of "discourse ethics" that Habermas has in mind, in that the issues that are subject to contestation (in this case, the validity of paranormal phenomena *per se*) are "bracketed" from discussion, and the focus instead is on the manner in which those issues are addressed.

But even with an approach that focuses on methodology rather than subject matter (i.e. form over content), there is still potential for conflict in regard to the way that views on the paranormal are formulated and presented. Skeptics, for example, have consistently demanded that paranormal claims conform to strict empirical demonstration, and have rejected the metaphysical approach and testimonial approach that paranormal proponents have tended to adopt. Also, other factions participating in the paranormal debate, such as Christian conservatives/fundamentalists, would be unlikely to see the value of opposing occult ideas based simply on their "rational" mode of presentation. Even if they did take the mode of presenting ideas into account, I suspect that their assessment of the validity of those ideas would still be based on different criteria to that employed by Skeptics. Christians, for example, would tend to base their assessment on the degree to which the ideas conformed to Scripture or to church teachings. So while we might expect to see some improvement in the quality of dialogue from these sorts of changes — at least between some of the participants — they might not be sufficient, in and of themselves, to produce changes that could revolutionise the quality of dialogue between the majority of participants in the debate.

A change that might have a more profound impact on the quality of dialogue involves the influence of discourses such as postmodernism and democratisation that are able to modify or undermine the tendency for participants to exclude and demonise their opponents. For example, the discourse of democratisation tends to discourage elitist and uncivil behaviour, while postmodernism strives to dissolve the foundational truths and demonised conceptions of difference that underlie much of participants' strategic behaviour. So a discourse such as postmodernism (and I can hear the gasps of postmodern purists here, objecting to my reference to postmodernism as being itself a discourse!), while unlikely to completely discourage participants from seeing their opponents as misguided, could, nevertheless, cast an element of doubt on the validity of such perceptions — enough, perhaps, to discourage the more strategically motivated behaviour that tends to undermine a positive dialogue.

In order for discourses such as democratisation and postmodernism to have a far-reaching impact on the paranormal debate, it will require much more than the promotion of such discourses by just a few individuals. In fact, such promotion of conciliatory perspectives might actually be counter-productive, in that more hardline participants might see this as undermining their "cause" and could, as a result, harden their own stance against demonised opponents even further. Hence, the changes would need to be both far-reaching in terms of their effect and subtle enough to avoid the resistance that direct appeals for changes in "attitude" typically meet. It is for this reason that I would emphasise the importance of a subtle proliferation of such discourses into the paranormal debate. This perspective accords with Foucault's description of the way that "infinitesimal mechanisms" tend to be "invested, colonised, utilised, involuted, transformed, displaced, [and] extended" by "more general [discursive] mechanisms" (1980[1976]:99) that spread from "one point to another" (1979:138) in an ongoing process of mutation and proliferation.

A detailed discussion on the processes whereby discourses such as democratisation and postmodernism are able to proliferate in such a manner is beyond the scope of this book. Suffice to say that, in my opinion, such proliferation throughout society generally — and the paranormal debate in particular — would need to be accomplished through the legitimisation and link-making processes that I addressed in Chapter Four. For example, social analyst Jodi Dean (1998) explains that discourses related to aliens have gained considerable legitimacy in popular culture because of the way they resonate with certain sentiments associated with democratisation and postmodernism. Dean does not, however, see such proliferation as having a very positive effect on the quality of dialogue at present, mainly because she sees the appeal of alien imagery to the general public as being largely expressive of negative sentiments towards the Establishment and new technologies. For example, she argues that the alien abduction emphasis on deception, powerlessness and uncertainty resonates with widespread feelings of paranoia and despondency, brought about by the largely passive and uncertain role that most people feel that they now play in the exchange of information (1998:171ff). Such feelings, she explains, are the remnants of a Cold War "containment" mentality (1998:34ff) that craves security in an age of postmodern uncertainties, which aliens and new decentralised technologies have come to reflect—even symbolise. Dean believes that, presently, such a mentality is stifling the more democratic dialogue that might otherwise result from new media such as the Internet. However, she argues elsewhere (1999) that if and when this "containment" mentality gives way to a more "postmodern" mentality that de-emphasises "foundational truths" and identity politics, then a more democratic dialogue could develop in regard to a whole range of topics and concerns.

While Dean's analysis is veiledly reductionist in its treatment of UFO beliefs as mere symbols of collective paranoia (a reductionism all too common among sociological accounts of paranormal beliefs), one of the legitimate points that Dean's analysis raises is the notion that the proliferation of ideals of democratisation are not sufficient by themselves to improve the quality of dialogue. In fact, it seems to me that in an arena such as the paranormal debate, where participants tend to debate in terms of foundational truths and established categorical identities, a discursive trend such as democratisation could actually *reinforce* divisions and a negative dialogue. The problem is that many partici-

pants tend to cast their opponents as demonised Others who
are obstructing such ideals, and justify their own "undemo-
cratic" behaviour as a form of redress to such breaches.
Therein lies one of the great dilemmas faced by champions of
liberalism, for if they perceive that liberal ideals are not being
observed by their opponents, they can feel tempted to
employ non-liberal tactics to protect their freedoms. Consequently, an improved dialogue will also require participants
to place substantially less importance on the foundational
truths and demonised conceptions of others.

Postmodernism's value as a facilitative mechanism lies in
its suggestion that truth and identity may ultimately be con-
tingent (that is, have no objective or universal foundations),
which tends to cast a degree of doubt on cherished views.
This in turn may discourage participants from imposing
those views on others in a forceful manner. Such views are
already inherent in Skepticism, but Skeptics apply the principle of uncertainty to ideas other than their own. The effect of
postmodernism is to cast *all* ideas into some degree of doubt.

While more radical proponents of postmodernism (such
as Jean Baudrillard, 1988) might see postmodernism's effect
in terms of a *complete* dissolution of truths, I would argue
that in order to have a positive influence on the quality of
dialogue in the paranormal debate, postmodernism would
need to have only a *moderating* effect in casting doubt on the
validity of positions. This is because I see certain truths and
demonised conceptions as important components in a positive dialogue. For example, a democratic dialogue needs to
place importance on the moral principle of a "free" and
"participatory" dialogue, and it needs to demonise, to a certain extent, any behaviour that seeks to undermine that
principle (such as "tyranny", "elitism" and "discrimination").[8] Postmodernism's contribution to a positive dialogue in this respect is that it might make participants more
uncertain whether their opponents are in error and, con-

[8]   The tendency within postmodernism to discourage such activist
behaviour is one of the main difficulties that groups such as Marxists,
feminists and Skeptics have with postmodern ideology.

versely, whether their own ideas are unquestionably valid. Consequently, participants may feel less inclined to demonise and strategically attack their opponents, yet still be sufficiently committed to their position to abide by the liberal ideals that underlie their outlook. In this respect, then, we might expect to see the ideals of a positive dialogue upheld, and for participants to be on guard against any elitist or uncivil tendencies *within themselves* as well as others that might undermine such a dialogue.[9]

In fact, it is in this "self-surveillance" that I believe we can find a role for reflexivity – a practice that is a central tenet of both democratisation and postmodernism (in the form of critical deconstruction). Reflexivity can, I argue, help participants understand how their own views and behaviour might violate ideals related to a positive dialogue. Reflexivity is also important in helping participants understand the degree to which they actually do aspire to such ideals, because people are not always aware of the motives that underlie their thoughts and behaviour.

However, until enough participants in the debate acquire a sufficient commitment to, and proficiency in, reflexive practice, and until the type of discourses that I have outlined here (or ones like them) succeed in motivating enough participants to aspire to a more positive dialogue, then I believe we can expect to see a continuation of the type of negative, strategic behaviour that currently dominates the debate over the paranormal subject. At this point in time, few Skeptics would give much credit to postmodern conceptions. CSICOP chairman Paul Kurtz (2003) has been a vocal critic of postmodernism, arguing that its implication that science is "one methodology among others" is misguided. This opposition to postmodern ideas is not confined to Skeptics. During my research, the president of a pro-paranormal organisation warned me against taking a

---

[9] Postmodern purists would argue, however, that such self-surveillance is itself in need of dissolution, although, ironically, they seem to argue this point with the same critical, reflexive philosophy that they claim should be discarded (White 1988:35).

postmodern approach in my study (he did not know in fact whether I was taking such an approach, but had heard that sociologists were fond of this approach and so felt compelled to warn me). Undoubtedly, he felt that postmodernism undermined the truths with which they were seeking to establish (Goode 2000:51). Many Christian fundamentalists would readily share in such an assessment. Writes one evangelist:

> Contrary to the egotistical claims of postmoderns that they are on the cutting "edge" because of their subjectivist, relativist, existential view of reality, this concept was foisted upon the universe and world by Satan himself before the world was created (Simpson, 2005: online).

A shared opposition to the tenets of postmodernism is perhaps yet another element that participants share in common! But, in my opinion, the root of this opposition largely lies in the totalistic manner in which postmodern proponents have advocated their tenets and the unfortunate theoretical baggage (not to mention the flowery vocabulary) that has accompanied it, which is why I do not hesitate in categorising postmodernism as a discourse. Further, it seems that opposition to postmodern ideas is expressed most passionately by those gatekeepers deeply committed to promoting demonised views of opponents in the paranormal debate, whose commitment to a particular version of the truth is the most uncompromising and who perceive serious dangers should that truth be obscured.

What I am emphasising is the uncertainty principle contained within postmodernism expressed as a cautiousness towards truth-statements rather than their total dismissal. The uncertainty principle need not even be associated with postmodernism or any particular discourse in order to have an effect (indeed, other discourses circulate, such as a relativism, nihilism, philosophical scepticism, and even academic inquiry itself, that advocate the uncertainty principle). It is simply that postmodernism is presently the most recent discourse espousing this principle. What is fundamentally required, however, is a basic commitment to treat all truth-claims with some degree of uncertainty for the sake of debate and to subject those claims to as much interrogation as participants' reflexive capacities will allow. Without such an element of uncertainty, the assumptions underlying the demonisation tendencies within the debate will remain steadfast, and there will be little possibility of viewing other sides in the debate as anything other than misguided and dangerous adversaries who need to be corrected or silenced.

5. Concluding Remarks

In this book I have endeavoured to expose the underlying discursive processes that constitute the contemporary paranormal debate — in terms of *how* it functions, *why* it functions the way it does, and finally (in this final chapter) the potential for the debate to move in a more positive direction. But while the focus has been on the paranormal debate, I believe the ideas I have put forward in this book apply to far wider truth-making processes than those occurring in the paranormal debate alone. Here, I am not just talking about the processes underlying other controversial topics, such as Creationism. Rather, I see the findings to be relevant to the processes that underlie all knowledge construction and dissemination in Western society.

Yet, the paranormal debate does have something unique to offer in terms of understanding those wider processes, for it is an arena where some of the most basic issues involved in knowledge construction are contested in a relatively "raw" manner. As Foucault writes: "one should try to locate power at the extreme points of its exercise, where it is always less legal in character" (1980[1976]:97) — and the paranormal debate, I contend, represents just such a "point". It is a site where many (though not all) taken-for-granted truths are contested, and, consequently, where each discursive formation that relies on those truths must re-establish its legitimacy in a more forceful and transparent manner than is required in more "conventional" truth-negotiating arenas. As such, I see the paranormal debate as presenting a particularly clear platform for view-

ing the politics of truth that underlies the knowledge production processes of our Western society as a whole.
Consequently, a study such as this one may well help us
understand the way a whole range of non paranormal-related "truths" are contested, and how all utterances
are, at the end of the day, inherently political.

Appendix

2001 Gallup Poll of Paranormal Beliefs (by Subject)

The results on the opposite page are tabulated from a poll (Newport & Strausberg 2001) that questioned 1012 randomly selected American adults across the country on a range of paranormal topics.

Paranormal Subject	Believers %	Not Sure %	Disbelievers %
Psychic or spiritual healing or the power of the human mind to heal the body	54	19	26
ESP or extrasensory perception	50	20	27
That houses can be haunted	42	16	41
That people on this earth are sometimes possessed by the devil	41	16	41
Ghosts or that spirits of dead people can come back in certain places and situations	38	17	44
Telepathy, or communication between minds without using the traditional five senses	36	26	35
That extraterrestrial beings have visited earth at some time in the past	33	27	38
Clairvoyance, or the power of the mind to know the past and predict the future	32	23	45
That people can hear from or communicate mentally with someone who has died	28	26	46
Astrology, or that the position of the stars and planets can affect people's lives	28	18	52
Witches	26	15	59
Reincarnation, that is, the rebirth of the soul in a new body after death	25	20	54
Channeling, or allowing a "spirit-being" to temporarily assume control of a human body during a trance	15	21	62

Bibliography

Abell, George 1982 *Exploration of the Universe,* 4th edn. Philadelphia: Saunders College Pub.

Alcock, James 1981 *Parapsychology: science or magic? A psychological perspective.* Oxford, England: Pergamon.

Alcock, James 1987 "Parapsychology: science of the anomalous or search for the soul?", *Behavioral and Brain Sciences,* vol. 10: 553–643.

Alcock, James 2003 "Give the Null Hypothesis a Chance Reasons to Remain Doubtful about the Existence of Psi", *Journal of Consciousness Studies,* vol. 10, nos. 6–7:

Allison, Paul D. 1979 "Experimental Parapsychology as a Rejected Science." In Roy Wallis (ed.), *On the Margins of Science: The Social Construction of Rejected Knowledge.* Keele, Eng: University of Keele.

Aquinas, St. Thomas 1922 (1265/66-1273) *Summa Theologica,* vol. 5. Translated by the Fathers of the English Dominican Province. London: Burns Oates and Washbourne.

Aquinas, St. Thomas 1975 (1258–64) *Summa Contra Gentiles,* vol. III (Providence). Translated by Vernon J. Bourke. London: University of Notre Dame.

"Appeals Court: Nebraska city can't ban fortune-telling". 1998 *The Associated Press,* 14 May. Available online: http://www.freedomforum.org/speech/1998/5/14fortune.asp (Accessed 12 October 1999).

Appelle, Stuart 2000 Ufology and Academia: The UFO Phenomenon as a Scholarly Discipline. In David Jacobs (ed.) *UFOs and Abductions: Challenging the Borders of Knowledge.* Lawrence, KA: University Press of Kansas. (pp. 7–30).

Appignanesi, Richard & Chris Garratt 1995 *Postmodernism for Beginners.* Cambridge: Icon Books.

Aronowitz, Stanley 1988 *Science As Power: Discourse and Ideology in Modern Society.* Minneapolis: University of Minnesota Press.

Atkinson, Rita, Richard Atkinson, & Ernest Hilgard 1983 *Introduction to Psychology,* 8th edn. New York : Harcourt Brace Jovanovich.

Bacon, Francis 1898 (1605) *Advancement of Learning.* In *The Physical and Metaphysical Works of Lord Bacon.* Edited by Joseph Devey. London: George Bell & Sons.

Bacon, Francis 1898 (1620) *Novum organum*. In *The Physical and Metaphysical Works of Lord Bacon*. Edited by Joseph Devey. London: George Bell & Sons.

Balch, Robert & David Taylor 1977 "Seekers and Saucers: The Role of the Cultic Milieu in Joining a UFO Cult", *American Behavioral Scientist*, vol. 20, no. 6 (July/August): 839-860.

Barbell, Sharon 1993 "Play and the Paranormal: a conversation with Dr Raymond Moody", Available online: http://www.14850.com/14850/9311/interview.html (accessed 8 January 1997). Also published in *14850 Magazine*, November 1993.

Barnes, Barry & Donald MacKenzie 1979 "On the Role of Interests in Scientific Change". In Roy Wallis (ed.), *On the Margins of Science: The Social Construction of Rejected Knowledge*. Keele, Eng: University of Keele.

Barstow, Anne Llewellyn 1988 "On studying witchcraft as women's history: a historiography of the European witch persecutions", *Journal of Feminist Studies in Religion*, vol. 4 (Fall): 7–19.

Barth, Fredrik (ed.) 1969 *Ethnic Groups and Boundaries: The Social Organization of Culture Difference*. London: Allen & Unwin.

Basso, Keith 1979 *Portraits of "The Whiteman": Linguistic Play And Cultural Symbols Among The Western Apache*. Melbourne: Cambridge.

Baudrillard, Jean 1988 *Jean Baudrillard: Selected Writings*. Edited by Mark Poster. Cambridge: Polity.

Bay, David 1997 "God Has Now Been Reintroduced In American T.V. Today, But It Is Not The God Of The Bible; It Is The God Of Freemasonry!!" *The Cutting Edge*, no. 1071. Available online: http://www.cuttingedge.org/news/n1071.html (Accessed 15 September 2000).

Bay, David 2000 "Meet our Staff". The Cutting Edge home web page. Available online: http://www.cuttingedge.org/meet.html (Accessed 9 September 2000).

Beam, Alex 1995 "The Search for Intelligent Life at Harvard", *The Boston Globe*, April 12: 85.

Beattie, John 1964 *Other Cultures: Aims, Methods and Achievements in Social Anthropology*. London: Routledge & Kegan Paul.

Becker, Howard 1963 *Outsiders: Studies in the Sociology of Deviance*. New York: Free Press.

Beckford, James 1992 "Religion, modernity and post-modernity". In B.R. Wilson (ed.) *Religion: Contemporary Issues*. London: Bellew.

Bekker, Balthasar 1695 *The World Bewitched* (translated from a French Copy). London: Approved of and subscribed by the Author's own Hand.

Ben-Yehuda, Nachman 1985 *Deviance and Moral Boundaries: witchcraft, the occult, science fiction, deviant sciences and scientists*. Chicago: University of Chicago Press.

Berger, Peter & Thomas Luckmann 1967 *The Social Construction of Reality: a treatise in the sociology of knowledge.* Garden City, N.Y.: Doubleday.

Bischoff, David 1994 "Opening the X-Files: Behind the Scenes of TV's Hottest Show", *Omni Magazine*, vol. 17, no. 3 (December): 42-47, 88.

Blackmore, Susan 1986 *The Adventures of a Parapsychologist.* Buffalo, NY: Prometheus Books.

Blackmore, Susan 2001 "Why I have Given Up". In P. Kurtz (ed.), *Skeptical Oddyseys: Personal Accounts by the World's Leading Paranormal Inquirers.* Amherst, NY: Prometheus Books. Pp.85-94.

Blavatsky, Helena Petrovna 1952 (1888) *The Secret Doctrine: the synthesis of science, religion and philosophy.* Pasadena, Calif: Theosophical U.P.

Bloomberg, David 1993 "REALLity Check", *The REALL News* (The official newsletter of the Rational Examination Association of Lincoln Land), vol. 1, no. 8 (September). Available online: http://www.lysator.liu.se/skeptical/newsletters/REALL_News/REALL1-8.TXT (Accessed 9 September 2000).

Bohm, David & F. David Peat 1989 *Science, Order and Creativity.* London: Routledge.

Bolton, Lissant 1999 "Introduction (Using Multi-sited ethnography: Investigations of a Methodological Proposal)", *Canberra Anthropology*, vol. 22, no. 2 (Oct): 1–5.

Bourdieu, Pierre 1977 *Outline of a Theory of Practice.* Translated by Richard Nice. Cambridge: Cambridge University Press.

Brown, Richard Harvey 1994 "Rhetoric, textuality, and the postmodern turn in sociological theory". In Steven Seidman (ed.), *The Postmodern Turn: New Perspectives on Social Theory.* Cambridge: Cambridge University Press.

Brown, Wendy 1998 "Genealogical Politics". In Jeremy Moss (ed.), *The Later Foucault: politics and philosophy.* London: Sage Publications.

Brugger, Peter & Kirsten Taylor 2003 ESP: Extrasensory Perception or Effect of Subject Probability?, *Journal of Consciousness Studies*, vol. 10, nos. 6–7: 221–246.

Budapest, Zsuzsanna Emese 1989 *The Holy Book of Women's Mysteries.* Oakland, CA: Wingbow Publishers.

Bullard, Thomas E. 2000 "UFOs: Lost in the Myths". In David Jacobs (ed.) *UFOs and Abductions: Challenging the Borders of Knowledge.* Lawrence, KA: University Press of Kansas. pp. 141–191.

Burkholder, John Richard 1974 "'The Law Knows No Heresy': Marginal Religious Movements and the Courts". In Irving I. Zaretsky & Mark P. Leone (eds.), *Religious Movements in Contemporary America.* Princeton, NJ: Princeton University Press.

Buss, Arnold 1978 *Psychology: Behavior in Perspective*, 2nd edn. New York: Wiley.

Calvin, Jean 1960 (1559) *Institutes of the Christian Religion*, vol. 1. Edited by John T. Mitchell. Translated by Ford Lewis Battles. London: S.C.M. Press.

Campbell, Colin & Shirley McIver 1987 "Cultural Sources of Support for Contemporary Occultism", *Social Compass*, vol. 34, no. 1: 41–60.

Carter, Stephen L. 1998 *Civility: Manners, Morals, and the Etiquette of Democracy*. New York: Basic Books.

Cavendish, Richard 1977 *A History of Magic*. London: Weidenfeld & Nicolson.

Charmed (television series) 1998-2006 USA. The WB. Producer Aaron Spelling et al.

Christ, Carol 1998 *Rebirth of the Goddess: Finding Meaning in Feminist Spirituality*. New York: Routledge.

Clark, Jerome 2000 "The Extraterrestrial Hypothesis in the Early UFO Age". In David M. Jacobs (ed.), *UFOs and Abductions: Challenging the Borders of Knowledge*. Lawrence: University Press of Kansas (pp. 122–140).

Clark, Stuart 1997 *Thinking With Demons: The Idea of Witchcraft in Early Modern Europe*. Oxford: Clarendon Press.

Close Encounters of the Third Kind (motion picture) 1977 USA. Columbia Pictures & EMI Films Ltd. Producers Julia Phillips, Michael Phillips, Clark L Paylow & John Veitch.

Collins, Harry & Trevor Pinch 1982 *Frames of Meaning: The Social Construction of Extraordinary Science*. London: Routledge & Kegan Paul.

Collins, Harry 1983 "An Empirical Relativist Programme in the Sociology of Scientific Knowledge". In Karin D. Knorr-Cetina & Michael Mulkay (eds.), *Science Observed: Perspectives on the Social Study of Science*. London: Sage.

Corbin, Michael 1992 "John Lear Material", alt.alien.visitors, 12 Oct 1992. Available online: http://www.eagle-net.org/UFOSSI/special/jlear1.htm (Accessed 19 December 2000).

Could It Be A Miracle? (television series) 1996–1997 USA. Franklin Waterman (syndicated programme, broadcast on NBC).

Couliano, Ioan 1987 *Eros and Magic in the Reniassance*. Chicago: University of Chicago Press.

Couttie, Bob 1988 *Forbidden Knowledge: the Paranormal Paradox*. Cambridge: Lutterworth.

"CSICOP announces the Council for Media Integrity". 1996 *Skeptical Inquirer*, vol. 20, no. 5 (Sept/Oct): 8.

Currie, Elliot 1974 (1968) "Crimes Without Criminals: Witchcraft and its Control in Renaissance Europe". In Edward Tiryakian (ed.), *On the Margin of the Visible: Sociology, the Esoteric, and the Occult*. New York: John Wiley & Sons. Originally published in *Law & Society Review*, 3, 1968 (August): 7–32.

Cuvelier, Anne Ramsey 1997 "The Truth Is Still Out There", Letter published in the OPEN FORUM, *San Francisco Chronicle*, Friday, 11 April 1997: A25 ("Opinion" Section).

Davison, Gerald & John Neale 1994 *Abnormal Psychology*. 6th edn. New York: Wiley.

216   *The Paranormal and the Politics of Truth*

Dawson, Lorne L. 1998 "Anti-modernism, modernism, and postmodernism: struggling with the cultural significance of new religious movements", *Sociology of Religion*, vol. 59, no. 2 (Summer): 131–156.

Dean, Jodi 1998 *Aliens in America: Conspiracy Cultures from Outerspace to Cyberspace*. Ithaca, NY: Cornell University Press.

Dean, Jodi 1999 "Virtual Fears", *Signs*, vol. 24, no. 4 (Summer): 1069–1078.

Dempsey, David & Philip Zimbardo 1978 *Psychology & You*. Glenview, Il: Scott, Foresman.

Descartes, René 1968 (1637) *Discourse on the Method of Properly Conducting One's Reason an ofd Seeking the Truth in the Sciences*. In his *Discourse on Method and the Meditations*. Translated by F. E. Sutcliffe. London: Penguin Books.

Dews, Peter 1992 Editor's Introduction. In Jurgen Habermas *Autonomy and Solidarity: interviews with Jurgen Habermas*. Edited by Peter Dews. London: Verso.

Dirks, Nicholas; Geoff Eley, & Sherry B. Ortner 1994 Introduction. In their (eds.) *Culture/Power/History: a reader in contemporary social theory*. Princeton, N.J.: Princeton University Press.

Dobbelaere, Karel & Liliane Voyé 1990 "From Pillar to Postmodernity: The Changing Situation of Religion in Belgium", *Sociological Analysis*, vol. 51, no. S: S1–S13.

Dolby, R.G.A. 1979 "Reflections on Deviant Science". In Roy Wallis (ed.), *On the Margins of Science: The Social Construction of Rejected Knowledge*. Keele, Eng: University of Keele.

Donahue, Michael 1993 "Prevalence and correlates of New Age beliefs in six Protestant denominations", *Journal for the Scientific Study of Religion*, vol. 32, no. 2 (Jun): 177–184.

Duncan, David; William Donnelly & Thomas Nicholson 1992 "Belief in the Paranormal and Religious Belief Among American College Students", *Psychological Reports*, vol. 70: 15–18.

Easlea, Brian 1980 *Witch Hunting, Magic & the New Philosophy: An Introduction to Debates of the Scientific Revolution 1440–1750*. Sussex: Harverster Press.

Emery, Gene 1995 "John Mack: off the hook at Harvard, but with something akin to a warning", *Skeptical Inquirer*, 19(6): 4-5.

Emmons, Charles & Jeff Sobal 1981a "Paranormal Beliefs: Testing the Marginality Hypothesis", *Sociological Focus*, vol. 14, no. 1 (January): 49–56.

Emmons, Charles & Jeff Sobal 1981b "Paranormal Beliefs: Functional Alternatives to Mainstream Religion?", *Review of Religious Research*, Vol. 22, No.4 (June): 301–312.

Emmons, Charles F. 1982 *Chinese Ghosts and ESP: A Study of Paranormal Beliefs and Experiences*. Metuchen, N.J.: Scarecrow Press.

Emmons, Charles F. 1997 *At the Threshold: UFOs, Science and the New Age*. Mill Spring, N.C.: Blue Water Publishing.

Engler, Suzanne 1987 "ETs, Rafts, and Runestones: Confronting Pseudoarchaeology in the Classroom". In Francis Harrold & Raymond Eve (eds.), *Cult Archaeology and Creationism: Understanding Pseudoscientific Beliefs about the Past*. Iowa City: University of Iowa Press.

ET–the Extra-terrestrial (motion picture) 1982 USA. Amblin Entertainment & Universal Pictures. Producers Kathleen Kennedy, Steven Speilberg & Melissa Mathison.

Evans-Pritchard, Edward 1940 *The Nuer: A Description of the Modes of Livelihood and Political Institutions of a Nilotic People*. Oxford: Clarendon Press.

Eve, Raymond & Francis Harrold 1987 "Pseudoscientific Beliefs: The End of the Beginning or the Beginning of the End?" In their *Cult Archaeology and Creationism: Understanding Pseudoscientific Beliefs about the Past*. Iowa City: University of Iowa Press.

Felski, Rita 1997 "The doxa of difference (theories of sexual difference as a feminist thought)", *Signs*, vol. 23, no. 1 (Autumn): 1–21.

Fine, Alan & Jeffrey Victor 1994 "Satanic tourism: adolescent dabblers and identity work", *Phi Delta Kappan*, vol. 76, no. 1 (Sept): 70–72.

Fiske, John 1993 *Power Plays, Power Works*. London: Verso.

Flint, Valerie 1991 *The Rise of Magic in early Medieval Europe*. Oxford: Clarendon Press.

Flood, Samuel 1845 "On the Power, Nature, and Evil, of Popular Medical Superstition", *Lancet*, Aug 16: 179–181; Aug 23: 201–204.

Flynn, Bre 1997 "UFOs and the Bible: Aliens, Angels and Demons", Watcher Ministries website: Conspiracy & Prophecy Index. Available online: http://www.MT.net/~watcher/ufos3.html (Accessed 15 June 1997).

Fodor, Nandor 1966 (1934) *Encyclopaedia of Psychic Science*. New Hyde Park, N.Y.: University Books. Available online: http://www.tcom.co.uk/hpnet/fodor.htm (Accessed 13 October 1999).

"Forbidden Knowledge" 1986 Six part documentary series. Broadcast on BBC 4 Radio, England. Producer Bob Couttie.

Foucault, Michel 1970 (1966) *The Order of Things: an archaeology of the human sciences*. London: Routledge.

Foucault, Michel 1972 *The Archaeology of Knowledge*. Translated by A.M. Sheridan Smith. London: Tavistock.

Foucault, Michel 1979 *Discipline and Punish: The Birth Of The Prison*. Translated by Alan Sheridan. New York: Random House.

Foucault, Michel 1980 (1976) "Two Lectures". In his *Power/Knowledge: Selected Interviews and Other Writings, 1972-1977*. Edited by Colin Gordon. Translated by Kate Soper. Brighton, Sussex: Harvester Press. Originally published in his (1977) *Mircrofisica del Potere*.

Foucault, Michel 1980 (1977) "The Eye of Power". In his *Power/Knowledge: Selected Interviews and Other Writings, 1972-1977*. Edited and translated by Colin Gordon. Brighton, Sussex: Harvester Press. Originally published as Preface to 1977 edition of Jeremy Bentham's *Le Panoptique* (1791).

Foucault, Michel 1980 (1978) *The History of Sexuality, Volume 1.* Translated by Robert Hurley. New York: Vintage Books.

Fox, John W. 1992 "The Structure, Stability, and Social Antecedents of Reported Paranormal Experiences", *Sociological Analysis*, vol. 53, no. 4 (Winter): 417–431.

Frazer, James 1980 (1890) *The Golden Bough: A Study In Magic And Religion.* London: Macmillan.

Frazier, Kendrick 1981 *Paranormal Borderlands with Science.* Buffalo, N.Y.: Prometheus Books.

Frazier, Kendrick 1986 *Science Confronts the Paranormal.* Buffalo, N.Y.: Prometheus Books.

Freeman, Anthony 2003 "A Long Time Coming: A Personal Reflection", *Journal of Consciousness Studies*, vol. 10, nos. 6–7: 1–5.

Gallup, George, Jr. & Frank Newport 1991 "Belief in Paranormal Phenomena Among Adult Americans", *Skeptical Inquirer*, vol. 15 (Winter): 137–146.

Gardner, Martin 1981 *Science: Good, Bad and Bogus.* Buffalo, New York: Prometheus Books.

Garfinkel, Harold 1956 "Conditions of Successful Degradation Ceremonies", *American Journal of Sociology*, vol. 61 (February): 420–24.

Gauld, Alan 1968 *The Founders of Psychical Research.* New York: Schocken Books.

Gieryn, Thomas 1983 "Boundary-work and the demarcation of science from non-science: strains and interests in professional ideologies of scientists", *American Sociological Review*, vol. 48 (December): 781–795.

Godzich, Wlad 1992 "From the Inquisition to Descartes: The Origins of the Modern Subject". *Surfaces* (Internet Journal), vol. 2. Available online: http://elias.ens.fr/Surfaces/vol2/godzich.html (Accessed 27 March 1997).

Goffman, Erving 1974 *Frame Analysis: an essay on the organization of experience.* New York: Harper & Row.

Goldsmith, Barbara 1998 *Other Powers: The Age of Suffrage, Spiritualism, and the Scandalous Victoria Woodhull.* New York: A.A. Knopf.

Goodare, Julian 1998 "Women and the witch-hunt in Scotland", *Social History*, vol. 23, no.3 (Oct): 288-308.

Goode, Erich 2000 *Paranormal Beliefs: A Sociological Introduction.* Prospect Heights, Ill: Waveland Press, Inc.

Goode, Erich & Nachman Ben-Yehuda 1994 *Moral panics : the social construction of deviance.* Oxford, Eng.: Blackwell.

Gove, Walter 1980 *The Labelling of Deviance: Evaluating a Perspective.* Beverly Hills, Calif: Sage Publications.

Grabner, Ingo & Wolfgang Reiter 1979 "Guardians at the Frontiers of Science". In H. Nowotny & H. Rose (eds.), *Counter-Movements in the Sciences.* London: D. Reidel Publishing.

Gratian 1897 (c.1140) *Decretum.* Edited by Emil Friedberg. Leipzig: Tauchnitz. An English translation of the *The Canon (Capitulum)*

Episcopi appears in Henry Charles Lea (ed.), *Materials toward a history of witchcraft*, vol. 1:178–180. New York: Yoseloff. 1957.

Gray, T, & D. Mill 1990 "Critical abilities, graduate education (Biology vs. English), and belief in unsubstantiated phenomena", *Canadian Journal of Behavioural Science*, vol. 29: 162–172.

Greely, Andrew 1974 "Implications for the Sociology of Religion of Occult Behavior in the Youth Culture". In Edward Tiryakian (ed.), *On the Margin of the Visible: Sociology, the Esoteric, and the Occult*. New York: John Wiley & Sons.

Green, Karen 1998 "Does science persecute women? The case of the 16th-17th century witch-hunts", *Philosophy*, vol. 73, no. 284 (April): 195-217.

Gurevitch, Zali 2000 "Plurality in Dialogue: A Comment on Bakhtin", *Sociology*, vol. 34, no. 2 (May): 243–63.

Gurstein, Rochelle 1998 "Civility: Manners, Morals, and the Etiquette of Democracy", *The New Republic*, vol. 219, no. 14 (Oct 5): 40–45.

Habermas, Jurgen 1974 *Theory and Practice*. London: Heinemann.

Habermas, Jurgen 1976 *Legitimation Crisis*. Translated by Thomas McCarthy. London: Heinemann Educational Books.

Habermas, Jurgen 1979 *Communication and the Evolution of Society*. Translated by Thomas McCarthy. London: Heinemann Educational Books.

Habermas, Jurgen 1984a *The Theory of Communicative Action*, vol. 1. Translated by Thomas McCarthy. Boston: Beacon Press.

Habermas, Jurgen 1984b "Questions and Counterquestions", *Praxis International*, vol. 4: 229–49.

Habermas, Jurgen 1992 (1977) "Ideologies and Society in the Post-War World". In his *Autonomy and Solidarity: interviews with Jurgen Habermas*. Edited by Peter Dews. London: Verso.

Habermas, Jurgen 1992 (1981) "The Dialectics of Rationalization". In his *Autonomy and Solidarity: interviews with Jurgen Habermas*. Edited by Peter Dews. London: Verso.

Hall, Timothy & Guy Grant 1978 *Superpsych: The Power of Hypnosis*. London: Sphere Books.

Ham, Ken 1992 "Battles Behind the Scenes", *Acts & Facts* (Newsletter of the Institute for Creation Research). Available online: http://www.icr.org/pubs/btg-a/btg-041a.htm (Accessed 9 September 1999).

Harré, Rom 1981 Preface. In K. Knorr-Cetina, *The Manufacture of Knowledge: an essay on the constructivist and contextual nature of science*. Oxford: Pergamon Press.

"Harry Potter on list of controversial books" 2000 USA Today website (books). Available online: http://www.usatoday.com/life/enter/books/book846.htm (Accessed 1 Feb 2001).

"Harry Potter series again tops list of most challenged books" 2001 ALA News Release, American Library Association website. Available online: http://www.ala.org/pio/presskits/

midwinterawards2001/challenged.html (Accessed 1 February 2001).

Hayden, Brian 1993 *Archaeology: The Science of Once and Future Things*. New York: W.H.Freeman & Co.

Heelas, Paul 1993 "The New Age in Cultural Context: the Premodern, the Modern and the Postmodern", *Religion*, vol. 23, no. 2: 103–116.

Heelas, Paul 1995 "The New Age: Values and Modern Times". In Lieteke van Vucht Tijssen, Jan Berting, & Frank Lechner (eds.), *The Search for Fundamentals*. Dordrecht, Netherlands: Kluwer Academic Publishers.

Herrmann, Robert A. 1997 "A Scientific Analysis and True Significance of the Modern 'Psychic' and 'Paranormal' Movement". Available online: http://www.serve.com/herrmann/psychic.htm (Accessed 9 September 1999).

Hess, David 1991 *Spirits and Scientists: Ideology, Spiritism, and Brazilian Culture*. University Park, Pennsylvania: The Pennsylvania State University Press.

Hess, David 1993 *Science in the New Age: The Paranormal, Its Defenders and Debunkers, and American Culture*. Madison, Wisconsin: University of Wisconsin Press.

Hickman, John; Dale McConkey & Matthew Barrett 1996 "Fewer Sightings in the National Press: A Content Analysis of UFO News Coverage in the New York Times, 1947-1995", *Journal of UFO Studies*, 6 (1995-96): 213-226.

Hopkins, Budd 2000 Hypnosis and the Investigation of UFO Abduction Accounts. In David M. Jacobs (ed.), *UFOs and Abductions: Challenging the Borders of Knowledge*. Lawrence: University Press of Kansas (Pp.215-240).

Howe, Ellic 1967 *Uranias Children*. London: Kimber.

Hume, David 1963 (1741) "Of Superstition and Enthusiasm". In his *Hume on Religion*. Edited by Richard Wollheim. London: Collins.

Hyman, Ray & Charles Honorton 1986 "A joint communique: The psi ganzfeld controversy", *Journal of Parapsychology*, vol. 50: 351–364.

Hyman, Ray 1993 "Proper Criticism", *The REALL News*, vol. 1, no. 2 (March): Available online: http://www.reall.org/newsletter/v01/n02/index.html (Accessed 9 September 2000). Originally published in *Skeptical Briefs*, May 1987.

Hyman, Ray 1994 "Anomaly or Artifact? Comments on Bem and Honorton", *Psychological Bulletin*, vol. 115, no. 1: 19–24.

In Search Of (television series) 1976-82 USA. Alan Landsburg Productions. Producer: Alan Landsburg.

"Interview with Carl Sagan" 1996 Conducted by the Science Unit at WGBH Boston for *NOVA* (US television series broadcast on PBS). Available online: http://www.pbs.org/wgbh/nova/aliens/carlsagan. html (Accessed 1 October 1997).

Irwin, Harvey J. 1993 "Belief in the paranormal: A review of the empirical literature", *Journal of the American Society for Psychical Research*, vol. 87: 1–39.

Irwin, Harvey J. 1994 "Childhood Trauma and the Origins of Paranormal Belief: a Constructive Replication", *Psychological Reports*, vol. 74:107–111.

Jacobs, David 1975 *The UFO Controversy in America*. Bloomington, Indiana: Indiana University Press.

Jacobs, David 2000a Introduction. In his (ed.) (2000) *UFOs and Abductions: Challenging the Borders of Knowledge*. Lawrence, KA: University Press of Kansas. (pp. 1–6).

Jacobs, David 2000b The UFO Abduction Controversy in the United States. In his (ed.) (2000) *UFOs and Abductions: Challenging the Borders of Knowledge*. Lawrence, KA: University Press of Kansas. (pp. 192–214).

Jaki, Stanley 1975 Introduction. In Giordano Bruno (1584) *The Ash Wednesday Supper* (translated by Stanley Jaki). The Hague: Mouton.

James VI/I, King 1597 *Daemonologie*. London: John Lane The Bodley Head Ltd.

Jung, Carl G. 1961 *Memories, dreams, reflections*. New York: Vintage Books.

Kant, Immanuel 1950 (1783) *Prolegomena to Any Future Metaphysics*. Translated by L. W. Beck. Indianapolis: The Bobbs-Merill Co. Inc.

Kant, Immanuel 1990 (1781) *The Critique of Pure Reason*. Translated by J.M.D. Meiklejohn. Amherst: Prometheus Books.

Karr, Barry 1995 "The Geller case ends: 'psychic' begins court-ordered payment of up to $120,000 to CSICOP", *Skeptical Inquirer*, vol. 19, no. 3 (May-June): 3–4.

Kauffman, L.A. 1995 "Small change: Radical Politics since the 1960s". In Marcy Darnovsky, Barbara Epstein, and Richard Flacks (eds.), *Cultural Politics and Social Movements*. Philadelphia: Temple University Press.

Keefer, Michael 1996 "The dreamer's path: Descartes and the Sixteenth Century", *Renaissance Quarterly*, vol. 49, no. 1 (Spring): 30–76.

Kieckhefer, Richard 1989 *Magic in the Middle Ages*. Cambridge, England: Cambridge University Press.

Kilbourne, Brock & James T. Richardson 1989 "Paradigm Conflict, Types of Conversion, and Conversion Theories", *Sociological Analysis*, vol. 50, no. 1 (Spring): 1–21.

Koestler, Arthur 1960 *The Watershed*. Lanham, MD: University Press of America.

Kors, Alan & Edward Peters (eds.) 1972 *Witchcraft in Europe, 1100–1700: A Documentary History*. Philadelphia: University of Philadelphia Press.

Kuhn, Thomas 1970 (1962) *The Structure of Scientific Revolutions*, 2nd edn. Chicago, Il.: University of Chicago Press.

Kurtz, Paul 1976 "Committee to Scientifically Investigate Claims of Paranormal and Other Phenomena", *Humanist*, vol. 36: 28.

Kurtz, Paul 1996 "CSICOP at Twenty", *Skeptical Inquirer*, vol. 20, no. 4 (July/August): 5–8.

Kurtz, Paul 2003 *Science and Religion: Are They Compatible?* Amherst, NY: Prometheus Books.

Lakoff, George & Mark Johnson 1980 *Metaphors We Live By*. Chicago: University of Chicago Press.

Latour, Bruno 1993 *We Have Never Been Modern*. Translated by Catherine Porter. Harvester Wheatsheaf: Hertforshire.

Leibniz, Gottfried Wilhelm 1934 (1702-3) *New Essays on the Human Understanding*. In his *Philosophical Writings*. Translated by Mary Morris. London: J.M. Dent & Sons.

Leonard, Bill J. 1999 "American spirituality", *Religion and American Culture*, vol. 9, no. 2 (Summer): 152-7.

Lett, James 1991 "Interpretive Anthropology, Metaphysics, and the Paranormal", *Journal of Anthropological Research*, vol. 47: 305-330.

Lifton, Robert 1970 "Protean Man". In Robert Lifton (ed.), *History and Human Survival*. New York: Random House.

Lodge, Oliver 1927 *The Case for and against Psychical Belief*. Worcester, Mass.: Clark University.

Lowney, Kathleen S. (1995). Teenage Satanism as oppositional youth subculture. *Journal of Contemporary Ethnography*, 23(4): 453-484. Reprinted in Lorne L. Dawson (ed.) (1998) *Cults in Context: Readings in the Study of New Religious Movements*. (pp. 313-337). New Brunswick, N.J.: Transaction Publishers.

Luckmann, Thomas 1991 "The New and Old in Religion". In Pierre Bourdieu & James Coleman (eds.), *Social Theory for a Changing Society*. New York: Russell Sage Foundation.

Luhrmann, Tanya 1989 *Persuasions of the witch's craft: ritual magic and witchcraft in present-day England*. Oxford: Basil Blackwell.

Luke, Timothy W. 1996 "Identity, Meaning and Globalization: Detraditionalization in Postmodern Space-time Compression". In P. Heelas, S. Lash & P. Morris (eds.), *Detraditionalization*. Cambridge, Mass.: Blackwell Publishers.

Lyotard, Jean-Francois 1984 *The Postmodern Condition: a report on knowledge*. Translated by Geoff Bennington and Brian Massumi. Minneapolis: University of Minnesota Press.

Lyotard, Jean-Francois 1992 *The Postmodern Explained to Children: correspondence 1982-1985*. Edited by Julian Pefanis & Morgan Thomas. Translated by Don Berry *et. al*. Sydney: Power Publications.

McClenon, James 1982 "A survey of elite scientists: their attitudes toward ESP and parapsychology", *Journal of Parapsychology*, vol. 46: 127-52.

Mack, John 1994 *Abduction: human encounters with aliens*. New York: Scribner's.

Mack, John 2000 How the Alien Abduction Phenomenon Challenges the Boundaries of Our Reality. In David M. Jacobs (ed.), *UFOs and Abductions: Challenging the Borders of Knowledge*. Lawrence: University Press of Kansas (pp. 241-261).

Mack, John 2002 "Messengers from the Unseen", *Oberlin Alumni Magazine*, 98(2). Reprinted at: http://www.johnemackinstitute.org/ ejournal

Mackay, Charles 1841 *Memoirs of Extraordinary Popular Delusions*. London: R. Bentley.

Mackenzie, Brian 1987 "Parapsychology's critics: A link with the past?", *Behavioral and Brain Sciences*, vol. 10, no. 4: 597.

McNeil, Elton & Zick Rubin 1977 *The Psychology of Being Human*, 2nd ed. San Francisco: Canfield Press.

Malinowski, Bronsilaw 1954 (1948) *Magic, science and religion and other essays*. Garden City, N.Y: Doubleday.

Marcus, George 1995 "Ethnography in/of the World System: the emergence of multi-sited ethnography", *Annual Review of Anthropology*, vol. 24: 95–117.

Markovsky, Barry & Shane R. Thye 2001 "Social Influence On Paranormal Beliefs", *Sociological Perspectives*, vol. 44, no. 1 (Spring): 21–44.

Marx, Melvin 1976 *Introduction to Psychology: Problems, Procedures, and Principles*. New York: Macmillan.

Mather, Cotton 1868 (1692) Letter to John Richards, Boston, 31 May. Reprinted in *Massachusetts History Society Collection*, 4th series, vol. 8.

Medium (television series) 2005- USA. NBC. Producer Craig Sweeny.

Moody, Edward 1971 "Urban Witches". In J. Spradley & D. McCurdy (eds.), *Conformity and Conflict: Readings in Cultural Anthropology*. Boston: Little-Brown.

Moore, E.G. 1983 "Introduction: A Consideration of the Gift of Sensitivity or Mediumship in a Christian context". Pamphlet published by The Churches' Fellowship for Psychical and Spiritual Studies.

Moore, R. Laurence 1977 *In Search of White Crows*. New York: Oxford University Press.

Moore, R. Laurence 1994 *Selling God: American Religion in the Marketplace of Culture*. New York: Oxford University Press.

Murray, Stephen O. 1980 "The Invisibility of Scientific Scorn". In Richard de Mille (ed.), *The Don Juan Papers: further Castaneda controversies*. Santa Barbara, CA: Ross-Erikson.

"Music that's out of this World!" 1990 Available online: www.ufobbs.com/ufo (file: UFO399). (Accessed 19 April 1997).

Myers, Greg 1990 *Writing Biology: texts in the social construction of scientific knowledge*. Madison, Wis: University of Wisconsin Press.

Newport, Frank & Maura Strausberg 2001 Americans' Belief in Psychic and Paranormal Phenomena Is up Over Last Decade. Available online at http://www.gallup.com/poll (Accessed 9 June 2005).

Nierenberg, Gerard I. 1973 (1968) *Fundamentals of Negotiating*. New York: Hawthorn Books.

Northcote, Jeremy 2004 "Objectivity and the supernormal: The limitations of bracketing approaches in providing neutral accounts of supernormal claims", *Journal of Contemporary Religion*, Vol. 19, No. 1: 85–98.

Nowotny, Helga 1979 "Science and its Critics: Reflections on Anti-Science". In H. Nowotny & H. Rose (eds.), *Counter-Movements in the Sciences: the sociology of the alternatives to big science*. Dordrecht: D. Reidel.

Olson, David 1994 *The World on Paper: the conceptual and cognitive implications of writing and reading*. Cambridge, NY: Cambridge University Press.

Oprah Winfrey Show (television series) 1986– U.S.A. Harpo Productions/King World Production. Producer: Diane Atkinson Hudson.

Otis, L.P., & J.E. Alcock 1982 "Factors affecting extraordinary belief", *Journal of Social Psychology*, vol. 118: 77–85.

Palmer, John 2003 ESP in the Ganzfeld: Analysis of a Debate, *Journal of Consciousness Studies*, vol. 10, nos. 6–7: 51-68.

Paracelsus 1894 *Hermetic Astronomy*. In *The Hermetic and Alchemical Writings of Paracelsus*, vol. 2. Translated and edited by Arthur Edward Waite. London: James Elliott & Co.

Parsons, Arthur S. 1989 "The secular contribution to religious innovation: A case study of the Unification Church", *Sociological Analysis*, vol. 50, no. 3 (Fall): 209–227.

Parssinen, Terry M. 1979 "Professional Deviants and the History of Medicine: Medical Mesmerists in Victorian Britain". In Roy Wallis (ed.), *On the Margins of Science: The Social Construction of Rejected Knowledge*. Keele, Eng: University of Keele.

Pasachoff, Jay 1978 *Astronomy Now*. Philadelphia: W.B.Saunders.

Pasachoff, Jay & Marc Kutner 1978 *University Astronomy*. Philadelphia: W.B.Saunders.

Pater, Walter 1983 (1873) *The Renaissance*. New York: Chelsea House.

Pazameta, Zoran 1999 "Science vs. Religion", *Skeptical Inquirer*, vol. 23, no. 4 (Jul/Aug): 37-39.

Pfeffer, Leo 1974 "The Legitimation of Marginal Religions in the United States". In Irving I. Zaretsky & Mark P. Leone (eds.), *Religious Movements in Contemporary America*. Princeton, NJ: Princeton University Press.

Pflock, Karl 1996 letter to the editor, *Saucer Smear*, vol. 43, no. 3 (1 April). Available online: http://www.martiansgohome.com/smear (Accessed 4 October 1998).

Pico della Mirandola, Giovanni 1969 (1557-1573) *Opera omnia*, vol. 1. Hildesheim: Olms.

Pinch, Trevor 1987 "Some suggestions from the sociology of science to advance the psi debate", *Behavioral & Brain Sciences*, vol. 10, no. 4: 603–605.

Pliny the Elder 1963 (AD 77) *Natural History*, vol. VIII. Translated by W. H. S. Jones. London: William Heinemann Ltd.

Poltergeist (motion picture) 1982 USA. MGM (Metro-Goldwyn-Mayer). Producers Frank Marshall, Steven Speilberg & Kathleen Kennedy.

Popper, Karl 1972 (1959) *The Logic of Scientific Discovery*. London: Hutchinson.

Possamai, Adam 2000 "A profile of New Agers: social and spiritual aspects", *Journal of Sociology*, vol. 36, no. 3 (November): 364–377.

Price, Richard, M. Glickstein, D.L. Horton, & R.H. Bailey 1982 *Principles of Psychology*. New York: Holt, Rinehart, and Winston.

Rahtz, Philip 1991 *Invitation to Archaeology*, 2nd edn. Oxford: Blackwell.

Randall, Tom 1991 "Is Supernaturalism a Part of Authoritarianism?" *Psycholgoical Reports*, vol. 68: 685–686.

Rao, Ramakrishna 1994 "Anomalies of consciousness: Indian perspectives and research", *The Journal of Parapsychology*, vol. 58, no. 2 (June): 149–187.

Redfield, James 1994 *The Celestine Prophecy*. Sydney: Bantam Books.

Renfrew, Colin & Paul Bahn 1991 *Archaeology: Theories, Methods and Practice*, 2nd edn. London: Thomas & Hudson.

Riesman, Paul 1980 "Fictions of Art and Science". In Richard de Mille (ed.) *The Don Juan Papers: further Castaneda controversies*. Santa Barbara, Calif.: Ross-Erikson.

Ripp, Bobby 1996 *End Time Deceptions. An Expose on: Medjugorje (Marian Apparitions), the New Age Movement, UFO Phenomenon, and Others*. Mandeville, LA: True Light. Available online: http://www.nternet.com/~ripp/ten.htm (Accessed 16 June 1997).

Robbins, Dale A. 1997 "When Sin Persists in the Church". Victorious Living bible study pamphlet. Available online: http://www.victorious.org/excomun.htm (Accessed 9 September 1999).

Roe, Chris A. 1999 "Critical thinking and belief in the paranormal: a re-evaluation", *British Journal of Psychology*, vol. 90, no. 1 (Feb): 85–89.

Ross, Andrew 1991 *Strange Weather: Culture, Science and Technology in the Age of Limits*. London: Verso.

Russel, Jeffrey 1984 *Lucifer: The Devil in the Middle Ages*. Ithaca, N.Y: Cornell University Press.

Said, Edward 1978 *Orientalism*. New York: Pantheon Books.

Saler, Benson 1977 "Supernatural as a Western Category", *Ethos*; vol. 5, no. 1 (Spring): 31–53.

Salter, C.A. & L.M. Routledge 1971 "Supernatural beliefs among graduate students at the University of Pennsylvania", *Nature*, vol. 232: 278–279.

Scarre, Geoffrey 1987 *Witchcraft and Magic in 16th and 17th Century Europe*. London: Macmillan.

Schmitt, Carl 1996 (1932) *The Concept of the Political*. Translated by George Schwab. Chicago: University of Chicago Press.

Schouten, S. (1993) "Are we making progress?" In L. Coly and J. McMahon (eds.), Psi Research Methodology: A Re-examination, Proceedings of an International Conference. New York: Parapsychology Foundation. (pp. 295–322).

Seeds, Michael 1986 *Foundations of Astronomy*. Belmont, CA: Wadsworth.

Seligman, Adam B. 1997 *The Problem of Trust*. Princeton, NJ: Princeton University Press.

Sharer, Robert & Wendy Ashmore 1987 *Archaeology: Discovering Our Past*, 2nd edn. Mountain View, CA: Mayfield.

Shermer, Michael 1997 *Why People Believe Weird Things: pseudoscience, superstition, and other confusions of our time*. New York: W.H. Freeman.

Sightings (television series) 1992 USA. Ann Daniel Productions. Producers Ann Daniel, Michelle A Davis, Steve Kroopnick, Henry Winkler.

Silver, Nina 1992 "Radical mediumship", *New Internationalist*, no. 237 (November). Available online: http://rightsforall-usa.org /ni/issue237/radical.htm (Accessed 14 December 2000).

Simpson, Sandy 2005 "Satan, The First Postmodernist". Available online: http://www.deceptioninthechurch.com/satan postmodernist.html (Accessed 18 April 2006).

Snow, D.A. & R. Machalek 1982 "On the presumed fragility of unconventional beliefs", *Journal for the Scientific Study of Religion*, vol. 21: 15–26.

Snow, Theodore 1993 *Essentials of the Dynamic Universe: An Introduction to Astronomy*, 4th edn. St Paul: West Pub. Co.

Speiser, Jim c.1987 "UFOs and the Press: An Assessment of Current Media Attitudes". Available online: http://totse.com/en/fringe/ flyingsaucers_from_andromeda/ufopress.html (Accessed 19 April 1997).

Stallybrass, Peter & Allon White 1986 *The politics and poetics of transgression*. Ithaca, N.Y.: Cornell University Press.

Star Trek (original television series) 1966-69 USA. Desilu Production Inc, Norway Corporation & Paramount Television. Producer Gene Roddenberry (plus various episode producers).

Staude, John 1970 "Alienated Youth and the Cult of the Occult". Mimeographed. Reprinted in Morris Medley & James Conyers (eds.), *Sociology for the Seventies*. New York: Wiley.

Sturrock, Peter A. 1994 "Report on a Survey of the Membership of the American Astronomical Society Concerning the UFO Problem: Part 1", *Journal of Scientific Exploration*, vol. 8, no.1: 1–45.

Sullivan, Walter 1972 "Influence of the Press and Other Mass Media". In Carl Sagan & Thornton Page (eds), *UFO's – A Scientific Debate*. Ithaca: Cornell University Press.

Supernatural (television series) 2005- USA. The CW. Producer Cyrus Yavneh.

Sutcliffe, Thomas 1996 "Evolution, Mystery and the X Files: How do you talk science with a generation that yearns for miracles?", *The Independent*, November 13, 1996. Available online: http://www.milligan.edu/communications/Library/Articals1/xdawkins.htm (Accessed 19 April 1997).

Swords, Michael D. 2000 UFOs, the Military, and the Early Cold War Era. In David M. Jacobs (ed.), *UFOs and Abductions: Challenging the Borders of Knowledge*. Lawrence: University Press of Kansas (pp. 82–121).

Tambiah, Stanley 1990 *Magic, science, religion, and the scope of rationality*. Cambridge, England: Cambridge University Press.

Taylor, Eugene 1994 "Desperately seeking spirituality", *Psychology Today*, vol. 27, no. 6 (Nov-Dec): 54–53.

Thomas, David 1998 *Archaeology*, 3rd edn. Fort Worth : Harcourt Brace College Publishers.

Thomas, Keith 1971 *Religion and the Decline of Magic*. London: Weidenfeld & Nicolson.

Thompson, W.N. 1944 "Discussion and debate: A re-examination", *Quarterly Journal of Speech*, vol. 30: 288–299.

Tiryakian, Edward (ed.) 1974 *On the Margin of the Visible: Sociology, the Esoteric, and the Occult*. New York: John Wiley & Sons.

Tobacyk, Jerome; M. Miller & G. Jones 1984 "Paranormal beliefs of high school students", *Psychological Reports*, vol. 55: 255-261.

Tolbert, Jane T. 1999 "Fabri De Peiresc's quest for a method to calculate terrestrial longitude", *The Historian*, vol. 61, no. 4 (Summer): 801–19.

Travisano, Richard V. 1970 "Alternation and Conversion as Qualitatively Different Transformations". In G.P. Stone & H.A. Faberman (eds.), *Social Psychology Through Symbolic Interaction*. Massachusetts: Ginn-Blaisdell.

Trocco, Frank 2000 "Encouraging Students To Study Weird Things", *Phi Delta Kappan*, vol. 81, no. 8 (April): 628–31.

Truzzi, Marcello 1974 "Definition and Dimensions of the Occult: Towards a Sociological Perspective". In Edward Tiryakian (ed.), *On the Margin of the Visible: Sociology, the Esoteric, and the Occult*. New York: John Wiley & Sons. Originally published in *Journal of Popular Culture*, vol. 5, no. 3 (Winter, 1971): 635/7–646/18.

Unsolved Mysteries (television series) 1988–99 USA. Cosgrove/Meurer Productions. Producers Raymond Bridgers, John Cosgrove, Terry Dunn Meurer, Tim Rogan, Stuart Schwartz & Timothy Stone.

Van Syckle, Richard 1995 C/Net interview with Chris Carter. 12 August 1995. Available online: http://www.scibernet.com/xfiles/misc/cnet.html (Accessed 28 January 1997).

Virato, Sw. 1996 "Extraterrestrial Research: An Interview with Steven Greer". *New Frontier Magazine*. Available online: http://www.newfrontier.com/2/extrater.htm (Accessed 8 January 1997).

Volz, Carl 1997 *The Medieval Church: From the Dawn of the Middle Ages to the Eve of the Reformation*. Nashville: Abingdon Press.

Wagner, M.H. & M. Monnet 1979 "Attitudes of college professors towards extrasensory perception", *Zetetic Scholar*, vol. 5: 7–16.

Wallace, Patricia M., Jeffrey H. Goldstein, Peter E. Nathan 1990 *Introduction to Psychology*. Dubuque, Iowa: Wm. C. Brown.

Walker, Teri 1988 "Whose Discourse?" In Steve Woolgar (ed.), *Knowledge and Reflexivity: New Frontiers in the Sociology of Knowledge*. London: Sage Publications.

Weber, Max 1930 *The Protestant Ethic and the Spirit of Capitalism*. Translated by Talcott Parsons. London: Harper Collins Academic.

Weber, Max 1947 *The Theory of Social and Economic Organization*. Translated by A. M. Henderson and Talcott Parsons (ed.). London: William Hodge & Company Ltd.

Webster, A.J. 1979 "Scientific Controversy and Socio-Cognitive Metonymy: The Case of Acupuncture". In Roy Wallis (ed.), *On the Margins of Science: The Social Construction of Rejected Knowledge*. Keele, Eng: University of Keele.

Webster, Charles 1982 *From Paracelsus to Newton: Magic and the Making of Modern Science*. Cambridge, Eng.: Cambridge University Press.

Westrum, Ron 1977 "Social Intelligence about Anomalies: The Case of UFOs", *Social Studies of Science*, vol. 7, no. 3: 271–302.

Westrum, Ron 1978 "Science and Social Intelligence about Anomalies: The Case of Meteorites", *Social Studies of Science*, vol. 8, no. 4 (Nov): 461–493.

White, Stephen 1988 *The Recent Work of Jurgen Habermas*. Cambridge, N.Y.: Cambridge University Press.

Wildermuth, Mark 1999 "The edge of chaos: structural conspiracy and epistemology in *The X-Files*", *Journal of Popular Film and Television*, vol. 26, no. 4 (Winter): 146–157.

Williams, Barry 1994 "From the President", *The Skeptic*, vol. 14, no. 2: 3.

Williams, Barry 1999 "Dialogue with an alien intelligence", *The Skeptic*, vol. 19, no. 2 (Winter): 40–42.

Willis, Paul 1977 *Learning to Labour*. London: Saxon House.

Wilson, Fred L. 1996 "Galileo and the Rise of Mechanism". *History of Science*. Available online: http://www.rit.edu/~flwstv/galileo.html (Accessed 9 September 2000).

Wilson, Keely M. & Michael L. Frank 1990 "Persistence of Paranormal Beliefs", *Psychological Reports*, vol. 67: 946.

Wooffitt, Robin 2000 "Some Properties of the International Organisation of Displays of Paranormal Cognition in Psychic-Sitter Interaction", *Sociology*, vol. 34, no. 3 (August): 457–479.

Woolgar, Roger 1987 *Other Lives, Other Selves: a Jungian psycho-therapist discovers past lives*. New York: Bantam Books.

Wuthnow, Robert 1976 "Astrology and Marginality", *Journal for the Scientific Study of Religion*, vol. 15, no. 2: 157–168.

Wynne, Brian 1979 "Between Orthodoxy and Oblivion: The Normalisation of Deviance in Science". In Roy Wallis (ed.), *On the Margins of Science: The Social Construction of Rejected Knowledge*. Keele, Eng: University of Keele.

X-Files, The (television series) 1993– USA. 20th Century Fox Television & Ten Thirteen Productions. Producer Chris Carter (plus various episode producers).

Yeager, Jennifer A. 1993, "Opportunities and limitations: female spiritual practice in nineteenth-century America", *ATQ (The American Transcendental Quarterly)*, no. 7 (Sept): 217–28.

Zusne, Leonard 1981 "On Conducting a Zetetic Discussion", *Zetetic-Scholar*, vol. 8 (July): 118–122.

Zusne, Leonard & W.H. Jones 1982 *Anomalistic Psychology: A Study of Extraordinary Phenomena of Behavior and Experience*. Hillsdale, NJ: Lawrence Erlbaum.

Index